T0244476

AMERICAN POLY

AMERICAN POLY

A HISTORY

CHRISTOPHER M. GLEASON

OXFORD
UNIVERSITY PRESS

OXFORD
UNIVERSITY PRESS

Oxford University Press is a department of the University of Oxford. It furthers
the University's objective of excellence in research, scholarship, and education
by publishing worldwide. Oxford is a registered trade mark of Oxford University
Press in the UK and certain other countries.

Published in the United States of America by Oxford University Press
198 Madison Avenue, New York, NY 10016, United States of America.

© Oxford University Press 2024

All rights reserved. No part of this publication may be reproduced, stored in
a retrieval system, or transmitted, in any form or by any means, without the
prior permission in writing of Oxford University Press, or as expressly permitted
by law, by license, or under terms agreed with the appropriate reproduction
rights organization. Inquiries concerning reproduction outside the scope of the
above should be sent to the Rights Department, Oxford University Press, at the
address above.

You must not circulate this work in any other form
and you must impose this same condition on any acquirer.

CIP data is on file at the Library of Congress

ISBN 978-0-19-765914-4

DOI: 10.1093/oso/9780197659144.001.0001

Printed by Sheridan Books, Inc., United States of America

In memory of Dr. Joshua Hodge

Contents

Acknowledgments

This book has been a byproduct of my own intellectual journey, and I am greatly indebted to the many people who have helped me navigate that process. Its seeds were first planted in the Religious Studies department at Georgia State University by Katherine McClymond, Eric Rovie, and John Iskander, each of whom was pivotal in helping me begin to think critically about religion. I am forever grateful for their influence, and particularly for John who, despite imploring me to consider grad school over seminary, supported me in my youthful assuredness and has since.

Though I did not know it yet, the foundation for this project was laid during my time as a seminarian at Liberty University. Witnessing first-hand the inner workings of the Religious Right awoke me to the inconsistencies of my own worldview in ways that my liberal arts education had been unable. It was there that I left behind the fundamentalism of my youth and began to really ask questions.

I must thank John Shouse at Golden Gate Seminary. Though he would certainly not approve of where this journey has led, his willingness to take in an intellectual refugee kept me from giving up my academic pursuits. Though he was unable to preserve my future as a Baptist minister, his willingness to work independently with me, to read books, to criticize ideas, and to eventually recommend me to programs where I would fare better has left sweet memories. While those long hours did not convince me to stay, they did awaken within me an obsession with the evolution of ideas that has remained ever since.

This book also owes a great debt to James Moorhead and Wentzel van Huyssteen at Princeton Theological Seminary. At a time when

I was rethinking history, philosophy, religion, and culture from the ground up, they not only accepted me with open arms, but also taught me rigor. I took that with me when I eventually ventured across the street to Princeton University and into Daniel Rodgers's seminar on intellectual and cultural history, a defining experience that solidified within me the historical methodology present in this work.

This book owes the greatest debt to David Sehat. Not only was he a forthright and honest doctoral advisor, but he has remained an ongoing source of guidance and support. When I wanted to rehash older debates over science and religion, he encouraged me to do something fresh and new. Without his direction, this project would not only lack its novelty, but likely would not exist.

I would also like to thank my editor, Susan Ferber, who believed in this project from the beginning and has remained committed to it throughout rounds of revision spread over a trying pandemic. I would also like to thank Alex Cummings and John McMillian at Georgia State University for their ongoing encouragement and support.

In addition, I am deeply indebted to many archives and archivists. The bulk of the material that makes up this book, as well as the parts that did not make it in, were mined from the archives of the University of California Santa Barbara and Santa Cruz, Emory University, Hamilton College, and, of course, the Kinsey Institute. I am particularly thankful to the Kinsey Institute and their kind, supportive, and wonderful staff, especially Liana Zhou and Shawn C. Wilson. A thank you must also go to Christian Goodwillie at Hamilton College for his help with photos and Edsel Llurador, the graduate student working in the archives there, who photocopied hundreds of letters for me when I could not go to New York.

I am also deeply thankful to the numerous individuals within this narrative who have spoken with me. Their willingness to engage with me is forever appreciated. Among these I must give specific mention to Oberon Zell, Ryam and Brett Hill, Barry Northrop, Eve Furchgott, Dave Gallo, Robyn Trask, Crystal Byrd Farmer, and Dr. Ken Haslam.

I would like to give a very special thank you to my daughter Autumn for her patience throughout this project. Many of her early memories are of sitting at my feet as I typed away at a computer. I am happy now to take some time and make different ones with her. I want also to thank my old friend Brandon Dillard at Monticello for his ongoing encouragement. Perhaps Autumn and I will begin by coming to see you and the Shenandoah.

Lastly, a thank you goes to my friend Dr. Ryan Prechter, who lent me the quietness of his apartment in Atlanta through summers and holidays while he was home in New Orleans. Many of these chapters were composed there.

AMERICAN POLY

Introduction

Piper Joy Mayfield was born in San Diego, California, in 2017. Despite a very short stint in the newborn ICU over concerns about her ability to breathe on her own, her birth was unremarkable. Yet if Piper's physical birth was routine, the events surrounding it were not. Her three fathers, Ian Jenkins, Alan Mayfield, and Jeremy Allen Hodges, had made history as the first polyamorous "throuple," or mutually consensual romantic relationship between three people, to have all three of their names listed as parents on their child's birth certificate. At the time, Jenkins and Mayfield had been in a committed relationship for almost a decade and a half, with Jeremy joining them eight years in as their third. Even though the three men had long been in a committed relationship, the legal battle they fought to secure a surrogate, finance in vitro fertilization, and then obtain legal recognition as co-parents cost more than $120,000. Initially the judge who presided over their case was reluctant to bestow legal recognition on such a novel and non-traditional familial structure, arguing that alterations to the law were first needed to accommodate the validity of their union. Yet the throuple's emotional pleas, combined with the promise of the financial and emotional security that a three-income, multi-parent household could provide, eventually persuaded the judge. Because the decision was not made in appellate court, it did not set future legal precedent for polyamorous families, a fact that aided the judge in her decision to grant their request. Although the three fathers subsequently indicated their desire to live private lives going forward, they made a few media appearances and Jenkins has penned a memoir of their journey, hoping to inspire other polyamorists to seek out legal protections for their own families.[1]

Despite the ongoing threat of social ostracization, other polyamorists have been less reluctant to step into the limelight. Take, for instance, Angelica, Lori, and Brian, a throuple who appeared on a 2020 episode of *House Hunters*, a popular reality show that follows families searching to purchase their ideal home. Despite being unable to lawfully wed in the United States, the throuple had recently joined in a commitment ceremony in Aruba, remarking that, "This has nothing to do with church and state; it's a commitment between the three of us. We are all equals in this relationship." Once united, they turned their attention to finding a home that included a triple sink vanity in the master bedroom. While many of the program's viewers lauded the show for its positive portrayal of polyamorous families, critics, including conservative Princeton law professor Robert George, lamented the episode as the latest example of the erosion of American sexual ethics.[2]

Moral evaluations aside, the controversy sparked by the episode, much like the San Diego throuple's legal struggle, represents polyamory's increasing public exposure and the cultural conflict that has accompanied it. Yet while those anxious over the revision or decline of American family values have expressed sharp disdain for polyamory, other Americans have embraced its legitimacy. The past two decades have witnessed mainstream media outlets such as *Time*, *The Atlantic*, *Esquire*, *Rolling Stone*, and *TED* bestowing favorable attention on the lifestyle, further attesting to its growing popularity. This has led some cultural commentators to ask whether polyamory represents a new stage in an ongoing sexual revolution.[3]

Polyamory's emergence in the public square has attracted academic attention as well. In 2016, the American Psychological Association (APA) established a task force on consensual non-monogamy. According to the APA, the goal of this initiative was to generate research, education, and training that would lead to increased awareness and acceptance of consensually non-monogamous lifestyles, including but not limited to polyamory. That same year, researchers at Indiana University, in conjunction with the Kinsey Institute, published a study claiming that as many as one in five Americans have experimented with some form of consensual non-monogamy at some point in their lives.[4]

Polyamory's mainstream novelty raises the question: What exactly is polyamory? The term, originally coined in the early 1990s, tacks the Greek prefix *poly* onto the Latin *amor*, translating to "many loves." Providing a concise answer beyond that can be difficult, with experts disagreeing over its practice, aims, and significance. Sociologist Mark Regnerus has argued that polyamory is really about cheap sex. According to Regnerus, polyamorists have negotiated relationships that allow for low-stakes sex, void of commitment, outside of their primary relationship. Primarily concerned with "sex and dinner dates," polyamorists, he argues, have a general disdain for marriage and typically do not share children or homes with their polyamorous lovers. This absence of commitment, Regnerus believes, leads inevitably to sexually transmitted infections, dead-beat dads, and patriarchal misogyny.[5]

Yet such conservative alarmism negligently overlooks polyamory's ideals and its practice. It certainly does not describe Piper Mayfield's three dads or the *House Hunter* throuple. A deeper look reveals that, over the past thirty years, "polyamory" has become an umbrella term used to describe a host of romantic or intimate relationships that provide an ethical framework for various forms of non-monogamy. As sociologist Mimi Schippers writes, polyamory refers to "committed, emotionally and sometimes sexually intimate relationships involving more than two persons." It presupposes that all parties consent and either know or are at least hypothetically aware of one another. Polyamory prizes commitment, honesty, trust, mutual consent, open communication, and equality among all sexes and sexual orientations. These common themes and commitments demarcate polyamory from other forms of non-monogamy, such as polygamy, that have historically rejected gender equality and LGBTQ+ lifestyles.[6] Thus, polyamory should be understood as a subcategory of the much larger category of ethical non-monogamy. Not all ethical non-monogamy is polyamory. But polyamory is inherently ethically non-monogamous.

Though polyamory entails these ideals, it manifests in diverse ways, making further definition difficult. It means different things to different people. For some polyamorists the term denotes a type of extended family structure where multiple individuals have made life-long commitments to one another and all live together. For others, polyamory means having one central committed relationship with the potential for a revolving set of secondary or tertiary relationships outside of that primary relationship. For still others, it might mean simultaneously enjoying several intimate relationships without ever sharing assets or living spaces with anyone else.

For some polyamorists, their relationships are deeply rooted in religion or spirituality, with the lifestyle sometimes thought of as a microcosm representing the greater interconnectedness of ultimate reality. For others, the lifestyle holds no spiritual basis at all, representing instead a freethinking mode to transcend religious or culturally constructed notions of familial structures. When Crystal Byrd Farmer, editor of the magazine and online forum *Black and Poly*, was recently asked to provide a succinct definition of polyamory, her answer was that it is a relationship form falling under the larger umbrella of consensual non-monogamy where people engage in consenting relationships with multiple people. Outside of this general definition, Farmer assured, there was no fixed model for polyamory. Practitioners may adapt it to fit their individual needs alongside the desires of the other individuals involved. Though many contemporary polyamorists take Farmer's pragmatic approach and even oscillate between variant forms of polyamory, more dogmatic polyamorists often ostracize forms of the lifestyle they deem illegitimate.[7]

This book aims to provide a history of polyamory in the United States as an idea and as a lifestyle. This is not to say that polyamory is a purely American phenomenon. It is now practiced throughout the world. But polyamory's central terms and concepts, including the word itself, were forged in the United States and their early proponents were products of American sexual dissent. By providing this historical context for polyamory, this book also intends to underscore that, at its core, polyamory is far more than an attempt to jettison commitment for hedonism. More than cheap sex, it is a detailed and often costly rethinking of the social, religious, and ethical foundations of intimate relationships.[8]

Historically, the very notion of ethical non-monogamy was a contradiction in terms within mainstream American culture. From the colonial period, monogamous matrimony was inextricably linked to the moral and social order. American families were seen as microcosms of the larger political order, with men at its head and women and children placed under their authority. This structure tied private life intimately to the public good, solidifying in both law and culture what historian Nancy Cott has described as "a particular marriage model: lifelong, faithful monogamy, formed by the mutual consent of a man and a woman, bearing the impress of the Christian religion and the English common law in its expectations for the husband to be the family head and economic provider, his wife the dependent partner."[9]

For early Americans, the consensual nature of heterosexual monogamous marriage bestowed upon the institution the same legitimacy American citizens were thought to grant their government. Yet, in practice, many Americans, particularly women, knew that the institution fell short in many respects. The most glaring of these shortcomings was the legal notion of *coverture*, which subsumed the citizenship of wives into that of their husbands, legally suspending their own civic identity and robbing them of their ability to accrue property or enter contracts. Coverture mirrored the biblical notion of the patriarchal family held in such high esteem by America's moral establishment. Christianity gave credence to established law, providing religious justification when the preservation of female personal autonomy was compromised. Deviations from this normative vision of matrimony, particularly those that challenged Christian morality, monogamy, the hierarchy of the sexes, or heterosexuality, were seen as threats not just to the public order but also to divine mandate. Such deviations were met with swift censure from both the American legal and moral establishments, or what historian Michael Bronski has aptly termed America's "persecuting society." Polyamory directly or indirectly challenges each of these assumptions.[10]

Because the most striking feature of polyamory is its rejection of monogamy, the most obvious starting point for this history would be an analysis of American traditions that have rejected monogamy. Polygamy is the most obvious example. Polygamy in America has a rich history predating European colonization. Even after the nation's founding, it existed among indigenous communities, slave populations, and, most infamously, within Mormonism. Yet while indigenous polygamy sometimes offered its female practitioners social benefits, including property rights, access to divorce, and even political power often not enjoyed by women living within the American mainstream, polygamy has predominately entailed a commitment to male patriarchy that is explicitly disavowed by polyamorists. Because of their commitment to gender equality and queer sexual orientations, polyamorists have all but unilaterally distanced themselves from American forms of polygamy, particularly that historically practiced by Mormons. They do not adopt polygamist concepts and often disdain the practice as unethical. For this reason, attempts to link the two based on their shared rejection of monogamy are typically based on shallow analysis and cannot hold up to historical scrutiny. Though polygamy is a form of ethical non-monogamy, polyamory is a distinct branch on that family tree.[11]

Another way to think about polyamory's beginnings is to frame it within the longer history of challenges to conventional marriage more closely situated within the American mainstream. From the nation's founding, subsets of American women have resisted the coercive and unequal effects of heterosexual monogamous matrimony. On the eve of Independence, the future First Lady Abigail Adams famously implored her husband that, when constructing the nation's new code of laws, he would "remember the ladies." Adding her conviction that all men were inherently tyrannical, she made it known that women

were determined to form their own rebellion against what she believed was an unlimited tyranny. Pleading with him to shun laws that
would perpetuate such indignity, she exhorted him to willingly trade
the tyranny of the master for the tenderness of an endearing friend.
Though it is certain that Abigail entertained no notions of ethical
non-monogamy, she clearly understood the potentially oppressive nature of the institution of marriage as it was practiced.[12]

Despite Abigail's hopes, her endeavor to stifle the need for rebellion
was ineffective. Well before women gained the right to vote nationally, women much more forthright than Adams publicly challenged
the male hegemony enshrined in marriage and supported by both
religion and law. In 1848, the iconoclastic reformer Elizabeth Cady
Stanton again drew a parallel between the nation's Independence and
the struggle between the sexes. In her Declaration of Sentiments, she
railed against a host of inequalities, from property rights to access to
jobs and education, decrying man's usurpation of Jehovah's authority
in his oppression of women in both civic life and marriage.[13] For the
next half-century, Stanton and other women's rights advocates, would
vie vigorously for equal treatment within the bounds of matrimony as
well as within the public square. Yet, in its mainstream forms, the pre-
feminist women's movement of the nineteenth century rarely went
so far as to advocate for the consensual sustainment of multiple intimate partners. Pragmatically, such notions were detrimental to the
more pressing goals of acquiring access to equal education, careers,
and suffrage.[14]

A closer nineteenth-century analogy to contemporary polyamory
can be found in the sex radicals from whom most feminists of the
period sought to distance themselves. Though the term "free love"
conjures images of Bay Area hippies during the 1960s in the minds
of most Americans, the tradition has a much a longer history. The
earlier free love dates to the 1820s and 1840s, when the ideas of the
freethinking religious critic Robert Owen and the utopian socialist
Charles Fourier began infiltrating the newly formed American middle
class. Originally efforts to ride the wave of early American reform,

both Owenism and Fourierism were attacks on the evils of unbridled capitalism that took aim at the injustices of wealth inequality. Such efforts had some short-lived success, as exemplified by the establishment of utopian communal experiments such as the Owenite New Harmony in Indiana and the originally Transcendentalist Fourierite stronghold of Brook Farm in Massachusetts. Though these early experiments failed to institute major marital reform, they did serve as spaces for rethinking traditional marriage and reshaping it along more secularly progressive lines. In the 1850s, a network of sexual dissenters took up these critiques. Heirs of the Second Great Awakening, these Americans rejected the orthodoxy of their youth, instead combining nineteenth-century spiritualism with notions of individual sovereignty that rejected systemic authorities, whether civil or ecclesiastical. The implications for marriage were unavoidable. By the early 1850s, free love proponents were drawing parallels between matrimony and slavery. Pointing to the endless agony of an unhappy marriage, free lovers decried the isolation and subjugation matrimony imposed on women and claimed it promoted infidelity, marital rape, and the seeking of prostitutes by men. To alleviate such evils, they promoted intimate unions rooted in individual autonomy that ensured marriages based on mutual attraction, gender equality, and spiritual affinity.

Free lovers became advocates of more liberal divorce laws that would offer a method of reprieve to Americans trapped in marriages that did not live up to these ideals. On the matter of sustaining relationships with multiple partners, however, free lovers often differed. On the more conservative side of the spectrum, many free lovers practiced serial monogamy, prizing the ability to vacate intimate unions when they no longer benefited the parties involved. Some would have disdained the notion of maintaining multiple partners simultaneously, and many, with sexual ethics rooted in contemporaneous spiritualist sensibilities, followed in the tradition of early American health reformers that downplayed the need for regular sexual intercourse. On the more liberal side of the spectrum were those who advocated for unlimited variance in lovers. The best-known example is Victoria

Woodhull, a self-proclaimed Savior and Prophetess who gave up her career as a fortuneteller to become the first woman stockbroker in New York City (along with her sister) before running for President of the United States. Woodhull's brand of free love was much less restrictive, railing against any law that would interfere with her ability to change lovers at any whim, a characteristic that led to popular artistic depictions of her as Satan.[15]

Though there are numerous parallels between the early free love movement and contemporary polyamory, there is no traceable historical connection between the two. At its heart, nineteenth-century free love was a countercultural movement that sought liberation from middle-class Victorian sexuality. Both it and polyamory were built on a rejection of Judeo-Christian orthodoxy and the belief that the state should refrain from regulating intimate relationships. Both share deep commitments to individual autonomy and gender equality, and both, at their zenith, were deeply spiritualist. Despite these shared characteristics, there appears no clear line of succession between these two manifestations of ethical non-monogamy. Though one of America's most influential polyamorists later received an award from the Woodhull Freedom Foundation (est. 2003), references to her or other contemporaneous free lovers are glaringly absent from early polyamorous writings. When such references are made, they usually show up in later work and appear to be ad hoc attempts to create a historical lineage.[16]

Rather than creating non-existent historical connections between polyamory and its precursors based on the shared rejection of monogamy or critiques of traditional marriage more broadly, this book originates in a study of the central personalities prominent within American polyamory and uncovers the ideas that influenced their thought, setting those ideas within their larger historical context. The key agitators who produced a coherent notion of polyamory and promoted that notion effectively within American society were children of the 1960s, hippies and communalists who experimented with alternative spiritualities, drugs, and free love during their youth. But the cultural shifts that allowed for such dissent predate the counterculture of the 1960s. When set within its proper historical context, it becomes clear that polyamory is a unique manifestation of the twentieth century.

The turn of the twentieth century was a watershed in the evolution of American sexual culture. By the late 1800s, the combination of immigration, urbanization, and industrialization was radically transforming American society, drawing together diverse groups of individuals in tighter proximity and arming them with newer technologies to spread their ideas. Growing populations of eastern and southern European immigrants combined anarchist and socialist political philosophies with pockets of homegrown progressives to produce new notions of free speech, gender equality, and sexual freedom that both intrigued and scandalized American moral sensibilities. These bohemian dissidents concentrated in America's growing metropolises, New York's Greenwich Village in particular, where they heralded the death of the repressive Victorian era while practicing a revitalized version of free love that celebrated sexual variety. The most infamous was Russian-born Jewish freethinker and anarchist Emma Goldman, who maintained a romantic foursome with her lover Alexander Berkman and another couple before conspiring political assassination, being arrested for distributing birth control material, and eventually being deported to Russia for encouraging draft dodging during the First World War.[17]

Though Bohemian sexual morality failed to liberalize American sexual mores wholesale, it did serve as a harbinger of greater change. By the 1920s, mainstream culture had coopted a watered-down version of Bohemian sexuality bereft of its political extremism and radical embrace of free love. Magazine ads and billboards commodified images of the New Woman, with her short hair, cigarettes, and economic independence. As sexual modernism trickled into the mainstream, American sexual culture began to evolve. The mass influx of rural Americans into cities radically altered family dynamics, and many young Americans found themselves in a world drastically different from that of their parents a few decades earlier. Access to automobiles, amusement parks, petting parties, and speakeasies provided new spaces for intimate interactions, both heterosexual and homosexual. Young Americans around the nation seized on such opportunities, becoming increasingly at ease with premarital sexual contact. In the political sphere, the passage of the Nineteenth Amendment in 1920 encouraged activists led by Alice Paul to introduce the Equal Rights Amendment (ERA) to secure the new age of gender equality for which so many American women had long hoped. Simultaneously, Margaret Sanger established the American Birth Control League, forerunner to Planned Parenthood. The group decried the oppressive moralism of the Comstock Laws that forbade the transmission of sex education material, typically deemed pornographic, through the mail. The shift in youth sexual culture, the ERA, and Sanger's war for birth control all pushed sex and family to the forefront of national dialogue, dividing progressives and conservatives in a manner that has led recent historians to argue that both the sexual revolution and the ensuing culture wars began during the Roaring Twenties.[18]

For many Americans enthusiastic about the liberal trajectory of American sexual mores during these years, hope seemed short-lived. The Great Depression and the New Deal's many attempts to remedy it not only meant that Americans' need to survive eclipsed preoccupations with sexual liberation but also that the federal government would have a more expansive role in American life. Though the passage of the Nineteenth Amendment had begun the long dismantlement of coverture, economic hardships reinvigorated the role of feminine domesticity. New Deal programs prioritized both marriage and white male employment, reinforcing the notion that a husband's civic identity was tied to his role as provider and a wife's to her role as mother.[19]

More than anything, the Cold War reshaped American notions of intimacy and domesticity. The rise of the Soviet Union as a superpower coupled with the detonation of the atomic bombs over Hiroshima and Nagasaki weighed heavily on the American family, producing a cultural paranoia that combined fears of the spread of godless communism with the psychological horror of imminent nuclear destruction. Such trepidation pushed Americans toward a desire for stability and order. Exacerbated by the rapid suburban-ization of its cities, these Cold War anxieties produced an American consensus concerning family life that further reinforced the notion that lifelong heterosexual monogamy was an integral linchpin of social order.

Though the nuclear family that emerged during the postwar years, with its isolated families made up of a husband, wife, and 2.5 children, was a deviation from the more geographically centralized family of previous decades, it functioned in mainstream America as a symbol of American unity, stability, and morality. Buttressed by law, culture, and a stable economy, the American consensus that emerged linked sexual conformity to the character and prosperity of the nation. Modesty and prudent talk were prized. Divorce, as well as procreation out-side of marriage, was highly disparaged, while interracial marriage remained illegal. Homosexuality, branded a mental disorder in 1952 by the APA, not only ensured social exclusion and loss of livelihood for queer Americans, but could also mean loss of freedom as both state and federal agencies systematically rooted out homosexuals for arrest.[20]

Yet where there is culture there is always counterculture. Even as America's midcentury consensus was forming, there were already signs of its collapse. In the wake of the century's most sexually op-pressive years, subsets of the American public were already pushing back against the culture of sexual coercion that permeated American society. Both the nascent homophile movement, led by the gay men of the Mattachine Society and the Daughters of Bilitis, their lesbian counterparts, made great strides in legitimizing queer lifestyles during the most dangerous years of the antigay McCarthyite witch-hunts. Simultaneously, the Beatniks of the late 1950s represented a swath of American youth who rejected the conformity and ease of Cold War suburban life for a more transient, drug-induced, and sexually experimental lifestyle, paving the way for the counterculture of the 1960s. Equally significant was the publication of the best-selling Kinsey Reports, *Sexual Behavior in the Human Male* (1948) and *Sexual Behavior in the Human Female* (1953), written by Indiana University zoologist Alfred Kinsey and his group of researchers. These studies belied the façade of the American consensus on sexuality with their claims that masturbation, premarital and extramarital sex, and homosexuality permeated American life to an extent unappreciated by most Americans.

Ironically, the same generation that produced the consensus culture of the mid-twentieth century also birthed the children who dismantled it. By the early 1960s, it was clear that the postwar baby boom made possible by the monotony of American domesticity would prove its undoing. Those seeking sexual liberation began looking to the organizational strategies of the Civil Rights Movement. By the end of the decade, increased access to the birth control pill, the emergence of second-wave feminism, the legalization of interracial marriage, and the first sparks of a more militant Gay Liberation Front all signaled an undeniable sexual revolution occurring in American society.

One group within this larger cultural stream were the hippies, young Americans who, like the Beats before them, rejected conformity to mainstream values in lieu of existential experience. Beginning in the 1960s, thousands of these American youths left home and migrated toward the West Coast. Following the dictate of Harvard professor and psychedelic evangelist Timothy Leary to "tune in, turn on, and drop out," these youths established a host of countercultural communities that promoted experimentation with religion, drugs, and sex. Polyamory's most influential figures were active within these communities, and it was there that their ideas began to take shape.[21]

Using polyamory as a lens through which to view sexual dissent in the second half of the twentieth century provides a unique perspective on American sexual counterculture. The polyamorist impulse that emerged during the 1960s was already more than youthful appeals to jettison prudish morality for unchecked hedonism. Dovetailing the counterculture's critiques of the American sexual order, polyamorists took aim at the traditional Christianity on which that order was based. But they did not become more secular. Early polyamorists were as drawn to the plethora of new religious movements that arose from within the counterculture as they were to its emphasis on sexual experimentation. Their search for a new spiritual foundation on which to rebuild a moral and social order in the absence of Judeo-Christian mores opened them up to a host of alternative spiritualities. Many of these spiritualities were eclectically fabricated from diverse sources, including eastern religious traditions, pre-Christian paganism, and even science fiction novels. This history testifies to that deeply religious, though anti-Christian, character of early polyamorous thought.[22] It also uncovers how early polyamorists married these new religious notions with a right-wing political disposition typically uncharacteristic of the larger American counterculture.[23]

During the 1970s, polyamorists remained on the cultural periphery. As the optimism of the 1960s waned, many hippies and others sharing their ideals reluctantly reintegrated into mainstream society. Radical notions of sexual liberation, including those challenging monogamy, did seep into American culture. More privatized manifestations such as swinging parties among aging baby boomers replaced older public performances like those embodied in the infamous 1967 Summer of Love. However, polyamory's key players held on. Rather than reintegrating into the American mainstream, they tended to remain in either formal communes or other isolated countercultural communities where their ideas continued to develop. As the Civil Rights Movement, gay liberation, and second-wave feminism continued to make gains within the mainstream, polyamorist impulses remained on the fringes within these disparate communities. Not until the 1980s would their ideas make their way into more public forums.[24]

The emergence of polyamory in the public square during the 1980s provides insights into divisions within queer sexual dissent. The polyamorist agitators who coalesced in the 1980s saw themselves as working within the same tradition as the many other liberation movements of the 1960s and 1970s. Initially hoping to build political alliances among gay and lesbian communities, they were disappointed when many queer Americans shunned the promotion of polyamory as detrimental to their political aims for social acceptance. Finding that bisexuals were also shunned within gay and lesbian communities, polyamorists harnessed this shared sense of alienation to form alliances with bisexual activists.[25]

In addition to these alliances, polyamory is distinct in the way proponents framed their message in the face of moral detractors during the decisively conservative shift of the 1980s. For conservatives, the 1960s represented a break from the perceived unity and stability of the American commonweal. By the 1980s, this uneasiness had incited an all-out backlash among Christian conservatives who saw the sexual revolution of the 1960s and 1970s as catastrophic for America's destiny, as well as its very soul. In subsequent decades, these cultural warriors took aim at liberal gains in censorship laws, birth control, sex education, gay liberation, and women's rights.[26]

In the face of this conservative counter-revolution, polyamorists tirelessly organized, leading conferences, making public appearances, and printing a deluge of material. But they did not chide conservative reverence for family values. Rather, they internalized the conservative emphasis on stability and commitment, reframing the sustainment of multiple intimate partners not as an undoing of family values but as a necessary evolution in familial dynamics that better safeguarded the family from the alienation, isolation, and economic hardships of the post-nuclear age. Their focus on religiosity and family values, along with their consistent distrust of the state, allowed polyamorists to argue that they, not the Religious Right, were the true defenders of spirituality, family, and freedom. They naïvely believed that their new vision for the American family might become readily accepted as a

moral corrective rather than an erosion of family values. Though in
the end they failed to produce a cohesive social movement, their ideas,
aided by the internet revolution of the 1990s, diffused into American
society, ensuring that an unsuspecting link to the 1960s, reshaped by
the culture wars of the 1980s and 1990s, became increasingly popularized in twenty-first-century mainstream culture.

I

Paganisms

To deny or denigrate sexuality in humanity is to deny or denigrate
Nature, and, therefore, Divinity.

—Council of Themis (1971)

The sexual revolution of the 1960s and 1970s ignited a war
against mainstream sexual mores. During that time, the counterculture rejected traditional monogamy in lieu of a more laissez-
faire approach to experimentation and promiscuity. This project was
not merely destructive. Many American youths wanted more than
simply to tear down the sexual traditionalism of their parents' generation. There were also those who wished to erect it its place a re-
formulated sexual ethics built on novel moral foundations. Rejecting
the Judeo-Christian basis on which mid-century sexual ethics were
based, they often looked to other religious traditions to supply new
spiritual foundations for the sexual mores they created for themselves.
For some this meant looking to Eastern religious traditions. Traditions
predating Christianity in the West appealed to others. Throughout the
1960s and 1970s, thousands of young Americans experimented with
these non-Christian traditions, eclectically synthesizing new syncretic religious movements that incorporated religiously based ethical
systems that rejected monogamy on spiritualist grounds. Instead of
embracing models of spirituality that pitted the immanent against the
transcendent, these traditions often sought to harmonize all realms of
human experience, interpreting the well-being of the individual in

terms of being in sync with the divine. By the early 1970s, it was clear
to those who were paying attention that the counterculture fostered a
unique environment where such traditions could thrive, enabling this
impulse to proliferate.[1] It was from within this spiritualist wing of the
counterculture that one of the most colorful and influential streams of
American polyamory emerged.[2]

Science fiction writer Robert Heinlein called religion and sex the
two sacred cows of Western civilization. Heinlein was an agnostic
with mystical leanings who took a libertarian approach to sexual
freedom. By the 1960s, he had made it his personal mission to undermine blind devotion to those twin pillars of American culture. His
most well-known effort to achieve that end was his novel *Stranger in
a Strange Land*.[3]

Stranger follows the life of Valentine Michael Smith, a human child
left behind as the last survivor of a failed colonization effort on Mars.
Raised on the red planet, Smith learns telepathic and telekinetic abilities during his adolescence spent among the Martians. Upon his return to earth, Smith imparts Martian culture to the friends he meets.
He initiates them into the Martian ritual of "water-sharing," which
binds individuals together as "water-brothers." This ritual requires
that, after drinking water together, the participants commit to a relationship of complete honesty and loyalty for the rest of their lives.
He also introduces the Martian term "grok," meaning to comprehend
something in its fullness. Smith's conversations with his new earthly
water-brothers regarding the nature of religion and reality lead him to
the statement "Thou art god," which he takes to apply to himself as
well as his friends. Smith then founds his own church, the Church of
All Worlds. The church, made up of carefully selected individuals separated into clusters called "nests," all subscribe to Smith's pantheistic
article of faith and practice a form of ritualistic free love. Factions on
earth reject Smith's unorthodox message, and at the end of the story,
he is martyred.[4]

By the mid-1960s, *Stranger* was mandatory reading for anyone seriously involved in the American counterculture. Heinlein's neologism,

grok, spread throughout the collective consciousness of a generation aching to shed the cultural homogeneity of its predecessor. Soon nests and water-brotherhoods popped up across the country as a subset of American youths looked to Valentine Michael Smith's example. Yet few were as inspired by the Martian Smith as Oberon Zell, the founder of the neo-Pagan Church of All Worlds (CAW). During the late 1960s, Zell created an entire religion in St. Louis, Missouri, modeled on and named after Smith's church in *Stranger*. Zell followed the novel's example closely. He organized his movement into nests, adopted the rituals of water-sharing and open sexuality, and centered his new belief system around the Smith's pantheistic dictum, "Thou art God."[5]

During the mid-60s, Zell's band of cultural misfits appeared much like other discontents looking to Heinleinian texts for inspiration. They were anti-authoritarian hippies who embraced the typical staples of 1960s counterculture, including free speech, free love, and drug use, characteristics that made them a thorn in the side of the administration of Zell's alma mater, Westminster College, in Fulton, Missouri. Their presence there is evidence of the extent to which the counterculture, so visible on the East and West Coasts, had penetrated the interior of the country.

Zell and his church members were not ordinary hippies. Before discovering *Strangers*, Zell cut his teeth on the writings of Ayn Rand. Much like Heinlein, Rand used fiction to undermine the Judeo-Christian foundation of American culture. Her novels, *The Fountainhead* (1943), *Anthem* (1945), and *Atlas Shrugged* (1957) each attacked collectivist thought, taking special aim at religion. In its place, Rand erected a libertarian ethics of selfishness that rejected spiritualist metaphysics and prized the primacy of the individual above all else. Deriding any strictures on personal autonomy, whether imposed by traditional morals or the state, Rand's materialist philosophy offered young Americans an alternative to the Judeo-Christian moral consensus. Zell's early infatuation with Rand's libertarian gospel of anti-religious individualism shielded him from the leftist ideology so common among others in the American counterculture. Later in the 1960s, Zell's increasingly mystical outlook led him to favor Heinlein over Rand. During the 1970s, Zell combined Heinleinian elements from *Stranger* with a swath of other occultic themes to become a leader in the emerging neo-Pagan movement. The sexual ethics he and his lovers crafted during these years deeply influenced American polyamory for decades and residual aspects of their contributions still permeate it today.[6]

"Neo-Paganism" is an umbrella term that encompasses several new religious movements that sprang up during the 1960s and 1970s. Closely tied to witchcraft, these diverse traditions share several general commitments, most notably a tendency toward anarchy, pantheism/ polytheism, ecological concern, and goddess worship. Neo-Paganism as a movement often includes the practice of ritual magic, and many of its adherents trace their belief systems back to the old pagan religions of pre-Christian Europe. By the end of the 1960s, Zell's ongoing commitment to neo-Pagan religion prevented him from following the path of so many other ex-hippies who became jaded by the era's unfulfilled utopian promises and eventually returned to the American mainstream. Instead, Zell formulated an enduring form of ethical non-monogamy that persisted long after the optimism of 1960s free love had waned among most of his contemporaries.[7]

Oberon was born Timothy Zell on November 30, 1942. He spent his earliest years with his mother in St. Louis while his father fought in the Second World War. Although he was baptized as a Presbyterian, his family never regularly attended church. Instead, Zell remembered his early religious education coming from the *Childcraft* series of books, published by *World Book Encyclopedia*. He gravitated toward the Greek and Roman mythologies portrayed in those volumes, later claiming that it was that introduction to polytheism that inoculated him from the infection of Christian monotheism. Zell remained fascinated with Greco-Roman mythology throughout his youth and his preoccupation with it sparked his interest in mystery and magic. Soon after, Zell discovered Heinlein's juvenile science fiction stories, which furthered his obsession with nature's secrets. As an adult he fondly remembered mimicking the psychic exercises described in Heinlein's stories, hoping to develop telepathic and telekinetic abilities. An eccentric youth, he did well in school, and, after graduating high school in 1961, he left to study psychology at Westminster College.[8]

It was an early college friend who introduced Zell to both Rand and *Stranger*. Despite feeling out of place in traditional social settings, Zell pledged a fraternity, where he met fellow freshman Lance Christie. Christie, like Zell, initially had difficulty fitting into college life. Their shared sense of alienation drew them together, and they formed a lasting friendship. Christie was an avid science fiction fan raised on Heinlein's juveniles, as well as an adherent of Ayn Rand. Prior to arriving at Westminster, Christie started a high school chess club based closely on the community of innovators described in *Atlas Shrugged*. Upon arriving at college, he set out to establish "Christie House," an institute dedicated to producing Randian self-actualized heroes. He and Zell used one another as a sounding board in their discussions about competing conceptions of what constituted an ideal humanity. Zell's interest in psychology drew him to the work of American psychologist Abraham Maslow. He believed that Maslow's emphasis on self-actualization dovetailed with the concepts he found in Rand, and he joined Christie in his adulation of the Russian novelist. But Christie's dreams of creating an assembly line for Randian supermen were sidelined that first year of college when he encountered a copy of Heinlein's *Stranger*. Both men quickly became obsessed with the book.[9]

Christie received *Stranger* via a science fiction book club in the autumn of 1961. After reading it over Christmas break, he passed it on to Zell. The concepts of nests, water-sharing, grokking, open relationships, non-jealousy, and social nakedness all resonated deeply with him. But, most important, the novel introduced Zell and Christie to the Martian Smith's pantheism. The two felt as though they had found a model that encompassed their social goals and decided to actualize *Stranger's* principles in real life. During the spring of their freshman year, Zell and Christie mimicked the water-sharing ritual, each drinking water and committing always to remain honest with one another. A few weeks later, in May, they shared water with their girlfriends, officially birthing their water-brotherhood.[10]

Zell and Christie sought a name for their new community that symbolized their marriage of Randian and Heinleinian notions. They called their new water-brotherhood, *Atl*, Aztec for water and, according to Christie, a derivative form for the Greek mythological Titan Atlas, the namesake of Rand's infamous novel.[11] The model set by *Stranger* soon enveloped every aspect of the young men's lives. After Zell's girlfriend Martha became pregnant, they married in early 1963. They rented an apartment off campus where they established a "nest." Their home quickly became known for its libertine environment of sexual openness and social nakedness. They even posted a sign for those leaving on the inside of their door, copied straight from the Martian Smith's church that read, "Did You Remember to Dress?"[12]

Despite their free-spirited approach to sexuality, those early years of sexual liberation were not without their hardships. When the birth of their child, Bryan, strained the Zells' relationship, they relied on their open marriage to compensate for what was lost between them. The cold Missouri winters were spent at home, and the summer nights were filled with campfires, skinny-dipping, and an abundance of marijuana. Young and idealistic, they married the counterculture's infatuation with sex and drugs with Heinleinian mysticism and the anti-religious libertarianism they had learned from Rand. The two even adopted the nicknames of Rand's heroes from *Anthem*, Prometheus and Gaia.[13]

Zell followed Rand in her militancy against Judeo-Christian morality. To share their ideas, Atl published an underground newsletter, the *Atlan Torch*, that promoted itself as an organ of free speech and open dialogue. Though the newsletter called for submissions from opposing viewpoints, the *Torch* was highly critical of Christianity, reprinting articles from the likes of British philosopher Bertrand Russell and atheist activist Madalyn Murray (O'Hair). Zell was pointed in his critiques and used *The Torch* to rail against what he believed to be the

destructive history of the Judeo-Christian tradition. Christianity, for
Zell, was irrational dogma, snake oil sold to repress the autonomy of
the individual. It was Christie's position that *The Torch* should be a
neutral place for asking questions, and he even hinted that perhaps
Christianity could be reformed. But his appeal for objectivity did
little to tame the newspaper's largely anti-Christian ethos.[14]

The Torch's anti-authoritarian focus on autonomy gave it a decisively conservative political bent. For example, the first article the
newsletter published was an unabashed call for Barry Goldwater for
president, urging all water-brothers to vote for his nomination. The
article painted Goldwater as a freedom fighter who sought to protect individual liberties against the oppression of an ever-encroaching
state. Critical of fascism, communism, and the New Deal, Christie
later remembered *The Torch* as a means for fighting for student's rights,
promoting free speech, and making fun of campus socialists. "We are
allergic to bigbrotherism," Christie wrote. Whether it was taxes or
censorship, the Atlans had little regard for political oversight.[15]

Soon the combination of *The Torch's* content and Zell's reputation
as a libertine drew him into conflict with Westminster's all-female
sister college, William Woods, which Martha had attended. The newsletter was banned on the Woods campus. This exacerbated the attacks
of its writers, who depicted Woods' administration as infringing on
the rights of its students. Eventually the controversy faded as the administration ceased responding to provocations and Zell moved to
attend graduate school in 1965 at Washington University at St. Louis.[16]

During his first year of graduate study in psychology, Zell decided
that the program's focus on behavioral psychology did not align with
his interests in more humanistic approaches. He left academia the
following year, securing a job as a social psychologist through the
Human Development Corporation, one of President Johnson's War
on Poverty programs. Despite entering the workforce in St. Louis,
Zell remained committed to building the community he and Christie
had founded. The pair remained in close contact, and Zell continued
to contribute to *The Torch*.[17]

By 1966, however, it was becoming apparent that Zell's and
Christie's visions for the future of Atl were beginning to diverge. Over
the following year the co-founders decided to devote themselves to
creating two similar but distinct movements, although they disagreed
over the nature of the split. Zell believed Christie was devoted to
keeping Atl a clandestine organization committed to changing the
world by working outside of the public eye. This was not something
he was inclined to do. Christie remembered things differently. For
him, the split followed naturally from the differences in their personalities, Zell being the more extroverted, communal, and passionate.
Christie's vision for Atl was more of a confederation of lone wolves.
It was not so much that he wished to work undercover as he simply
had no desire to participate in Zell's propensity for "guerrilla theater."
As Christie put it, he was more of a Spock-like figure, while Zell was
more of a Captain Kirk.[18]

Despite his aversion to Zell's growing inclination toward theatrics,
Christie noted that Atl was public in its ongoing ecological work. He
continued to share Zell's metaphysical worldview and a deep commitment to pantheism, self-actualization, and harmony with nature.
But Christie was increasingly uncomfortable with Zell's outspokenness, particularly when it came to sexual liberation. He believed that
most Atlans felt themselves practically, emotionally, and spiritually sa-
tiated with monogamy.[19]

Zell decided to split from Atl in 1967, during the Summer of Love.
Again mimicking the Martian Smith's example, he named his new
splinter organization the Church of All Worlds (CAW). He soon en-
rolled in correspondence courses at Life Science College, a small
Christian seminary in Rolling Meadows, Illinois. After becoming
CAW's High Priest, he received his Doctor of Divinity degree.
Emboldened, Zell reached out to the St. Louis community to seek out
others who shared his intellectual interests and countercultural proclivities. He spoke at beatnik coffee houses on local college campuses,
eventually attracting a small following. In the spring of 1968, CAW
moved into a five-story Victorian mansion, where they constructed a

temple upstairs and ran a coffeeshop out of the basement. In March, CAW's state incorporation was finalized, and later that month they published the first issue of their new magazine, *Green Egg*.[20]

Green Egg quickly became one of CAW's most successful endeavors. Originally a one-page newsletter, the magazine grew over the next decade into one of the country's leading neo-Pagan publications. From its inception, *Green Egg* clearly portrayed CAW's anti-authoritarian ideological heritage. CAW was presented as a life-affirming pagan religion that proclaimed the divinity of all persons while simultaneously rejecting the validity of all formal creeds. There were only three basic commandments: know yourself, believe in yourself, and be true to yourself. New initiates could move up in the church's hierarchy by reading and reporting on a short list of books, most notably *Anthem* by Rand and *Stranger* by Heinlein.[21]

Prior to 1970, CAW's ideology was not religious in any traditional sense. Zell remained deeply critical of the Judeo-Christian tradition in *Green Egg*, just as he had been in *The Atlan Torch*. He had yet to develop an overarching vision to unite his church, and he lacked any desire to create a fixed metaphysical system. The cultivation of homogeneity was antithetical to CAW's ethos. His inclinations at this point are more aptly described as anti-metaphysical. Questions regarding the afterlife were disregarded as inconsequential, and CAW members had diverse and conflicting opinions regarding them. Zell simply wished to promote a combination of Maslowian self-actualization and Randian individualism, loosely held together by a vaguely defined Heinleinian pantheism.

What united CAW members was little more than their shared belief in their own divinity and the pursuit of the individual freedoms that that divinity granted. Beyond that, there was only a rough ethical reasoning that prevented individual liberties from turning into interpersonal abuses. According to Zell, since sin historically meant going against the will of god, and since each person was god, hypocrisy was the only possible sin. Constant betterment of the self was encouraged. The only way fidelity to oneself presented a problem was if it harmed someone else, since that person was also god. Even then, harm of others was not sin, but a crime that had to be dealt with personally between the offender and the offended. While Zell's aggressiveness toward Christianity, as well as his tireless promotion of individualism, continued to sound very Randian, the Heinleinian pantheism that undergirded his worldview set boundaries around what was morally permissible. The Martian Smith's teachings mitigated the potential abusiveness of any Randian underpinnings.[22]

In the early 1970s, CAW underwent an ideological shift that led to its emergence as one of the most influential religious groups within American neo-Paganism. As historian Margret Adler commented,

> The real story of CAW is how contact with the ecology movement and other groups and research into the history of ancient and "primitive" peoples (the worship of Mother Goddess, etc.), transformed into a Neo-Pagan religion an organization originally based on the vision of a science fiction writer, a psychologist, and a right-wing philosopher who hated with a passion all forms of reverence for nature and all forms of religion.[23]

Adler attributes this shift to Zell reading Kerry Thornley's 1966 article, "Functional Religion." Thornley, writing under the pseudonym "Young Omar," focused on the ancient pagan religions that predated Christianity. He not only believed that these inherently countercultural religions were devoid of any strict doctrines or dogmas, but also that they were more congruent with modern scientific discovery than was Christianity.[24]

Thornley's example of a modern pagan religion was Kerista, a loosely organized and libertine new religious movement that sprang up in lower Manhattan in the late 1950s.[25] While Kerista in its early manifestation rejected dogma and advocated for almost unlimited personal freedom, particularly in the sexual sphere, its use as a modern example of an ancient and freeform version of Paganism is ironic given that the religion eventually adopted strict dogmas. Furthermore, Kerista's founder, Jud Presmont, rejected the term. When Zell met Presmont years later, he greeted him as a fellow neo-Pagan leader.

Presmont, annoyed with the designation, rebuffed Zell, claiming instead that he was a genuine Hebrew prophet.[26]

Kerista aside, the application of the term "Pagan" to refer to historical religions that pre-dated Christianity made a significant impact on Zell. Prior to this point, Zell used the word simply to mean non-Christian. After reading Thornley, Zell no longer used it solely as a negation of Christianity but as an umbrella term that positively denoted a host of pantheistic or polytheistic pre-Christian nature religions. Once he embraced Thornley's definition, he began seeking out other like-minded groups.[27]

The most significant influence on CAW's shift was the Los Angeles based neo-Pagan group, Feraferia. While Thornley's ideas structured Zell's conception of Paganism, it was Feraferia that filled it with content. Feraferia's founder, Fred Adams, was both a utopian and a revivalist. Adams believed in the existence of a primordial paradise, free from violence and suffering. During his graduate studies at Los Angeles State in the late 1950s, Adams underwent a religious epiphany that convinced him that the divine was feminine. According to Adams, within the center of existence, there was a nameless maiden referred to as *Arretos Koura*, ancient Greek for the "ineffable bride." He taught that only her worshippers could re-instantiate the primordial paradise that was lost to modern industrial mechanization and violence. It was up to them to usher in a religious reunification with nature and actualize a renewed Luddite, nudist, nonviolent, and vegetarian utopia. Ecology, sensuality, eroticism, and ritual were all bound up in Feraferian theology and sealed with an authoritative appeal to ancient pagan history. Increasingly insistent on the veracity of his teachings, Adams came to require belief in their detailed tenets from all his followers.[28]

Just as Zell was drawn to the idea of pre-Christian religions, most other neo-Pagans saw themselves as reviving an ancient nature religion that was violently suppressed by what they believed was the militant religious coercion of the Judeo-Christian era. This idea was first promoted by Egyptologist and folklorist Margret Murray, who

published *The Witch-Cult in Western Europe* in 1921. Murray concluded
that there existed a highly structured pre-agricultural fertility cult
among the uneducated and rural populace of pre-Christian Europe.
Murray's thesis, since discredited, was briefly influential and laid the
foundation for the myth of a unified pre-Christian nature religion.
Notable among those influenced by Murray was poet Robert Graves
and amateur archaeologist Gerald Gardner, both of whom were integral to the emergence of Wicca and neo-Paganism in England and
the United States. Graves's *The White Goddess* (1948) was an ambitious tome arguing that a pre-Christian tradition of goddess worship
was usurped by the emergence of a rigid and patriarchal Christianity.
Graves also presented a pre-Christian Celtic seasonal cycle represented by the goddess's sacred tree astrological calendar. Later neo-
Pagans adapted various versions of this notion to restructure their
calendar according to festivals correlating with seasonal equinoxes and
solstices. While some scholars have argued that Graves completely fabricated his "tree calendar," its appropriation, particularly in America,
was often based on the fervent desire to throw off the cultural shackles
of Christianity and revive its pagan predecessor in its place.[29]

English amateur anthropologist and archaeologist Gerald Gardner
was also deeply influenced by Murray's thesis. Gardner believed there
was an unbroken line of succession connecting ancient paganism to
the present, and he sought initiation into what he believed was a sur-
viving witch cult with roots stretching back to antiquity. Allegedly
successful, Gardner became a public advocate for the revitalization
of ancient European witchcraft and published several works on the
topic during the 1950s. Although his account of the nature of the
ancient religion differed somewhat from Murray's, Gardner was instrumental in publicizing the old religion's focus on ritual, nature reverence, and goddess worship, and many see him as the grandfather of
modern Wicca. Along with Graves and Murray, Gardner contributed
to the myth of a unified ancient pagan religious tradition replete with
pre-Christian rituals and cosmology. As neo-Paganism in America
emerged in the twentieth century, many of its leaders held fast to this

myth, not only because it produced a sense of historical legitimacy, but also because it provided them with ritualistic and cosmological content. Feraferia was one such manifestation of this tendency.[30]

Fereferia was exactly what Zell was looking for. While Adams's insistence on the veracity of his intricate theological system was much too dogmatic for him, Zell was nonetheless captivated by many of Adams's arguments about the divine feminine, ecology, and ritual. CAW's pantheistic focus on the immanent already made it sympathetic to ecological concerns, and it took little to bring Zell over to full-blown nature worship. He quickly assimilated much of Adams's source material. He followed Adams's appropriation of Graves's "tree calendar" and adopted a new nomenclature for seasons based on pagan festivals that coincided with the solstices and equinoxes. Zell initially hoped to mesh this new liturgical cycle with CAW's preexisting devotion to Heinlein by resetting the first year of the common era to 1961, when *Stranger* was first published. Although CAW did adopt the new pagan seasonal cycle, it did not reset the calendar. Regardless, Zell's newfound liturgy and sense of religious historicity stoked his already communal spirit, and he set out to unite his fellow nature worshippers. By the summer of 1970, CAW partnered with Feraferia to establish the Council of Themis, a non-authoritarian ecumenical coalition of neo-Pagan religions based on a shared commitment to Pagan values such as polytheism/pantheism, ecology, freedom in worship, spiritual eroticism, and sacred myth. Soon other neo-Pagan groups joined the coalition, and, by late 1971, thirty groups had become members.[31]

During the first half of the 1970s, CAW's belief system matured in ways that had a profound and lasting impact on its sexual ethics. These changes were attributable to three major factors. The first was its interaction with other neo-Pagans. By 1970, Feraferia's influence on CAW was explicit within the pages of *Green Egg*, and Zell's newfound commitment to the larger neo-Pagan movement was reshaping his vision for his church.[32] Second, Zell's own theology was rapidly evolving. As eagerly as he appropriated the thought of figures such as Adams and Graves, he was just as committed to adding his own contributions. Finally, Zell's personal relationships intimately affected CAW's development during these formative years.

By the late 1960s, Martha Zell had become uncomfortable with the changes that were taking place within CAW. She did not share her husband's interest in neo-Paganism. While she did not protest outright, she remained largely aloof, electing to remain in another room or to go out on dates when the other members conducted rituals. As she put it, "Tim became more pagan, and I didn't." But the couple's problems ran deeper than Martha's alienation from Zell's new religious orientation. Aside from her general discontent with CAW's direction, Martha was dissatisfied with their open marriage. She was more prone to jealousy than Tim, and, despite her own sexual escapades, she secretly hated their sexual openness. If given the chance, Martha would have both done away with Paganism and embraced monogamy. By contrast, Tim was interested in witchcraft, LSD, and threesomes. As Zell's philosophy toward sex became increasingly melded to his evolving pantheistic theology, the couple's relationship became estranged.[33]

Over Labor Day weekend, 1970, Zell underwent a life-altering experience that cemented his unwavering commitments to neo-Paganism and non-monogamy. He had spent most of the summer reading Graves's *The White Goddess* and engaging in environmental activism. For the first Earth Day, on April 22, 1970, Zell created a presentation of Graves's tree calendar to promote the idea that spirituality and environmental concern were inherently unified. It was there that he met a young "witchy" woman named Julie Carter who became his lover. Eventually, Martha moved out of their house, and Carter moved in. But at the end of that summer, Carter was only eighteen and about to go to off to college. Hoping to show her one last good time before she left, Zell obtained some LSD for them to enjoy together over the holiday weekend. After taking a few hits, they went to the backyard, undressed, looked up to the sky, and waited for the drug to kick in.[34]

Over the next few hours Zell experienced a vision that has defined his thought ever since. According to his own testimony, he saw a cell dividing. He then began to experience time in reverse. He watched the complexity of terrestrial life rewinding, becoming less and less complex until it reached the primordial simplicity of the first living cell. He came to the realization that all life on earth was once condensed into that first cell. The process of its initial division, which resulted in life's present complexity, he likened to the Big Bang. When once again replayed forward, Zell witnessed the construction of all life on earth, from primordial protoplasm through the emergence of divergent species. Evolution was embryology writ large.[35]

After watching the deconstruction and reconstruction of life on earth, Zell reasoned that, just as all the cells within an individual body make up one sentient being, all sentient creatures on earth must aggregately constitute a single being as well. Zell claims that as soon as he came to this realization, he looked down at the atemporal terrestrial drama he was witnessing, and this unified being opened her eyes, smiled, and told him, "Now you know me." Deeply moved, Zell decided to devote the rest of his life to serving this personal, feminine, unified consciousness made up from the conglomerate of all biological life. He had personally met the goddess Adams and Graves had spoken of.[36]

Zell's vision immediately reframed his message. Over the next week Zell composed a written account of his drug-induced revelation and presented a formal sermon to his nest. Many in his congregation were uneasy with this new revelation. Up until that point, CAW was united in its emphatic rejection of anything resembling dogma. Divinity of the individual, self-actualization, and personal responsibility were the only tenets that earned universal assent from CAW members. Many were worried that Zell's revelation might calcify into a normative belief system. They did not want CAW to end up like Feraferia, with dogma and doctrine that members must accept. But Zell was no Fred Adams. He had no intention of creating a rigid belief system or mandating fidelity to his own spiritual revelations, no matter the depth of his personal commitment to them. He was too inclusive. As real as his experience seemed, Zell wished the vision to unify, not divide, his members. Unity in diversity was, after all, the very spirit of its message.[37]

Although Zell refused to enshrine his new belief into CAW scripture, he was not reluctant to use *Green Egg* to espouse his new convictions. During the early 1970s, he published several articles to explain the implications of his new theology. The first of these articles, "TheaGenesis: The Birth of the Goddess," published in the summer of 1971, presented Zell's construction of a unified history and theory of religion. He began by arguing for the subjective truth of all religions. All religions are real in the sense that they deeply affect the behavior and worldview of their respective adherents. However, Zell believed that it was the duty of the individual to strive to uncover as much of the objective world as can be known. Ancient Paganism, he argued, subjectively apprehended the goddess's reality, the truth of pantheism, the importance of seasonal celebrations, and the necessity of nature veneration that flowed from those truths. But lacking the insights of modern science, ancient Pagans could not objectively demonstrate this spiritual knowledge. Twentieth-century science provided new insights into evolution, embryology, and cellular development, affording neo-Pagans scientific tools well beyond those of the Pagans of old. Drawing on his Labor Day vision, Zell argued that the origin of all biological evolution was one primordial cell from which all of life's diversity originated. Just as the cells of an embryo divide, so, too, did this original cell continue to split, each new division specializing along different lines, making up the body of the goddess.[38]

Zell's goddess theology continued to evolve in the following months. He initially referred to her as *Terrabios*, Latin for "earthlife." However, he eventually adopted the name *Gaia*, which was used by British biochemist James Lovelock to refer to the idea that the entire earth was one living organism. Zell had little trouble mapping this new theology onto the Heinleinian pantheism that already undergirded CAW's ethics. He concluded that all nonliving aspects of the planet worked alongside the biosphere to make up the goddess's body. Rocks and minerals were her skeleton, oceans were her blood, the air her breath, and the sun her food. Most significantly, Zell believed that mankind, as the first intelligent species, was intended to constitute the goddess's mind. This was the destiny of humanity. As evolution progressed, Zell believed mankind would become telepathically connected into one unified mind that would have power over natural occurrences such as hurricanes and earthquakes. That was mankind's rightful end, its collective self-actualization. It was the only way for Gaia to mature into the adult form of her divinity. Zell had only to slightly tweak the Martian Smith's statement, "Thou art God," to fit his new revelation. The dictum was no longer merely descriptive, but teleological, referring to any discrete entity within the biosphere. Divinity, Zell came to believe, was the self-actualization of any living thing, whether plant or animal. By participating in their true purpose, all living objects partook in divinity, with the aggregate total of all seemingly discrete beings constituting the goddess.[39]

Zell continued to emphasize the compatibility of Heinleinian pantheism and his new neo-Pagan theology in subsequent months. In the next issue of *Green Egg*, he further elaborated the metaphysical and ethical implications of his vision in another article, "Biotheology: The Neo-Pagan Mission." There he reiterated that Heinlein's ideas could be expanded to encompass this new vision. The term "grok," he argued, should be redefined, once again on teleological grounds, to refer to the self-actualization of individual entities, human or otherwise. To grok was no longer to merely understand something deeply; it was a living thing partaking of its own divinity. Neo-Paganism as a movement was no different. It, too, had a specific purpose. Synthesizing Heinleinian pantheism, Maslowian psychology, and a neo-Pagan view of religious history, Zell concluded that the Christian era had rejected the truth of immanent divinity in its obsession with the transcendent. Like a phoenix, neo-Paganism was rising from the ashes of suppression. With this discovery, however, came great responsibility. The destructive tendencies of mankind were like a cancer in Gaia's brain, preventing humanity from becoming what it was meant to be. It was the duty of the neo-Pagan community to awaken those unaware of their destiny and promote peace and harmony with nature and each other. Grokking, or partaking in the divine, could never be simple assent to occult truth. It was a blueprint for social action.[40]

As Zell developed his Gaian theology, Rand's influence on CAW was waning. While Rand's novels were still included in the expanded reading lists printed in *Green Egg*, Zell's positive commentary on her thought had dramatically diminished. Throughout the early 1970s, her influence remained apparent in the magazine, which often included articles on libertarianism and anarcho-capitalism and even select quotes from *Atlas Shrugged*.[41] But after Zell's goddess vision, Randian notions fell under increasing scrutiny. Years later, Zell reflected on his growing distaste for the Russian author who was once so pivotal to his early thought.

> The further we investigated her thinking, the more we came to see behind the curtain to her appalling racism and anti-environmentalism. Her position that European colonists had the right to develop land stolen from indigenous peoples (whom she referred to as "savages"). . . . Her ferocious advocacy of sexual possessiveness and jealousy. . . . Calling homosexuality "immoral" and "disgusting." Her championing of pollution as an indicator of "progress". . . . Her contempt of all things metaphysical and spiritual. . . . Her general distain towards Pagan values and traditions, and to all things natural. . . . And just her general meanness. . . . It became a case of "know thy enemy."[42]

By the mid-1970s, Zell's gospel of ecological pantheism and spiritualist sexuality was completely at odds with Rand's materialist philosophy.

While Zell's budding belief system drew him further from his Randian foundations, it only reinforced his rejection of monogamy, instilling it with a new sense of divine purpose. He and Julie Carter continued to grow closer, and he regarded her as his second wife. She often published under his last name, though they never had a legalized marriage. Carter was invaluable to Zell during this transitional period, both professionally and personally. A gifted writer and artist, she often wrote for and edited *Green Egg*. Their shared talents, coupled with the romantic nature of their relationship, naturally led the two to collaborate on the meaning of neo-Pagan sexuality. One of the most significant of these joint efforts was a co-authored article, "Erotheology: Sexual Communion as Worship." In many ways, the article was merely an extension of the sexual ethics that already undergirded CAW's practices prior to Zell's goddess vision. It strongly promoted a liberated and libertarian approach to sexuality, citing thinkers such as Maslow, Bertrand Russell, and Heinlein. However, it also drew explicitly on Zell's vision, arguing that a full comprehension of mankind's sensual potential required a knowledge of the goddess.

According to Zell and Carter, the Judeo-Christian focus on reproduction obscured the sensual function of sexual relations, robbing it of its liberating properties. For Christians, the need to have sex constituted a type of carnal slavery, which they interpreted as man's greatest weakness. For neo-Pagans, sex was a means for individuals, or each of Gaia's discrete cells, to transfer libidinal energy from one to another. Because each person is god, as the Martian Smith taught, sex is an act of worship in which individuals intimately partake in the divinity of one another and thus, by extension, the divinity of the goddess. The implication was that monogamy suppresses this energy flow, robbing it of its natural pathways and impeding true worship. Zell argued that sex should be a communal act, tribal, and essential for unity. All consensual sexual acts conducted openly and honestly were inherently good for the community and thus for the goddess.[43]

Armed with their new sexual theology, Zell and Carter worked tirelessly throughout the early 1970s to bring like-minded neo-Pagans together through *Green Egg*. By 1972, the tenth anniversary of Zell and Christie's first water-sharing, CAW was publishing eight issues a year, following the eight Sabbats of the neo-Pagan calendar. *Green Egg* secured a national readership, and Zell made the publication of each issue a communal endeavor by throwing "clothing optional" parties to collate the issues. By midyear, CAW was on its way to becoming the first governmentally recognized neo-Pagan religion, a status that was not easily earned (Figure 1.1).

Zell previously applied for tax exempt status in Missouri but was denied on the grounds that his church was unconcerned with conventional matters of religious significance, including, but not limited to, the existence of heaven and hell, sin, and the afterlife. CAW appealed the decision, seeking the help of the American Civil Liberties Union (ACLU) on the basis of religious discrimination. CAW's recalcitrance gained the attention of local media outlets, which covered its battle against the state. The *St. Louis Globe-Democrat* and the *St. Louis Post-Dispatch* both published articles on the conflict, which Zell reprinted in *Green Egg* to encourage similar activism among the national neo-Pagan community. He and Carter were also invited to appear on local news shows, which gave CAW positive publicity. The legal struggle lasted two years, but, with the help of the ACLU, CAW

Figure 1.1 A "clothing optional collating party" for *Green Egg* magazine, early 1970s.
Photo courtesy of Oberon Zell.

gained tax exempt status in March of 1974. Zell again reprinted the local newspaper report in *Green Egg* for the edification of the larger neo-Pagan community.[44]

During this period Zell also contacted Robert Heinlein. For almost a decade, he had deliberately refrained from reaching out to the science fiction master despite having created an entire religion based directly on his work. But as Zell matured and his confidence increased, he wrote a letter to Heinlein in January of 1972. He was forthright about being intimidated. He admitted that his adulation for his older hero, Rand, had fallen by the wayside upon discovering her true character, and he hoped this would not be the case with Heinlein. Although Heinlein had a reputation for ignoring fan mail, he responded, assuring Zell that, though he never intended *Stranger* to serve as the basis for any new religions, he was not antagonistic toward CAW. As for Rand, Heinlein told Zell that the difference between his work and hers was that he merely wished to ask meaningful questions, whereas she was intent on providing inflexible answers. His novel, he told Zell, was never meant to be a how-to manual for saving the world, but rather a fictional parable meant to provoke thought within the individual. Nonetheless, Heinlein expressed interest in CAW and asked Zell for more information about his church. This sparked an epistolary friendship that lasted for several years. Heinlein read Zell's and Christie's histories of their movement and he even sent Zell money for issues of *Green Egg*. He told Zell that he continued their correspondence because Zell gave as much as he took from their exchange and because *Green Egg* provided him with new perspectives and content that he could not find elsewhere. Despite his interest in CAW and his affinity for Zell, he did not wish Zell to quote him in CAW publications.[45]

Zell's increasing notoriety as a neo-Pagan leader, coupled with the success of *Green Egg*, connected him to a wide range of countercultural eccentrics, some of whom found their way into his inner circle. Many of these thinkers became influential for him as well as *Green Egg*'s wider readership. During the early 1970s, three of these individuals were particularly important to the history of CAW: Robert Rimmer, Robert Anton Wilson, and Diane Moore. Each of them connected Zell to larger communities and furthered the ongoing evolution of CAW's sexual ethics.

Zell met novelist Robert Rimmer while traveling the country to speak at neo-Pagan events. Despite their twenty-five-year age gap, their shared interests made the two fast friends. Rimmer had gained notoriety after he published *The Harrad Experiment* in 1966. The novel, a critique of traditional sexual mores, follows several fictional Ivy League students placed together in an intimate co-ed living arrangement. After graduation, they form a group marriage. The novel sold millions, secured Rimmer's reputation as a literary fixture within the sexual counterculture, and was made into a movie starring Don Johnson in 1973. Rimmer's lesser known first book, *The Rebellion of Yale Merritt*, follows a man who remarries after he is convinced his wife is dead. When he later discovers her to be alive, the man decides that he loves both women and tries to fight laws preventing bigamy. *Proposition 31*, published in 1968, was also Rimmer's fictional plea to amend the legal restraints against multiple marriage.[46]

The preoccupation with marriage reform that permeated most of Rimmer's work arose from his own personal life. He and his wife were a part of a four-person relationship that lasted for over two decades. It was Rimmer's hope that one day he would live in a world that could accept such an arrangement. Although Heinlein thought Rimmer was working in the same vein as Rand, attempting to provide ready-made answers, Rimmer was much less dogmatic and lacked many of Rand's more offensive characteristics. Rimmer donated boxes of his novels to Zell, who then dispersed them among *Green Egg*'s readership. Zell and Rimmer collaborated during the 1970s and went on to become pivotal figures within American polyamory after its mainstream emergence in the 1980s.[47]

Another key figure in *Green Egg*'s early history was Robert Anton Wilson. Wilson, a somewhat enigmatic figure, was a countercultural journalist who worked as an editor at *Playboy*. He was also a libertarian and a mystic. During the 1970s, he popularized the satirical religion known as Discordianism. Discordianism, not unlike CAW in its infancy, rejected the notion that objective religious dogma was knowable. Instead, it promoted the underlying premise that the nature of reality was inherently chaotic. The religion was co-founded by Kerry Thornley, who wrote the paper that initially inspired Zell to adopt the term "Pagan."[48]

Given their shared proclivities, the friendship between Wilson and Zell was natural. Wilson was an agnostic and a libertarian who was drawn to both Zell and Discordianism due to their emphases on individual autonomy and agnosticism concerning the transcendent. His and Zell's interests drew them into the same circles during the early 1970s, and they sometimes attended the same events. The two officially met and became water-brothers at the Annual Gnostic Aquarian Festival in Minneapolis in 1974. From that point on, Wilson became a frequent writer for *Green Egg*. His contributions to the magazine helped preserve CAW's libertarian foundations and promote its newer tendency to marry spirituality and sexuality. CAW's antiauthoritarianism permitted its members to hold diverse political views, which by the mid-70s ranged from Marxism to John Birchism. Wilson's anti-statist skepticism was manifested in articles containing sharp critiques of a host of governmental actions, ensuring that the magazine continued to promote the libertarian ethos reminiscent of its Atlan precursor. In addition, Wilson shared the sentiment that Judeo-Christian puritanism was a plague preventing mankind from living out its true sexual identity in the modern age. Like Zell, Wilson taught that modern Pagans were uniquely equipped to understand the sexual and spiritual implications of modern scientific discovery.[49]

While Rimmer and Wilson proved great assets to Zell both professionally and personally, no one was more influential on Zell and the trajectory of CAW than Diane Moore. Zell met Moore during a time of revelation and expansion as well as great personal difficulties. By 1971, Zell's first wife had remarried, and, influenced by her new Catholic husband, she successfully sued Zell for full custody of their son on the grounds that Zell's nudism made his home unfit. Not long after that, the Council of Themis, which Zell had co-founded with Fred Adams as an ecumenical brotherhood of like-minded neo-Pagans, determined that, because CAW was founded on a science fiction novel, it had no legitimate connection to ancient Paganism and that Zell could no longer possess a leadership role within the group. Even more painful than that betrayal was Julie Carter's departure during the summer of 1973. Carter embraced Zell's open sexuality in ways his first wife, Martha, never could. However, when CAW members shared a sexually transmitted infection after engaging in extended group sex, Carter became irritated. Their fighting escalated, and, when Zell became violent, Carter left. By the summer of 1973, the Council of Themis had disbanded, and Zell was without his son and his partner.[50]

Emotionally distraught, Zell decided to go on a sabbatical. In June of 1973, citing the pain caused by the loss of Carter and his son, Zell resigned from his position as priest of CAW. However, his decision to leave his leadership role did not dim his prestige within the larger neo-Pagan world. He continued to edit *Green Egg* and to accept speaking invitations periodically. That fall, he was invited to give the keynote address on the concept of TheaGenesis at the Gnostic Aquarian Festival in Minneapolis, where he met Diane Moore.[51]

Moore was everything Zell was looking for in a woman, and his recollections of their meeting are almost hagiographical. They were alike in many ways. She was iconoclastic and visionary, with a propensity for witchcraft. Moore had an unstable childhood. Her mother introduced her to Pentecostalism and early on she gravitated toward that form of Christianity. As a child, her father's failing health caused her family to experience financial precarity. After losing their home, they became indefinitely transient. As her father's condition worsened, he became physically abusive. Moore sought refuge in the church, but, after her pastor told her that she and her mother were to submit to her father, even to the point of death, she left the faith. It was then she started reading Ayn Rand and became an outspoken atheist.[52]

While Rand helped cure Moore of her Christianity, she did little to satisfy her innate mystical tendencies. Searching for a body of literature that could meet that need, she made her way through a host of religious and philosophical texts, including Graves's *The White Goddess* and other works that directed her toward ancient pagan goddess worship. Though Moore was not the typical middle-class youth running from the monotony of midcentury suburbia, she, like so many other young discontents during the 1960s, became enchanted with hippie culture and was lured to the West Coast. It was there that she found love and acid. In Big Sur, on the northern California coast, Moore had an acid-induced ecstatic experience that resulted in her lifelong devotion to the divine feminine. The next day, she renamed herself Morning Glory. After a brief stint trying to return to the mainstream, Morning Glory realized such efforts were futile. With her pet boa constrictor in tow, she and a friend set out for San Francisco. Along the way, they picked up a young hitchhiker named Gary who became her first husband and the father of her daughter, Rainbow. The two embraced a hippie lifestyle and had an open marriage.[53]

Gary and Morning Glory eventually found their way to Eugene, Oregon, where they tried, but failed, to establish a hippie commune. While living in an apartment in Eugene, Morning Glory became increasingly aware that she was different from her new family and friends. Neither Gary nor any of her other new friends shared her predilections for witchcraft and the occult. She read tarot and offered small classes on witchcraft locally, but she could never find the community she sought and soon became discouraged. Early in 1973, she learned that a Gnostic Aquarian Festival was happening that fall in Minneapolis. With the encouragement of her husband and her neighbor, she traveled there, hoping to meet other like-minded people.[54]

By both of their accounts, Zell and Morning Glory were deeply connected from the first time they saw each other. She was seeking a priest and he a priestess. Following his keynote address on TheaGenesis, the two spent hours getting to know each other before they declared that they were to be married within the next year. This was tricky, but not impossible, given Morning Glory's open marriage with Gary.

While Morning Glory had decided not to return to Gary, she had no intention of coupling up solely with Zell. She confessed her innate aversion to monogamy.

> I must be honest with you, I can never be in a monogamous relationship; for one thing I already have a family. Monogamy is just not in my nature and I don't want to deceive you. I want to be free to have other lovers, and you're free to do that as well. I'll give you my whole heart and soul, but I cannot give you monogamy. There are other people in my life, and there always will be other people. Yet what we have is special and unique beyond any measure; nothing will take away from that.[55]

Despite her fears, Morning Glory had little to worry about. She and Zell were in perfect agreement. He had found a woman who shared both his passion for magic and his vision for the way intimacy should function. Morning Glory, along with Rainbow and her boa constrictor, followed Zell back to St. Louis from Minneapolis. Her presence rejuvenated Zell, who resumed his position as High Priest of CAW. While she still cared deeply for her husband Gary, she knew she would always feel out of place living around people who did not share her occultic interests.

Despite the excitement sparked by her newfound circle of friends, Morning Glory did not take well to life in St. Louis. The nest offered little privacy, and she missed the rural freedom of the Pacific Northwest. She knew this would likely be the case and, among her stipulations for moving to St. Louis, was that Zell would eventually accompany her west. She took solace in the fact that Missouri would not be their home forever. In the meantime, Morning Glory immersed herself in Gaian theology and wedding plans (Figure 1.2).[56]

Tim and Morning Glory were married on April 14, 1974, at the Gnostic Aquarian Festival where they had met the previous year. A public event held on a Sunday afternoon at the local Holiday Inn, the wedding ceremony consisted of a neo-Pagan "handfasting" rite

Figure 1.2 Tim Zell and Morning Glory engaging in a pagan ritual just after their first meeting. St. Louis, Missouri, 1973.
Photo courtesy of Oberon Zell.

the two created together. The ritual incorporated neo-Pagan traditions alongside the Heinleinian elements so dear to CAW. The couple came together in a consecrated circle before a High Priest and High Priestess. After declaring their devotion to the goddess and each other, they exchanged rings. They then pierced their hands with a knife and united them together, mingling the blood. Afterward, they each fed the other a piece of bread, declaring to one another, "Thou art God" and "Thou Art Goddess," respectively. Then they shared water. Finally, they pledged in unison that, upon one of their deaths, the dead would live on in the survivor's body, partaking in the greater consciousness they had co-conceived together.[57]

The marriage rite culminated in a four-day celebration reported on by local newspapers. Never one to miss out on an opportunity for positive publicity, Zell welcomed the coverage. He plugged CAW as a holistic, ecological, goddess-centered alternative to Western culture that simultaneously prized both individual autonomy and responsibility.[58] Morning Glory, on the other hand, used the media attention to promote the sexual dimension of their religious views. In an interview with the *Minnesota Daily*, she explained the nature of their intimacy.

> We are marrying to declare before all the world that we are one with each other, but there is also room in our lives for more than just us. . . . We see ourselves as the beginning of a collective consciousness—like two raindrops coming together. The more raindrops you add, the larger the pool becomes. There's no limit to how many people can share consciousness. In this context, monogamy isn't even in the running.[59]

Events soon put Morning Glory's philosophy to the test. Just as it was time to consummate the marriage, a chronic stomach condition she suffered from flared up. Initially unable to engage in the intimate act, she invited three other women from their inner circle into their marital bed to act on her behalf. According to Morning Glory, the positive energy generated by the foursome her new husband was enjoying alleviated her pain, and she was eventually able to join, making it five.[60]

Over the next few months, Morning Glory deeply immersed herself into her new role within CAW, preparing to become a Priestess. She became a frequent contributor to *Green Egg* and was officially ordained on August 3, 1974.[61] For the next year, she co-edited *Green Egg* with Zell and collected articles that brought together libertarian and ecological ideals with neo-Pagan sacred sexuality.[62] Sharing her husband's ecumenical spirit, Morning Glory wrote favorably about other similar traditions, such as Discordia, which she judged to be CAW's natural allies. Despite being happy in her marriage and with her new role within CAW, Morning Glory remained discontent with life in St. Louis. In November of 1975 she reminded Zell of his promise to move west. He quit his job and bought an old school bus they painted red and named the Scarlett Succubus. He slowly rebuilt the interior and the engine, turning it into a motor home. That following May the

Zells heeded what *Green Egg*'s new editor, Tom Williams, poetically referred to as "the siren call of the Western Lands."[63]

After the Zells' departure from St. Louis, CAW continued to publish *Green Egg* under Williams's leadership. The Zells contributed to the publication as they embarked on the next phase of their adventures together. However, without Tim's direction and standing within the larger neo-Pagan world, the magazine soon lost momentum. In mid-1977, Williams published the last issue of *Green Egg* before he, too, decided to move west. More than a decade later the Zells would resurrect the influential magazine. In the meantime, they focused on building a new life and gaining CAW adherents in the west. They lived in hippie communes, made friends with other neo-Pagans, and continued to live out their ecologically informed sexual theology, disseminating CAW's ideas on the West Coast and taking many new lovers along the way.[64]

Margret Adler has described the death of *Green Egg* as a tremendous blow to the vitality of neo-Paganism that took years for the movement to overcome.[65] Though CAW outlasted the magazine, the Zells' sabbatical from publishing undoubtedly robbed the community of a consistent organ for promoting both shared values and opposing viewpoints. However, the Zells' attenuated influence continued in the absence of *Green Egg*, and neo-Paganism persisted as a countercultural movement.

The evolution of the CAW's ideology throughout the 1960s and 1970s is emblematic of the counterculture's innate desire to rebuild a new American society. CAW's search for a sexual ethics built on a foundation other than Judeo-Christian morality did not lead to a rejection of religion. Instead, its eclectic marriage of libertarianism, interpersonal psychology, environmentalism, pantheism, and goddess worship, united by a church modeled on a science fiction novel, exemplifies the religious pragmatism common to the American counterculture of the 1960s and 1970s.[66] This pragmatism shielded CAW from dogma while allowing it to rethink the relationship between the immanent and the transcendent, collapsing the two together. If men and women were divine, then sex was true worship and monogamy must be jettisoned. Such a perspective was palatable to many who were not yet ready to give up on the fleeting sexual idealism of the 1960s. CAW then normalized this religious form of ethical non-monogamy within neo-Paganism a decade before polyamory emerged as a coherent set of ideas.

2

Communes

It used to throw people for a real loop. On the one hand, here were
these people who were into this radically new family structure . . . on
the other hand, they were puritanical in a lot of their sexual attitudes.

—Eve Furchgott, "The Erotic Evolution of Kerista" (1987)

The year 1967 marked the high tide of hippiedom. That summer, an estimated 100,000 young hippies descended on San Francisco's Haight-Ashbury district to promote peace, unity, LSD, and free love as panaceas for the nation's sins of violence and prejudice. Branded the "Summer of Love," the event was covered by both national and underground media, further cementing the Bay Area's reputation as the epicenter of American counterculture. Nonetheless, contemporary onlookers, as well as recent scholars, have noted the adverse effects of such national attention on the idyllic utopianism of hip. The influx continued over the following months. By fall of 1967, the rapid arrival of thousands more American youths in this one neighborhood was already compromising visions of a new, free, and detached community. Along with the rush of newcomers came the larger social problems of violence, homelessness, and poverty, which were only exacerbated when the influx of hard drugs, including cocaine, speed, and heroin, began to replace earlier psychedelics. To make matters worse, the national attention further undermined hippies' aims as their ideas were co-opted and commodified by the mainstream. In response to such events, that autumn, the Diggers, an anarchist collective of hippies famous for their promotion of free services and socially critical "guer-illa theater," famously led a march in San Francisco, burning a casket filled with hippie memorabilia and declaring the "death of hip."[1]

After the death of hip, young hippies were often left feeling as though their social movement had failed to deliver on its promises. Many fell victim to violence and drug addiction. Most reintegrated back into the American mainstream. Others doubled down on their commitment to creating a new society. The countercultural ethos of the previous decade had spawned tens of thousands of communal experiments where hippies isolated themselves from larger society to perfect further their visions of a novel American utopia. After the deterioration of the Haight and the waning of hippiedom from the public eye, many of these communities continued to thrive, and many others formed. Within these communities, the countercultural im-pulse to experiment with sex, religion, and drugs continued.[2]

The communal experience became integral not only to the preser-vation of hip, but also foundational to the evolution of polyamorous thought. Communes provided isolated spaces where rudimentary no-tions of free love could be tested and reshaped into more coherent and enduring ethical systems. Within these spaces, residents forged many of polyamory's foundational concepts, seeking to build further on the foundations of sexual and religious experimentation that they had already laid.

The Church of All Worlds (CAW) may have been the most ardent countercultural appropriation of Robert Heinlein's concepts, but it was not the only one. Also significant for American polyamory was the San Francisco-based religious commune, Kerista. Kerista during the 1960s was a bulwark of drug use and free love, with a vaguely re-ligious overtone. Heinlein mentioned Kerista in a letter to his agent after one of its satellite groups contacted him to speak at one of their meetings. While he was no doubt intrigued, particularly by the asser-tion that some of its adherents accepted *Stranger* as their scripture, he declined their offer.[3] Although some Keristans looked to Heinlein's work as authoritative during this period, this was hardly true for all.

Kerista prided itself on its rejection of dogma to a degree that rivaled CAW. However, while CAW retained its anti-dogmatism, Kerista followed a very different path.

Kerista's history can be divided into two distinct eras. Its first manifestation, referred to as the "Old Tribe," existed throughout the late 1950s and 1960s, when the Kerista was a free-form hippie religion. During the 1970s, its leader, Jud Presmont, revamped it into a rigorously structured religious commune with an extended list of rigid dogmas. Keristans refer to this era, which lasted from 1971 to 1991, as the "New Tribe." Over this period, the commune became increasingly exclusive, isolating itself from any potential countercultural allies just as polyamory began to emerge as a coherent set of ideas. Nonetheless, Kerista's tireless promotion of ethical non-monogamy made it preeminent in the history of polyamorous thought. Though the commune failed to take a central role among polyamorous activism during the 1980s, its ideas permeated polyamory as influential polyamorists adopted Keristan concepts and inserted them directly into a coalition of which Kerista wanted no part.

As with many new religious movements, Kerista arose from the ecstatic vision of a charismatic leader. Its founder, Jud Presmont, or Brother Jud as he was commonly known, had served as an Air Force officer during the early 1950s. After receiving an honorable discharge, he turned his attention to religion, philosophy, and drugs. In 1956, while smoking marijuana and reading various religious and philosophical texts, Jud heard a voice telling him he was to establish a new religion. The voice assured him that he was going to become the "Pied Piper who would pull out the Swinging People."[4] Jud claimed he was initially skeptical of the voice. However, after it reassured him of his prophetic role and inevitable success, he began proselytizing throughout Manhattan's Lower East Side. He soon adopted the title of the Prophet of Kerista and began preaching a gospel of interracial free love and drug use. One of these tenets proved particularly problematic when Jud was arrested for large-scale marijuana possession in the fall of 1958. Despite this initial setback, he continued proclaiming his message after his release from jail. His gospel found fertile ground, and he rapidly attracted new followers throughout the early 1960s.[5]

While the day-to-day lives of early Keristans are not as well documented as their New Tribe counterparts, the Old Tribe was heavily influenced by the larger countercultural ethos of the 1960s. Equality and autonomy were the most basic of the early Keristan concepts. As one believer put it, "Kerisa *is* freedom and love." Beyond these abstract ideals, the Old Tribe maintained deep commitments to racial equality and sexual freedom. Jud was involved in many interracial relationships, and his community later prided itself on its interracial children.[6]

From its inception, Kerista rejected monogamy. Yet the Old Tribe's commitment to sexual freedom extended even to those who did not share a desire for promiscuity. They accepted monogamous couples and boasted at one point of having a member who was a virgin. However, most Keristans were non-monogamous, and Old Tribe members were infamous for their bisexuality and their practice of group sex. In a 1965 interview with Robert Anton Wilson, Jud claimed that Kerista was about total and complete sharing, both economical and sexual. He confirmed that most Keristans were bisexual and described the mutual consent of adults as the only requirement for ethical sexual engagement. Beyond that basic rule, there was little cohesion within the Old Tribe's ideology. Even when Kerista's lack of normative dogma began to concern Jud, he was unable to lay out anything resembling a fixed orthodoxy. An early attempt to fashion a list of tenets resulted in little more than an argument for the legalization of societal taboos such as abortion, miscegenation, group sex, polygamy, sodomy, homosexuality, and even incest. However, individual Keristans were not required to agree even on those beliefs. To enforce such adherence would undermine the autonomy of the individual.[7]

Old Tribe members could sexually engage with anyone they wished both within and without its circle of members. This was not the case with the New Tribe. One member of the Old Tribe was surprised to hear of the accretion of sexual rules and prohibitions that later defined Kerista, lamenting that when he was a member in the early 1960s "there was only one rule, and it wasn't so much a rule as it was a state-ment of truth: People don't belong to people." Of course, even before the onset of the AIDS epidemic, promiscuity often came at a price. Sex with outsiders meant that early Keristans often dealt with the oc-casional outbreak of pesky, if curable, sexually transmitted infections. Despite such perils, their commitment to individual liberty meant that the Old Tribe embraced a wide array of sexual orientations and practices. At least in theory, this meant that both sexual coercion and prohibitions were absent.[8]

The Old Tribe's laissez faire attitude meant that they were lax in screening their new members. This combination of open sexuality and minimal vetting added to Kerista's popularity. During the early 1960s, it spread from the Lower East Side of Manhattan to other major cities such as Chicago, Boston, Los Angles, and San Francisco, with Jud's message often breaching bohemian circles and bleeding into the ranks of middle-class college students. As Kerista spread, it attracted the attention of influential countercultural figures such as beatnik Allen Ginsberg. Ginsberg, who became enamored with Kerista dur-ing the 1960s, described it "as a bell that was heard all over the Lower East Side . . . and reverberated to San Francisco as a possibility for a new society."[9]

The Old Tribe's initial openness carried with it a downside. Its ability to draw attractive and sexually liberated young women meant that it was a magnet for young men who were often more inter-ested in having sex than building a utopia. One member recalled a young man who barely spent a few weeks in the community. During that short time he devoted himself to having sex with twenty or so women before moving on, without lending any aid to the cause. The threat of seedy characters and venereal infections vexed Jud, eventu-ally causing him to tighten up membership screening.[10]

Just as the Old Tribe promoted unbridled sexuality, they also em-braced the drug culture typically associated with 1960s liberation. Jud's initial vision occurred under the influence of drugs, and he continued to encourage the marriage of spirituality, sexuality, and intoxication

within the early community. One account recalled several couples
sitting around an idol, imbibing wine and smoking marijuana to ease
into a group sex session. When asked about the ritual, one young
girl casually described it as something that occurred a couple times a
week and felt completely natural. While the presence of harder drugs
was always present on the periphery, speed, cocaine, and heroin appear
to have been discouraged. Alcohol, marijuana, and a wide assortment
of hallucinations were either widely accepted or encouraged.[11]

As with their sexual practices, the Old Tribe's religious commitments were pluralistic and democratic. Jud was their prophet, bringing
a new religion made palatable by the burgeoning sexual revolution.
But individual members were able to draw on a host of philosophical concepts and religious texts to come to their own truths. While
this openness produced diversity of religious belief within the Old
Tribe, there were certain practices that functioned to promote uni-
formity. One of the most interesting was the Old Tribe's use of what
they called the "alphabet board," which functioned much like a Ouija
board. Initially members did not expect much to come from the practice, but, as time went on, the ritual gained traction and members
asked the board questions about a host of topics, from the spiritual
to the mundane. Many Keristans believed that diverse spirits, including those of deceased celebrities, guided them through the board's
messages. During the mid-60s the Old Tribe began the practice of
taking new names given to them by the alphabet board. One by
one, current members adopted communal pseudonyms they derived
from the board, while new members received their new names upon
initiation.[12]

The alphabet board and the acceptance of communal names promoted a sense of ritualistic cohesion among early Keristans that its
amorphous ideology failed to impart. However, there was a divisive
aspect to the practice as well. One member recalled that on the very
first night the board was used, it singled out roughly thirty people who
it deemed wastes of communal energy that should be evicted from
the group. Jud obliged the board, or more likely the board obliged

him. Either way, those members were expelled. This set a precedent. Over time, the alphabet board was used as a means of deciphering members' commitment to the group. Thus, the alphabet board functioned both to instill a sense of communal unity and to serve as a check in Keristan purity.[13]

By the late 1960s, Jud's hands-off leadership style gave way to a more unified vision. He tired of New York and wished to relocate. He initially looked to Berkeley as a potential location for a new headquarters. Given Berkeley's countercultural climate at the time, it seemed ideal. However, Jud possessed an inexplicable conservative streak for someone radical in so many other respects. Perhaps due to his earlier military service, Jud was an unwavering supporter of the Vietnam War. Unsurprisingly, this alienated many of his countercultural brethren who might otherwise have heeded his message. After deciding that Berkeley might not be the best fit, Jud turned his attention to establishing an island commune. In 1965, he aligned himself with an amateur sociologist, Desmond Slattery, who aided him in making his dream of an island utopia a reality. They eventually settled on Honduras, where they hoped to establish an idyllic get-away that would attract free love hippies. They believed the fees they charged visiting hippies and swingers would sustain the endeavor and legitimize Jud's prophetic position as the "Pied Piper who will pull out the swinging people."[14]

It was not just Jud's growing utopianism that made leaving the country seem like a good idea. The previous fall he and eighteen of his fellow Keristans had been arrested on charges of immorality and narcotics. According to *The New York Times*, Jud told the police that one of his main goals was to establish a colony to grow legal marijuana. Unfortunately for Kerista, such outspokenness earned the community ongoing police surveillance that severely hampered its members' activities. After serving a ten-month jail sentence, Jud, along with several of the original members, moved to Honduras. However, due to a combination of financial stress and interpersonal complications that accompanied the practice free love, the island excursion quickly came to an end. By 1971, Jud was in San Francisco, estranged from the Old Tribe's inner circle as well as his wife and children.[15]

Jud relocated in the Haight-Asbury district and redoubled his efforts to create a utopian commune. He had learned hard lessons from his previous failures and knew that any new sustainable incarnation of Kerista must incorporate fail-safes to prevent it from sharing the same fate as the Old Tribe. To implement such protections, he fine-tuned his message. He could jettison drugs at this point, at least officially, but he was not ready to embrace monogamy. Instead, he set out to create a new dogma that could save sexual freedom from the divisiveness, jealousy, and other emotional turmoil associated with free love. In the meantime, he needed new followers.[16]

Relocating to San Francisco was a calculated risk. On the one hand, the Bay Area was a veritable hothouse of countercultural activity and there were plenty of potential adherents ready to embrace new mixtures of spirituality and sexual liberation. Yet, Jud's more conservative views remained at odds with most of his possible converts' political sensibilities, just as they had when he previously pondered moving there. Nonetheless, he was adept at harnessing the disappointment shared by many that the radicalism of the 1960s had failed to deliver the personal fulfilment and systematic change it had promised. Jud was able to rebrand his message as a practical plan for implementing real-world change. By doing this, he attracted several key followers who proved extremely valuable in promoting his quickly evolving visions of utopia.

Jud's first convert, Eve Furchgott, was archetypical of the seeker to whom Jud wished to appeal. Smart, young, and attractive, Furchgott, who went by the name Even Eve, was the daughter of Nobel Prize–winning biochemist Robert Furchgott. She had spent the late 1960s as a hippie high schooler in Vermont and was bored with mainstream society. After graduating from high school, she tried to find fulfilment locally, experimenting in communal life throughout the Northeast before venturing to San Francisco in 1971. When she arrived on the West Coast, Eve was disappointed not to find the vibrant and unified hippie community she sought, but instead a divisive culture wracked by commercialization and heroin abuse. Turned off by Haight-Asbury's hollowness, she pondered what to do. Most of her friends had either fallen victim to drug addiction or reintegrated into the mainstream. Disillusioned, Eve considered capitulating to her parents' desire for her to come home and live a normal life. Just before giving up on discovering the community she sought, she met Jud. Encouraged by his promises, Eve decided to stay in San Francisco. Soon she was joined by a high school friend, another hippie discontent who went by the name of Bluejay Way. With the addition of Eve and Way, Jud resurrected Kerista as the New Tribe. Others soon followed, and the small first group of converts adopted the name The Purple Submarine (Figure 2.1).[17]

One of the first things Jud did to prevent the problems that plagued the Old Tribe was to prohibit free love. But the New Tribe had no intention of reverting to monogamy; sexual liberation was a core tenet

Figure 2.1 Kerista in San Francisco, 1978. From left to right: Jud, Geo, Pep (front), Lil (behind), Eve, Way, and Azo.
Photo by David Gallo. Communal Societies Collection, Hamilton College.

of what Jud and his new followers found appealing about American counterculture. To protect themselves from the emotional and physical perils of indiscriminate sexual engagement, the New Tribe agreed that sex was only permissible with other Keristans. This dictum, they believed, would serve to combat loneliness and deepen interpersonal relationships within the group while insulating them from the unwanted consequences of unbridled promiscuity. To solidify this commitment, Eve and her friends coined the term "polyfidelity," meaning that members of the New Tribe could have many lovers so long as they were faithful, or fidelitous, to the group.[18]

Jud liked the stability that polyfidelity brought to the group and decided that more rules were needed to ensure the commune's sustainability. He turned to the Old Tribe's trusted alphabet board to help in his task. The alphabet board laid out a blueprint for the New Tribe's religion. It advised the Keristans to cease drug use and focus on achieving the happiness that only proper religion could provide. It proclaimed that, while every detail of life was predestined, the Keristans should act as though they had free will. Righteous morality was essential to establishing utopia on earth, and religious communalism was the key to happiness. Only those living communally could achieve true contentment. It assured them that they were unique in their religious insight; no other group possessed the knowledge and truth that they did. To spread this truth, they were to focus on recruiting non-monogamous singles, whom they should admit one by one, excluding transient individuals or anyone committed to monogamy. Because romance bred division and jealousy, they must reject it in favor of rational, utopian ideals. To ensure that preferential treatment between members never occurred, the Keristans taught that group members were best friends, not romantic partners. They used the term "best friend identity cluster" (BFIC) to describe their communal arrangement. All relationships were to be egalitarian, and anyone unwilling to reject romantic attachments in favor of a rational commitment to the group's shared vision of egalitarian polyfidelity must be removed.[19]

Beyond forfeiting romantic attachments, each Keristan was required to confront and work out any contradictions that existed between Keristan ideals and personal opinions and behavior. Divided
interests were not tolerated, and anyone not completely committed
must be cut off. In stark contrast to the Old Tribe's free-form ethos,
the alphabet board lauded the cultivation of these fixed standards
and behavioral norms. It counseled that, while the Keristans should
keep the specifics of their religion esoteric, they would inevitably become a moral prototype for the world. Through the organic spread
of polyfidelitous communalism, Kerista would create a global utopia.
The board even presented the Keristans with a new term, "compersion," which they defined as "the positive emotion that comes from
seeing one's partners enjoying themselves together, the antithesis of
jealousy."[20]

In addition to establishing the basic framework of Keristan religious orthodoxy, the alphabet board sessions also conveyed Kerista's,
or rather Jud's, conservative political convictions. One session's log
focused on the likelihood of war with Russia. Despite affirming the
reality of such a danger, it warned against contacting the Department
of Defense, telling the Keristans that the government was unable to
provide sanctuary at a time of threat. Instead, it told them that it was
their patriotic duty to spread Keristan utopianism globally to thwart
the totalitarian menace. In the end, their utopian dream would prevail,
and communism would never overtake free enterprise. Emboldened
by the transcendent authority afforded by the alphabet board, the
Keristans passionately embraced their new gospel that brought sex,
psychology, capitalism, and religion together in a neatly packaged utopian communalism (Figure 2.2).[21]

As Kerista's ideology matured, its members shifted their focus toward evangelization. Most of their endeavors were devoted to outreach, and spreading the message of utopian communalism came
to define every aspect of Keristan life. They put on plays, seminars,
and talks throughout the Bay Area and published several newsletters,
pamphlets, and journals. By 1973, they were publishing *Far Out West*

Figure 2.2 A Keristan "alphabet board" ritual, San Francisco, California, 1978.
Photo by David Gallo. Communal Societies Collection, Hamilton College.

Comics, a comic strip illustrated by Furchgott to promote polyfidelity, as well as a more expansive publication, *Storefront Classroom*, that explicated Keristan ideology while addressing a host of relevant contemporary issues, from abortion rights to ecological concerns.[22]

Members found that minute controls were put on their personal and sexual lives. Healthy diets were mandatory; sweets, junk food, and excessive servings of meat were all prohibited. Outside interests deemed unhealthy or distracting were also not allowed. The Keristans' fear of romantic attachment caused them to institute a strict sleeping schedule whereby each member rotated nightly among all the others of the opposite sex. A more pessimistic view of the implementation of the sleeping schedule might take into consideration the fact that, by the time Jud had established the New Tribe, he was already in his late forties. Many of his restless hippie converts, men and women alike, were still very young and attractive. Jud may have implemented such a rule to ensure that he received as much "horizontal time" as the other members. This perspective is supported by Bluejay Way later telling a prospective convert that one of Jud's previous attempts to instate a sleeping schedule had resulted in his lover telling him she wanted to spend his night with someone else. Jud allowed it, but their relationship soon ended. Nevertheless, the official narrative of the sleeping schedule's significance was that it was a mechanism to promote even connections between members and to purify the community of the uncommitted. If a member did not want to sleep with another member, that person's commitment to Kerista was quickly called into question, and expulsion was a likely outcome.[23]

The meaning behind the sleeping schedule is debatable, but it was undeniable that Keristan theologizing on the principles laid forth by the alphabet board affected their religious outlook and sexual behavior. The alphabet board revealed that all of life's details were predetermined. Like many other religions based on determinism, the Purple Submariners quickly became adept at extrapolating from that starting point. The Keristans touted their religion as a unique blend of pantheism, science, freedom, and rationality that had divine origins. By this time, they referred to their benevolent deity as Allah, defining him as reality's consciousness. Bluejay Way wrote that Keristan utopianism was the commitment to a universal intelligence that teleologically ordered and guided all of existence. This marriage of pantheism and determinism was hard for some to swallow, and some detractors later pointed out that, given the existence of suffering in the world, such notions implied that Allah could not be benevolent. But such critiques caused few Keristans to doubt their faith.[24]

The teleology that undergirded the Keristans' determinism infiltrated all aspects of their lives, particularly sex. In the autumn of 1975, the Keristans published their "social contract." They heralded the document, which defined correct behavior within the group, as one of the most important documents in human history. The contract was initially composed of thirty-eight standards that new initiates must accept before becoming a Keristan. Included were a lifelong commitment to rational pantheism, accountability to the group in thought and actions, a balanced diet, shared parenting, democratic decision-making, and maintaining a good sense of humor. It also mandated that the Keristans must agree to what the social contract deemed "orthodox heterosexual relationships." Here it prohibited masturbation, public affection, voyeurism, homosexuality, sex toys, and both oral and anal sex. Sex, the contract proclaimed, was to be between a man and a woman, pure, and devoid of lust and desire. The misuse of sexual organs or the addition of sexual "additives," such as toys, compromised its purpose. The contract even dictated that Keristans were only to have sex in positions that were front facing so as not to degrade those engaged in the act. The contract stood in complete contrast to the Old Tribe's laissez faire approach to sexuality, a fact that Jud did not like to admit.[25]

By the mid-1970s, anyone who deviated from any of Kerista's quickly multiplying tenets was deemed unfit for intimacy, both intellectually and sexually. Although the social contract served as a barrier protecting the commune from uncommitted outsiders, the Keristans needed a stronger mechanism to ensure that members already among their ranks remained pure. To meet this need, they supplemented the alphabet board with a self-directed group counseling method that they termed "Gestalt-o-Rama." The name "Gestalt" was taken from a subbranch of psychology that originated in Germany in the second decade of the twentieth century. The philosophical foundations of Gestalt psychology reach back to the Kantian notion that the mind inherently orders individual subjective perceptions of the world. It is not surprising that the Keristans were drawn to such an approach. When pressed on the epistemological axioms of their belief system, Jud and his followers admitted that, while there was no scientific basis for belief in an intelligent designer that governed and ordered the cosmos, the belief made practical sense. Jud lauded Kant for critiquing the search for a scientific explanation of religion while eagerly accepting his deontological, or duty-based, approach to ethics. Following such an example allowed Keristans to remain epistemologically pragmatic in their religious speculations when it suited them, while remaining unbending in their normative ethics.[26]

The form of Gestalt psychology that the Keristans adopted was not derived directly from its original sources. The original form of Gestalt psychology made few inroads into American academia or mainstream culture. Instead, a derivative of the Gestalt approach, called "Gestalt therapy," was popularized by German-born immigrant and counter-cultural psychologist Fritz Perls. Gestalt therapy appropriated its predecessor's emphasis on the individual's role in organizing the chaos of the external world into a coherent subjective whole. Perls emphasized the active role the individual played in creating their experience. Gestalt therapy highlighted the contact between the therapist and patient, focusing on how a patient can actively transcend current anxieties, or blocks, rather than on the past traumatic experiences that may have caused those maladies. The original founders of Gestalt psychology repudiated Perls's version of Gestalt therapy. While they believed the mind ordered the world, they still attributed this to automatic neurological processes.[27]

Upon arriving in America, Perls made his way to the famed Esalen Institute in California's Big Sur, where he took up residence and began teaching and lecturing. During the 1960s and 1970s, Gestalt therapy became known as an approach to self-discovery, mixing psychoanalysis with existential philosophy. The American counterculture enthusiastically adopted it, with many who lacked any formal psychological training taking up the mantle of Gestalt therapist. When the Keristans referred to the intellectual foundations of their Gestalt process, it was Perls they cited.[28]

The Gestalt-o-Rama process was based on the presuppositions of Gestalt therapy but injected it with a specifically Keristan flavor. The process was intended to function as an in-house method to work out any perceived intellectual or behavioral discrepancies members might manifest. Any member could call upon another to defend minute thoughts and actions in front of the group. If taken to task, the member in question had to engage in a high level of open and honest verbal expression to purge any signs of internal contradictions, duplicity, or irrationality. If the member declined, the Keristans initiated a time of "graceful distancing" during which that individual could either repent or leave the group on their own accord. If they failed to do either, the community could simply vote them out. This increasingly intense drive for purity bred a relentless atmosphere of self-reflection and interpersonal interrogation. Not only was refusal to comply with the Gestalt-o-Rama process grounds for dismissal, but the Keristans also interpreted any failure to point out problems in others as a lack of dedication to the process and thus to the community.[29]

Despite its supposed good intentions, Gestalt-o-Rama proved a brutal process. It tended to entail pointed attacks on an individual's character, with interlocutors oscillating between affirmations that the individual in question should remain within the community and assertions that they were unfit. According to one ex-member, the process often mirrored the alphabet board's tendency to constantly undermine various members' commitments to the commune. Inherently aggressive, it often turned into group bullying sessions. Some less optimistic Keristans interpreted the process as a power play used specifically by Jud to maintain control over the rest of the commune. One ex-member lamented Jud's abuse of authority, recalling "the worst thing about Kerista was the endless nighttime gestalts, with someone . . . about anything."[30] Another ex-Keristan completely rejected the practice as an avenue for positive, two-sided communication, writing,

> A few select individuals of that group (far from all, just a few) had no problem justifying the expression of anger toward my person, but if I in turn expressed anger in return, here would come brother Jud, insulting my intelligence by implying anger was some kind of hideous character flaw, as if such things were only expressed by the mentally weak and retarded, and I would be tossed into yet another abusive gestalt session.[31]

Whatever its shortcomings, Gestalt-o-Rama quickly became synonymous with Keristan praxis. The Keristans believed it was the essential methodology for achieving both communal and individual perfection.

Armed with the social controls afforded by the alphabet board, the social contract, and the Gestalt-o-Rama process, Jud was able to focus on working out the specifics of his plan to spread Kerista throughout the world. This proved no easy task. The rigidity of the Keristan system, coupled with Jud's political conservatism, continued to turn off many would-be initiates. By the second half of the decade, many Keristans realized that their approach was too intense for most and that they were alienating potential members. To recoup their losses, they back-tracked on their prohibitions against oral sex and foreplay, hoping to make their message more palatable. Jud even committed to trying to be less abrasive and agreed to accept like-minded people who held slightly differing views. His inner circle, however, questioned if that was possible. Nonetheless, he knew that reaching a wider audience was essential to Kerista's success. In the summer of 1976, the Keristans wrote in *The Storefront Classroom* that they were focusing their ef-forts on researching economics and communicating with other indi-viduals who possessed the psychological freedom to reject romance and monogamy and embrace cooperative communalism. They were building an urban-rural "Eco-Village" in San Francisco and wanted to create a complex of centers that offered a wide array of services, including art, education, entertainment, and farming. An ad in the paper asked that anyone who fit the bill call.[32]

Jud understood that his commitments to communalism and capit-alism existed in tension, but he would bend on neither. To accommo-date the paradox, he looked toward international social experiments. This exploration led him to the Israeli Kibbutz movement, a collec-tion of like-minded communes devoted to a form of socialist Zionism practiced by young Jewish immigrants who fled Russia for Palestine after the failure of the 1905 revolution. Upon arriving in Palestine, the hardships of daily life forced them to work closely with one another, reinforcing their Jewish identity. The combination of both ideology and lived experience promoted a devotion to radical equality, group-centered morality, hard work, and asceticism. All Kibbutz members worked according to their ability and received equal provisions. Meals were shared, and child-rearing was a communal endeavor. While the Kibbutz movement made up only a small percentage of the Jewish population in Palestine, Kibbutz leaders often enjoyed an elite position within Israeli society. By midcentury, the classical Kibbutz model was reordered to address changing economic and political conditions. A strong focus was put on economic development and diversification. The mechanization of agriculture and the creation of a host of commercialized services drew the Kibbutz movement into the larger capitalist economy, where it functioned much like noncommunal entities. Nonetheless, the Kibbutz movement tried to remain culturally distinct from the outside world by creating intercommunal federations and private educational institutions.[33]

For Jud, the Kibbutz example was a godsend. *The Storefront Classroom* lauded the movement as the Western world's single successful example of a "collective settlement existing harmoniously within a larger capitalist, democratic society." Jud saw in it a successful blend of two different and largely irreconcilable philosophies that was a model to emulate, and he often used the term to refer to Kerista. Just as he did with religion, philosophy, and psychology, Jud did not adopt the Kibbutz model wholesale, but picked out what he thought was useful and discarded the rest. His vision of utopia remained distinctively his own.[34]

In the summer of 1976, Jud laid out his Utopian Worldplan of Kerista. According to him, this plan had been in the works for the past twenty years. It was very specific. Each member was to donate $7 dollars a month to advertising, $3 to audio materials, and $55 for tuition to the Performing Arts Social Society Experimental college, later rebranded a university, which was a collective dedicated to promoting Keristan ideology. The tuition, he claimed, was allotted to real estate acquisition. The college would establish 420 training centers with 120 adults at each, spread throughout the world. It would limit population growth, reducing the world population to two billion. After the birth of one child, each woman would undergo elective sterilization, a tenet that was later replaced with voluntary vasectomies for all men. In addition, each member would have to voluntarily limit personal wealth to a maximum of $600 dollars in personal savings. All other assets would be transferred to a trust, with the proceeds used to fund a nonprofit devoted to educational endeavors. Everyone would enjoy medical and dental benefits provided by professionals trained in utopian standards of living. Outside work was allowed, but the plan was designed to produce a self-sufficient society that afforded each member with one month off for every month worked. Free months were dedicated to education and personal development.[35]

Jud claimed the purpose of his plan was to build a democratic, egalitarian, and decentralized system free from bureaucracy. He believed the plan was inherently self-replicating. Its initial goal was twenty-four adults. After a group reached twenty-four, it would divide in half. The groups would continue dividing until there were 2,100 units of twenty-four adults. These would form clusters of five, living within 120 adult complexes, until there were 420 clusters. The cooperation of clusters, he proposed, would afford the purchase of a $1 billion estate to be used for vacation, retirement, and child education. The collective would engage with capitalism in the outside world. However, members would not need money because as they would have access to a computerized credit card system. Keristans would engage communally with one another, trading goods and services. All members would have to agree to actively proselytize, functioning as utopian sales agents. Of course, they would also have to agree to rid themselves of any internal contradictions in order to purge weaknesses in their personalities.[36]

With his blueprint for global salvation in hand, Jud turned his attention outward to recruitment. To the dismay of many Keristans, however, the process remained slow going. By autumn of 1979, the Purple Submarine had attracted only sixteen members. Yet they claimed a circulation of 60,000 for their journal, *Utopian Eyes*. While that number may seem inflated, Kerista's publications were certainly making waves within Bay Area counterculture. Their claim to have transcended jealousy attracted the attention of several social psychologists interested in studying jealousy within intimate relationships, leading to a feature on the community in the May 1980 issue of *Psychology Today*.[37]

The *Psychology Today* article mostly focused on the relationship between jealousy and self-esteem and jealousy's gender-varied expressions. Though there was skepticism about Kerista's claims, the piece was charitable and painted members in a largely positive light. It presented their ideas as a possible model for rethinking the necessity of jealousy within relationships. It described their concept of polyfidelity in detail, making it clear that it was the Keristans' rejection of romantic love to which they anchored their claim to be able to transcend jealousy. It mentioned in passing the Gestalt-o-Rama process but described it simply as a method of transcending past conditioning, including attachments to romantic love. The article proposed that the sleeping schedule was the most sensational of Kerista's tenets. It was not. While it may have been the most sensational concept relayed to the journalist who wrote the article, there was no mention of Kerista's origins, alphabet boards, or the intricate numerology entailed within Jud's world peace plan. In fact, the only mention of Brother Jud was his name as a member. Elliot Aronson, one of the social psychologists whose work the article featured, amicably described the commune's members as "not kooks."[38]

The article caught the attention of Phil Donahue, or at least his producers, who invited the Keristans to be guests on an episode of his popular daytime television talk show. Convinced of the virtue of their lifestyle, the Keristans agreed. All things considered, the appearance was rather tame. Jud was suspiciously absent, but Eve Furchgott and two other members, Ram and Lil, appeared alongside Dr. Gregory White, a psychologist whose work the *Psychology Today* article featured. The Keristans clearly wished to appear respectable in front of their audience. They presented polyfidelity as a rational option for anyone who wanted more than traditional marriage offered. They focused on the lifetime commitment that it entailed, arguing that it was at least, if not more, intentional and ethical than standard monogamy. While questions concerning the usual matters of jealousy and child-rearing led the Keristans to disclose their sleeping schedule and plans to self-educate their children, there was no mention of the more clandestine details of their religion. Again, there was no talk of the alphabet board, Gestalt-o-Rama, or Jud's grand world peace plan.[39]

Subtle hints of their latent numerology pointed to their deeper ideology. Lil mentioned that their families could grow to twenty-four individuals. When Donahue asked if she ever wondered if Mr. Right was yet to come along, she responded that she had found three Mr. Rights and had room for nine more. Humorous as the comment may have seemed, it belied a cultish undertone that did not sit well with many in the audience. When the discussion returned to shared child-rearing, one audience member charged the group with trying to start their own country. The Keristans skillfully turned the charge on its head, arguing that their endeavor originated from their patriotism. The freedom to do what they were doing was proof of America's greatness. They only asked for the tolerance they assured their listeners they would return. Despite restrained support from the psychologist, who argued that their cultural experiment seemed to imply that jealousy could be minimized, if not overcome, the overall performance did little to dispel the cultish feel the Keristans gave off.[40]

With their fifteen minutes of fame behind them, the Keristans returned to regional proselytizing. It was not yet time to go national. Instead, they focused again on attracting others who already shared their countercultural predilections, specifically those related to non-monogamy. One such figure was San Francisco radio broadcaster and founder of the Human Awareness Institute, Stan Dale. Dale was part of an extended group marriage and promoted alternative intimate relationships through workshops and radio broadcasts. An alliance with Dale could help the Keristans reach an audience that extended well beyond the Bay Area. Another target was Will Mahoney, an accountant in Denver, Colorado, who published a newsletter entitled *Beyond Monogamy*. Mahoney had written an article on Keristan ideology for his newsletter and proposed writing a book on the commune.

Kerista's interactions with both Dale and Mahoney contradicted
their claims to merely be seeking connections with like-minded people. The Keristans were more cordial with Dale, likely due to his platform in the city. However, the first correspondence letter they sent
to him gave little more than a one-line acknowledgment of his work
before devoting three long paragraphs to their own ideas, asking him
if he was sympathetic to their positions. It was clear that they were not
looking for friends so much as converts.[41]

Their letters to Mahoney were more characteristically Keristan.
Mahoney was willing to engage more deeply with the commune. He
not only showed interest in their ideas but was also willing to give
them subtle critiques, telling them that, while their concepts were
fascinating, their jargon, as well as Jud's abrasiveness, alienated those
who might otherwise be interested. His candor won him no pleasant-
ries. They quickly assured him that, as someone stuck in the romantic
paradigm, he was unable to comprehend the purity of their message,
which they exhaustively detailed, numerology and all. Furthermore,
his lack of critical intellectual engagement made him unfit to write
any book on their religion. They were, however, interested in knowing
if he would like to start a Keristan discussion group in his local area.
He declined. Undeterred, the Keristans pressed on. At one point, they
even wrote Gloria Steinem, pitching polyfidelity as a new form of
nonseparatist feminism, hoping that she would cover it in an article in
her popular feminist magazine, *Ms.* She did not.[42]

Luckily for Kerista, there were a small number of communally
minded individuals who were interested in their project. It was
through one of these connections made during the late 1970s that
Kerista's influence later infiltrated American polyamory. Allan Jensen,
like many of Jud's other followers, was never content with his intimate
relationships. He was promiscuous in his youth and unfaithful during
his first marriage. After he encountered Keristan literature, he became
mesmerized by the idea of polyfidelity. He followed Kerista's example
and started his own BFIC, replete with a social contract that rejected
romanticism in lieu of rational utopianism. He and his female partner,

Lynn, had several relationships with other men and couples before Jensen finally found the family he sought. Along the way, Jensen reached out to Jud, hoping that his BFIC could become a Keristan satellite in the Pacific Northwest. He even proposed partnering in a joint land venture. Jud was exceedingly pleased with such an idea and quickly wrote Jensen back with his own ideas about how to proceed. Unfortunately, Jensen's group quickly realized that, for them, physical attraction was just as essential to maintaining sustainable relationships as shared ideals. When they eventually lost physical interest in one another, the group fell apart. Allan and Lynn endured the breakup and continued looking for new partners to join them.[43]

By the early 1980s, Allan and Lynn were living in a land-based commune called Cerro Gordo, outside of Eugene, Oregon. There they met Mary and Barry Northrop, high school sweethearts who had relocated from Idaho after marrying. Before their move to Oregon, Mary became involved with another man. Rather than get a divorce, Barry befriended Mary's new lover. Although the relationship did not work out, Mary's desire for other lovers and Barry's desire for friendship led them west, to Cerro Gordo, where they encountered polyfidelity. Their shared interest in Keristan ideology drew the Northrops to Jensen and Lynn, and the two couples began courting in hopes of merging their families. Eventually Lynn left after deciding the situation was too emotionally taxing, and Jensen and the Northrops continued courting.[44]

Desiring a close relationship with Kerista, Jensen and the Northrops began promoting its ideas enthusiastically. In 1981, they traveled to San Francisco to meet the Purple Submarine. While Jud managed to convince the three to stop courting and form a committed polyfidelitous family, neither Jensen nor the Northrops were comfortable with the intensity of the Gestalt-o-Rama process. The visit ended with the Oregonians returning home for a period of "graceful distancing." Despite their tumultuous experience in California, the Oregonians were steadfast in their commitment and decided to remain together as a polyfidelitous BFIC. They named their new communal family

Syntony, started leading discussion groups at potlucks in Cerro Gordo to introduce polyfidelity to their local community, and reached out to the University of Oregon to set up workshops there on Keristan thought.[45]

Mary was particularly fascinated with Keristan ideas and took the lead in the ongoing correspondence between the two communes. Young and hopeful, she believed that, despite the Purple Submariners' abrasiveness, much of Keristan ideology could benefit the world. Shortly after returning from their visit to San Francisco, Mary wrote to Bluejay Way.

> We decided to use the Utopian concepts and vocabulary you've de-
> veloped as much as possible (rather than be divisive and quibble about
> terms) with the aim of joining together to put out the word. A spe-
> cific word I'm hot on right now is compersion—I've been giving it to
> everyone I talk with in hopes of strengthening the feeling it stands for.
> Everyone seems delighted with it. It fills a need.[46]

Mary's hope that the Keristans would be pleased with her use of their terms and concepts without wholesale acceptance of their world-view was tragically misplaced. A swift response informed Mary that Keristan ideals were part of a holistic system. This system, they reiter-ated, was based on the belief in a cosmic design in which each person had an essential and preordained role to play. The only method that led to this realization was the Gestalt-o-Rama process. There was no other way. Keristan concepts were part of a closed system that could not be cherry-picked.[47]

The problem was that, while Mary loved the practical applications of polyfidelity, she was turned off by many of the religious aspects of Kerista. She explained that she had long given up the Catholicism of her youth and no longer had a need, nor a desire, for organized religion of any kind. She did attend a church at Cerro Gordo, but it was a nonconfessional church focused on self-reliance and consisted mostly of people discussing their personal experiences. She did not believe in ideological rigidity. While Jensen was more prone to such structure, that was okay. She and Barry were much more pragmatic and were willing to alter their approaches as new information and circumstances arose. But, even if she was more disposed to a fixed ideology, she believed in free will.[48]

Mary's belief in free will incensed the Keristans. They castigated her for holding a belief they described as quaint, archaic, and unscientific. They railed that a belief in free will squelched self-esteem while promoting personal guilt and worry. Initially Mary was submissive and confessed that she was at a much earlier stage in her intellectual development than they were. While she hoped she would catch up, she currently needed them as a role model. In the meantime, she would study Gestalt psychology in hopes that she could adopt more Keristan practices.[49]

Despite her capitulations, Mary stood firm in her position on free will, maintaining that it was compatible with their notion of determinism in that she focused more on the relationship of cause and effect than on grander metaphysical speculations. Her firm but humble stance only incited lengthy rebuttals that contained both theological arguments and personal attacks on her and her husbands' characters. One Keristan wrote,

> There's absolutely no way, in our opinion, of you getting through your sick points and building a BFIC, when you're not involved with our Gestalt-o-Rama process here. We always thought deep down that it can't be done somewhere else, but wanted to give you encouragement and the benefit of the doubt. . . . The process is unique, participatory, and we are always developing it more deeply. I can't imagine it being replicated anywhere else and why would you even want to try? Your isolation from "Mecca" [Meaningful Equalitarian Cooperative Communities Alliance] indicates either stupidity, insincerity, or raw contrariness.[50]

The letter continued to alternate between personal affirmations and harsh critiques typical of the Gestalt-o-Rama process. Mary's husband, Barry, was not cowed by these characteristically Keristan tactics. He countered that their frequent mood swings and unwillingness to accept criticism called their sanity into question. Unable to get Jensen even to engage them at all at this point, the Keristans

charged him with a narcissistic superiority complex generated by
his good looks.[51]

As the Keristans continued to alienate Mary's two husbands, they
turned their attention more squarely to bringing her into their fold.
Again, this process oscillated between affectionate affirmations and
personal attacks. Jud told Mary she was a beautiful writer, but she was
bipolar in her split loyalties. Keristan utopianism was much more advanced than the polyfidelity Syntony practiced, so continued correspondence with her was likely a futile endeavor. But Mary was quickly
emerging as her own thinker, and the effectiveness of Jud's psychological tricks was waning. She was not just reconstructing her own
belief system, but her personal identity as well. In March 1982, Mary
changed her name to Ryam Nimziky, a reordering of Mary, followed
by a phonetic spelling of her maiden last name, Niemczycki. The first
name, Ryam, remained the same throughout her career. She eventually changed her last name to Nearing, the name she would publish
under as a public advocate for polyamory.[52]

While Nearing's personal reinvention was marked by a growing
self-assuredness, she did not believe she should make a clean break
from Kerista. She hoped the two groups could iron out their differences and maintain a good relationship. Despite Nearing's persistent
goodwill, the Keristans remained intolerant of Syntony's halfhearted
appropriation of their religious concepts. They claimed that their
unwillingness to capitulate was evidence that they remained stuck
in the romantic paradigm. They believed that if Syntony really cared
about communal utopianism, they must join Kerista. Syntony's unwillingness to do so proved they were unfit to transcend the romantic paradigm for the utopian. It was impossible to straddle the
two (Figure 2.3).[53]

Nearing tried to placate the Keristans. She assured them that she was
committed to utopianism, but, for her, romance and utopia were not
mutually exclusive. She appealed to analogy to make her point. While
Kerista saw commitment to a certain paradigm like a toggle switch,
either on or off, she believed that it was a continuum with "many

Figure 2.3 Syntony, in their home, Eugene, Oregon, 1984. From left to right: Allan Jensen, Ryam Nearing, and Barry Northrop.
Photo courtesy of Ryam Hill.

settings of intensity/amount/quantity, not just on and off," akin to a dimmer switch (rheostat). Syntony, she proposed, might exist closer to the romantic side of the continuum than Kerista, but they, too, were deeply committed to utopian values. The claim that they were less enlightened or evolved was an unfair critique. Her relationships were as intentional as theirs, and she was under no self-deception or romantic illusions. While she was resolved to building a lifestyle centered on polyfidelity, her main goal was to come "to terms with the fact that I am an active originator of my experience." She told them that she had learned early on that no relationships were better than negative ones, and she assured Jud that, rather than making excuses to stay together, she was more decisively herself than she had ever been.[54]

Of course, the Keristans rejected Nearing's analogy. They quickly proposed a new mantra "It's a toggle switch, it's not a rheostat." But Nearing argued that her position was justified by her own experience. She urged the Keristans to remember that metaphors were just guides, maps, and tools and that it was a mistake to hold to them too tightly at the expense of experiencing reality itself. While romance did not control her, she chose it freely. Rather than letting it shackle her, it brought her joy as she and her partners were "able to weave our individuality together and get yet MORE." Her increasingly self-assured and articulate responses only gained her ridicule. "I think you want me to cheer because you are not Jerry Falwell," one Keristan remarked. Submission to Gestalt-o-Rama was the only cure for romance. There was no other way.[55]

Despite the dissent between the two communes, Syntony continued to promote polyfidelity throughout Cerro Gordo. By the autumn of 1982, their efforts had borne fruit. They received invitations to do local television interviews, and their discussion groups gained converts, necessitating the formation of support groups for those practicing polyfidelity. The general social contract they crafted for those participating in the support groups sounded remarkably Keristan. Among its tenets were open communication, graceful distancing, non-preferentialism, democratic egalitarianism, and, of course, a commitment to polyfidelity. Gestalt-o-Rama was glaringly absent. Nearing explained that while she respected the practice, she was more interested in understanding others' experiences and coming to mutually beneficial compromises. Upon reviewing the contract, the Keristans declared that Syntony was neurotic and full of contradictions, a black hole no longer worthy of their energy.[56]

It is difficult to speculate how long the epistolary Gestalt-o-Rama might have continued between Kerista and Syntony had other factors not intervened. In an interesting turn of events, Jud became distracted from the correspondence. His obsession with his global peace plan had caused him to study global geopolitics. Jud had always feared the spread of communism, and, by 1980, he was convinced that the threat was greater than he originally believed and that the United States was losing its nuclear advantage in the Cold War. In several articles published in *The Storefront Classroom*, he speculated on Soviet infiltrations and the likelihood of nuclear war. He became increasingly radical.

Just as Kerista's attempts to convert Syntony were coming to a tense head, Jud backed off, telling Nearing that Kerista was through trying to rationalize with other groups based solely on a shared commitment to polyfidelity. They had more pressing concerns. He was convinced that Central and South America would likely fall to an international communist conspiracy before the American population awoke to the threat. In light of these concerns, most Keristans decided that Ronald Reagan best represented their interests, and they were switching their loyalties from the Democratic to the Republican Party. Global politics needed to take precedence over convincing other communes of their folly.[57]

Kerista's Cold War anxieties only intensified their commitment to their global peace plan. They believed it was their duty to invest money into Third World countries for education and practical assistance. This voluntary redistribution of wealth would not only promote Keristan values, but would also make teetering countries "immune to the lies of the communists who lured them with false promises of a better life." In the meantime, only an immense display of nuclear capability could thwart the threat of Soviet expansion. Anyone who believed in a nuclear freeze had bought into the lies of the KGB and was an enemy of global peace. Nearing, who was more concerned with the environmental destruction nuclear war would cause, fell into this camp. The Keristans informed her that her position made her an accessory to the spread of communism. They, on the other hand, were destined to become the new "Hip Right" in their countercultural support of "Peace through Strength."[58]

While Nearing remained in correspondence with individual Keristans, her patience with their coercive psychological tactics had come to an end. She composed a simple plea to disagree, writing,

> It seems unproductive to me to go point by point over all the letters, interactions, phone calls, etc. My perspective is that we see several of the major points quite differently and are both unlikely to change our views. My proposal is that we look where we are now (trade contact level) and at where we would like to be (based on a reasonable

assessment of ourselves). I'd like for us to be comfortable networking and sharing info that involves our mutual interests. I think we could manage this level, do you?[59]

Exhausted by Kerista's utopian psychology, geopolitical peace plans, and nuclear fears, Nearing had gleaned what she could from them. There would be no communal merger.

Nearing's choice to distance herself from Kerista had no bearing on her appropriation of many of their concepts. She remained true to her commitment to take up and disseminate their ideas as far as they were beneficial. In the end, Syntony was much more successful in spreading Keristan ideas than was Kerista. As her communication with its members diminished, her success as an ambassador of polyfidelity throughout the Pacific Northwest grew in inverse proportion. Syntony's polyfidelity discussion groups spread to the campus of the University of Oregon and soon far beyond it.

3

Collaborations

As we approach the 21st century and the emergence of a more
humane new civilization, many of us find that we have matured
beyond a blind acceptance of monogamy as the only legitimate sexual
love relationship. Yet we lack experience and support for creating
viable alternatives.

—Deborah Anapol, *A Resource Guide for the Responsible Non-Monogamist* (1989)

The 1980s marked a definitive conservative shift in American society. The "long 60s" (the late 1950s through the mid-1970s) was
defined by ongoing activism and social unrest, all of which belied
the myth of American unity. The Civil Rights Movement pushed racial issues to the forefront of the American consciousness, leading not
only to integration, but also birthing a more militant Black Power
Movement. Other ethnic splinter movements followed. The emergence of the New Left, its disparate factions held together by little
more than a shared anti-war sentiment, signaled a new age for political discourse. By the late 1970s, the fracture of the American commonweal was undeniable to liberals and conservatives alike, each hard
set on winning the "war for the soul of America."[1]

Sex played an undeniably central role in the destruction of the
façade of American unity. Increased access to birth control forced
the role of procreation to take a back seat in the intimate lives of
American women and paved the way for the legalization of abortion.
The publication of Betty Friedan's *The Feminist Mystique* in 1963 and

the emergence of second-wave feminism also marked a shift in the role of women in the household and in the workplace. Due to the liberalization of divorce laws, the divorce rate more than doubled between 1960 and 1980. Meanwhile, the Supreme Court's 1967 ruling in *Loving v. Virginia* banned laws against interracial marriage, tying the nation's racial strife to the sexual revolution. Equally as distressing to advocates of "traditional family values," the early 1970s witnessed the birth of thousands of gay liberation organizations, each following the militant turn in queer activism that lauded the aggressive tactics of the Stonewall riots of 1969. By the 1980s, however, the liberal march of the sexual revolution hit a wall.[2]

In the spring of 1984, *Time* magazine pronounced the death of the sexual revolution. Its April cover depicted an illustrated version of a visibly shaken Adam and Eve on each side of the forbidden tree of knowledge. As the serpent scaled its trunk, fruit shook to the ground. The article lamented the excesses of the 1960s and 1970s, attributing the popularity of the sexual revolution to an unfortunate combination of postwar affluence and wanton psychological theories that disproportionately fixated on self-actualization. According to *Time*, the end of the Vietnam War, the destabilization of the economy, and the threat of sexually transmitted diseases were swinging the pendulum of youth culture away from countercultural radicalism. College students were less interested in exploration than in finding stability in their finances and sex lives. However, for those who looked favorably on the gains of the sexual revolution, the news was not all bad. Conservatism was unable to resurrect Puritanism whole cloth. Society had not so much rejected the revolution as grown tired of its superficialities. According to *Time*, frank discourse had replaced reticence to speak candidly about sex and relaxed older prohibitions, as evidenced by the small but growing acceptance of homosexuality. Despite the increasingly ambiguous status of homosexuality in American culture, *Time* assured its readers that the more radical proposals of the revolution, such as the promotion of open marriages or group sex, had died along with

it. Such activities remained taboo for most Americans, as commitment
and intimacy were quickly coming back in vogue.[3]

Time's attribution of the conservative shift in the nation's sexual
ethics to a renewed search for economic and relational stability made
it appear that the American public had simply grown bored of the
frivolousness of the 1960s and 1970s. Yet this ignores the deeper tensions that the sexual revolution brought to the surface. That revolution had recast traditional gender roles and destabilized the place of
sex in human relationships. It also questioned the monolith of matrimony. For many progressives, marriage was a fluid institution, able to
be molded to fit modern understandings of human relations. For conservatives, the family was not just static, it was a sacred sanctuary that
the sexual revolution relentlessly undermined. As historian Daniel
Rodgers has noted, "above all, in ways that historians of these culture
clashes have only begun to realize, it was a battle over women's acts,
and women and men's natures. Of all the certainties whose cracking
seemed to culturally conservative Americans most threatening, the
destabilization of gender certainties set off the sharpest tremors."[4]

The sexual revolution ignited a counter-revolution throughout the
country that centralized the role of the family in the impeding culture wars. The battles that Jerry Falwell and Phyllis Schlafly fought
against abortion and the Equal Rights Amendment set boundaries
around the public discourse on sex. If a woman's rights over her own
body and her equality before the law were controversial issues that,
as conservatives claimed, undermined not just the sacrosanctity of the
traditional family, but the moral foundations of the country, there
was no place for a conversation over whether women might have
multiple husbands. As Ronald Reagan celebrated America's return to
God and family values, such discussions seemed impossible. Amidst
these debates, by the fall of 1984, San Francisco was shutting down
its bathhouses to prevent the spread of AIDS, the deadly new disease
that killed thousands by year's end. As one historian lamented, the explosion of the AIDS epidemic in the early 1980s arrived just in time

to serve as the political blessing the Religious Right needed to refute the last vestiges of 1960's sexual optimism.[5]

It was within these cultural tensions that polyamory emerged as a coherent set of ideas. This process was spearheaded by the collaboration of two women, Ryam Nearing and Deborah Anapol, who constructed a small but virulent coalition to normalize ethical non-monogamy in the face of a conservative backlash. Both women understood that to succeed they needed to counteract charges of hedonism with a coherent system of ethics that embraced commitment while rejecting monogamy. They believed this reconception was an essential step in mankind's social evolution. Rather than undermining the family, ethical non-monogamy was a vehicle for its salvation and was better suited to the strains of modern life.

The Church of All Worlds (CAW) and Kerista had been integral in formulating polyamorous concepts, but neither had created a unified coalition. By the late 1970s, CAW had all but disbanded and the Zells were chasing new adventures on the West Coast. They had effectively adapted Robert Heinlein's *Stranger in Strange Land* into a new religion and disseminated Heinleinian concepts into the neo-Pagan community. Yet their influence was largely confined within that sub-culture. Kerista's rigid ideology made its dreams of national influence impossible, despite its members' rigorous efforts. Without Nearing and Anapol's organizational work during the 1980s and 1990s, it is likely that both groups would have remained disparate and obscure manifestations of American counterculture.

Others made efforts to begin a national movement. Family Synergy, a volunteer-run nonprofit started in Orange County in 1971, presented itself as an educational organization committed to the promotion of non-possessive interpersonal relationships. The organization boasted of having members in every state as well as Canada, Australia, England, France, and West Germany. It printed a newsletter and held conferences and conventions. Despite building a rudimentary network, including substantial branches in Philadelphia and New York, Family Synergy was never able to unify its factions and achieve lasting results. Many of its members found their way into the larger poly-amorous coalition through the networking of Nearing and Anapol, rather than the other way around.[6]

Another significant component of early polyamory was the Human Awareness Institute, founded by radio personality Stan Dale. Established in 1968, Dale's institute offered workshops on love, in-timacy, and sexuality. His work was progressive enough to attract Kerista's attention and cause them to extend unrequited hopes that he would support their utopian ventures. His outspokenness about his own group marriage made him an inspiration to many, and he became a friend of Anapol's during the early 1980s. But Dale's efforts were not focused solely on promoting ethical non-monogamy. Although he contributed heavily to polyamory, it was largely through Anapol and Nearing's network. The Human Awareness Institute, like Family Synergy, was a preexisting component of a coalition that was brought together by the organizational efforts of Nearing and Anapol.[7]

Throughout the early 1980s, while Ryam Nearing was still in close contact with Kerista, she and her husbands established a close asso-ciation of Eugene residents interested in polyfidelity. They were out-spoken in their commitment to group marriage and tirelessly crusaded for the Keristan ideal of polyfidelity. They soon gained attention from others throughout the country inquiring about the pragmatic details of polyfidelitious living. This interest convinced Nearing that there was a need for an educational program with a national reach. In the summer of 1984, she founded Polyfidelitous Educational Productions (PEP), a nonprofit dedicated to establishing a national polyfidelitous network and disseminating information to its members.[8]

Nearing was uniquely suited to fight for ethical non-monogamy within the cultural climate of the Reagan era. The Catholicism of her early youth turned her off to traditional forms of organized religion, and she was impatient with religious fundamentalists who charged her with immorality. In her mind, her innately familial temperament, evidenced by her unwavering devotion to polyfidelity, made it impos-sible for her critics to level credible charges of promiscuousness. She argued that polyfidelity combined the best aspects of both monogamy and promiscuity while avoiding the pitfalls of both. She believed polyfidelity's emphasis on commitment and its emphatic prohibition against sex with anyone outside the family made her lifestyle traditional compared to both free love and swinging. Nearing was also a libertarian. While she was socially progressive, her economic and political conservatism enabled her to point out the contradictory beliefs of religious conservatives who believed in small government while insisting that the state should closely regulate matrimony. For Nearing, the state should have nothing to do with marriage.[9]

Nearing founded PEP and self-published the first edition of *Polyfidelity Primer*, a small newsprint tabloid, in 1984. There she presented a modified version of the polyfidelity she had learned from the Keristans. She argued that polyfidelity was the next evolutionary step in intimate relationships. It was a lifelong commitment, almost identical to monogamy, that entailed sharing all of life's joys and trials with one's partners. The mixture of enjoyment and responsibility embodied in sex, asset-sharing, and child-rearing were to be shouldered by multiple adults, none of whom receives preferential treatment. For Nearing, there were no superficial or secondary intimate relationships, only multiple committed egalitarian primaries (Figure 3.1).[10]

Nearing's conception of intimacy was Keristanity devoid of its metaphysical underpinnings and adapted pragmatically to fit her own social vision. Unlike Kerista, it accommodated a wide arrangement of sexual orientations. If heterosexual, like her and her two husbands, then same sex partners maintained nonsexual intimate friendships. Alternately, if gay or bisexual, they could choose whatever arrangement suited them. Like Kerista, Nearing argued that the idea of a fixed sleeping schedule was wise to preserve a sense of equality. To illustrate her vision, Nearing published an innocuous picture of a group of friends riding bikes in her *Primer*. Under it, she introduced the Keristan term *compersion*, defining it as the sense of contentment and joy that family members could experience from seeing their lovers enjoy one another. Jealousy, she noted, was its antonym.[11]

POLYFIDELITY PRIMER

FIRST EDITION $2.00

PICTURE
YOURSELF
WITHIN A
CIRCLE OF BEST FRIENDS

Figure 3.1 The first edition of Ryam Nearing's *Polyfidelity Primer*, published in 1984.
Photo courtesy of Loving More.

Nearing believed that the mainstream's overemphasis on romance was a mistake. But she did not categorically reject it. Instead, she offered a middle way, arguing that responsible relationships must stand on a bedrock of both attraction and shared ideals. It was too easy to make rash relational decisions when one was "blind and starry eyed" in the initial stages of infatuation. To remedy this, Nearing offered the Keristan solution of the social contract. She taught that writing down one's intellectual commitments promoted a soberness of mind that could offset the intoxicating pleasure of romance. When a potential partner was both stimulating and a practical fit, true and lasting intimacy was possible. She promised her readers that, while she was not offering them a simple ticket to paradise, the social contract made the journey much smoother.[12]

Though Nearing did not disparage monogamy, she believed that polyfidelity was an inherently superior alternative. She argued that the desire for commitment was completely natural, flowing from the need for intimacy, security, and stability. However, she argued that traditional monogamy was unable to sufficiently carry these burdens, and it often led to prolonged unhappiness and divorce. Polyfidelity more adequately provided for such needs. It offered sexual diversity, but, more importantly, it provided its practitioners with an expanded emotional support system, a greater sense of belonging within the home, and a better chance at achieving economic security. In addition, the sense of safety produced by an expanded emotional base and added physical resources provided the children of polyfidelitious families with a healthier and more stable environment. She pointed to the experiences of PEP's members as evidence, publishing an extended testimonial written by member Peter Hart chronicling his journey from an unhappy marriage to polyfidelity. Hart believed his life was changed after he heard Nearing speak at the University of Oregon. After years of struggling, Hart claimed polyfidelity's division of family responsibilities helped his own emotional well-being and gave his child greater stability.[13]

By the winter of 1984, Nearing had laid the foundations of her network. Her educational nonprofit was growing. She had published a succinct treatise enumerating the lifestyle's benefits, she sponsored courses at the University of Oregon on the tenets of polyfidelity, and she published a quarterly newsletter entitled *PEPTalk for the*

Polyfidelitous. By the end of the year, membership was growing, and she began advertising in alternative publications such as *CoEvolution Quarterly*, *New Age*, *The Progressive*, and Kerista's *Utopian Classroom*. She conducted presentations at her local library, organized monthly dinners, orchestrated weekly discussion groups, and even sponsored Kerista's television series, *Utopian Eyes*, through a local cable access station.[14]

A few hundred miles south of Nearing, Deborah Anapol had also devoted her life to ethical non-monogamy. Despite their shared goals, the two women were extremely different. In 1984, Anapol was a bisexual single mother in her early thirties with a PhD in clinical psychology. A self-described rootless maverick, Anapol had been a free spirit drawn to the counterculture in its various stages. Anapol devoted herself to the New Age spirituality that blossomed in the late 1970s and early 1980s. For Anapol, spirituality and sexuality were always intertwined. Just as she shunned orthodox religion, she also rejected sexual constraints. She later reminisced that even as a teenager she knew she was not built for the confines of monogamy. As a young hippie, Anapol often mixed psychedelics with promiscuity, hoping to reach new experiential heights. This youthful openness drew the ire of many of her peers, many of whom denigrated her as promiscuous. She periodically bent to societal pressures, but, though she tried multiple times to fit the mold of monogamy, such attempts were always short-lived.[15]

Anapol's first marriage was to her friend Steven. Despite their intellectual compatibility, Anapol was sexually unsatisfied and left Steven after their daughter's birth. As a struggling single mother trying to finish graduate school at the University of Washington, she soon latched on to a responsible man she met in town. This second marriage, which she admitted was one largely of convenience, also left her miserable and unfulfilled. After it failed, Anapol proposed never to make the same mistake again. From then on, she only dated people who were intentionally non-monogamous. This choice led her to the conclusion that she was inherently polygamous. She wished to have intimate relationships with all the people she loved. Monogamy, she believed, was weak and limiting in that it ruled out having these deep connections with more than one person, stifling freedom in the name of commitment. Anapol believed that this was a false dilemma that ethical non-monogamy could overcome.[16]

Given Anapol's academic training, it was natural that she decided to write a book on the benefits of ethical non-monogamy. In the autumn of 1984, as Nearing was laying the foundations of her Oregon nonprofit, Anapol mailed out proposals to publishers for her manuscript, *When One Is Not Enough*, a working title that changed multiple times before its publication. Anapol marketed herself as a participant observer, a polygamist, and a clinical psychologist. She pitched the project as the first popular nonfiction work to take an objective look at the diversity of Americans currently involved in "more than one ongoing, committed, non-monogamous relationship at the same time." It would focus on their personal stories, emphasizing the changing trends in familial structures occurring on the periphery of the American mainstream during the 1980s. After months of publisher rejections, Anapol shifted her focus to writing articles and doing local media appearances instead.[17]

Despite having difficulty finding a publisher, Anapol was able to connect with other ethical non-monogamists while conducting the research for her book. Having a PhD from a reputable academic institution helped. In January of 1985, Phil Donahue asked Anapol to appear on his popular talk show, along with Stan and Helen Dale of the Human Awareness Institute, to discuss the findings of her research. She agreed, hoping that it would interest potential publishers. It was a tumultuous experience. Stan and Helen, along with Stan's unofficial wife, Janet, and Helen's longtime lover, Hobart, made an honest attempt to portray their relationships as consensual, egalitarian, and healthy. Stan argued that, despite cultural norms, hundreds of thousands of people were presently living in such relationships and they deserved legal recognition. He presented the statistic without citation, and his plea for legal sanction was met with laughter from the audience. Nonetheless, the Dales and their extended family made every effort to show the benefits of their choices. They pointed to high divorce rates among monogamous couples and argued that the longevity of their relationships was evidence of the integrity of their lifestyle. They argued that their children were not only healthy and grounded but also enjoyed multiple stable and supportive parental figures. None of their arguments gained much acceptance from audience members, who were skeptical of the logistics of the Dales' relationships and the intentions behind them.[18]

When Anapol appeared, the conversation had centered on whether it was possible for non-monogamists to transcend jealousy. Anapol argued that one of the primary benefits of polygamy was that since there was no need to choose between lovers, it removed the need for jealousy. She believed that, while some people were naturally monogamous and others naturally polygamous, the problems occurred when polygamists were made to act like monogamists. She gained little sympathy from the audience, many of whom rejected the possibility of ethical non-monogamy as either impractical or, more often, morally reprehensible. Anapol later reflected on the experience, remarking that she was "thrown to the lions."[19]

Despite Anapol's negative experience, the *Donahue* appearance proved invaluable. Anapol received a deluge of fan mail from people across the nation who were interested in her research and wanted to know more about multiple committed relationships. This convinced her that she was in a unique position to start a national educational organization to promote ethical non-monogamy as a socially acceptable lifestyle. She established Intinet (intimate + network), a resource center for anyone interested in her ideas. For thirty dollars, members were given an annual membership that included information on resources, publications, and Anapol's newsletter, *Floodtide*.[20]

Ryam Nearing and Deborah Anapol met on the set of Playboy Channel's *Women on Sex* in the spring of 1985. The episode, co-hosted by sociologist Dr. Janet Lever and lawyer and former Playboy playmate Vicki McCarty, was entitled "Sex Without Jealousy." Anapol and

Nearing were joined by Vikki Powell, an advocate of open relationships. Anapol appeared first. Radiating a bookish yet liberated personality, she proposed that it was possible to conduct multiple intimate
relationships in a responsible and healthy manner. While she was currently living alone, Anapol admitted to seeing three different men,
each of whom she said she might continue to date indefinitely. When
questioned on how that was sustainable, Anapol stated that her lifestyle centered around trust and honesty in ways that monogamy never
could. To juggle these relationships, all parties had to be highly adept
at communication. Trust was constantly tested, and, if it faltered, the
relationships would fail. It was this trust and honesty, not sexual fidelity, that served as the moral foundation of the relationships.[21]

After Anapol gave her pitch, the hosts called Nearing out onto the
stage. Nearing's small frame belied the abundant confidence she projected when articulating the benefits of polyfidelity to the audience.
Gone were the insecurity and self-doubt present in her early interactions with Kerista. She did not waver in describing her preference
for fidelity. She affirmed her lifelong commitment to her husbands,
both of whom she referred to as her best friends. Nearing made it
clear that, for her, commitment was the crux of intimacy. It was morally inconsequential to her that her ideal conception of marriage happened to be a group of six, rather than two.[22]

The conversation among the three guests quickly clarified the differences between the women's worldviews. Each of the panelists rejected swinging as either undesirable or unethical. Beyond that, the
women had contrasting opinions about which intimate practices were
either preferable or most ethical. At one end of the spectrum, Powell
argued that what made her open marriage sustainable was the primary nature of her and her husband's relationship. While she could
have whatever experiences she wished outside of that relationship, all
other relationships were subordinate to that one and expendable in
comparison. In the middle was Anapol, who made the case for an in-
definite number of intimate relationships, each built on commitment
and honesty. At the other end, Nearing's indefatigable commitment to

sexual fidelity solely within the bounds of lifelong commitment made her seem relatively conservative despite her and her husbands' desire for three more family members.[23]

Anapol and Nearing's perspective was qualitatively different from that of Powell. While the two strongly disagreed on the level of commitment necessary for ethical sexual engagement, they both allowed for multiple primary relationships, whereas Powell did not. Anapol was not interested in relationships that hindered her freedom. Nearing was not interested in ones that hindered her commitment to her primary partners. Despite these differences, Nearing noticed the commonalties she and Anapol shared. She later relayed her experience to her *PEPTalk* subscribers, explaining,

> So on the show I sat between a woman who spoke for "open marriage" and Dr. Deborah Anapol who has a new organization called Intinet which is a center for idea exchange regarding "expanded options for quality intimate relationships." . . . The main hurdle on the show was for us to convince the interviewers . . . and audience you can have more than one partner without dying of jealousy. It worked well despite our quite different lifestyle choices.[24]

Nearing saw Anapol as a fellow traveler and a resource she was obligated to let her readers know about. The feeling was mutual. Anapol mentioned meeting Nearing on the set of *Women on Sex* to her readers, adding PEP's contact information for those who were interested.[25]

Anapol and Nearing's meeting on the program was a pivotal moment in the history of American polyamory. Both women were passionate and driven. Despite their differences, they knew they could work together to effect change on a larger scale. Each also functioned to offset the other's more extreme tendencies. While Nearing was a pragmatist compared to Kerista, her unwavering commitment to polyfidelity made her come across as an ideologue to many attracted to the libertine freedoms the rejection of monogamy offered. Conversely, Anapol's more laissez-faire approach gave the impression to many that her lifestyle was less ethical than she believed.

Though she was ambitious, Anapol was self-conscious about her inexperience. After the Playboy appearance she began seeking advice. In a letter to existential psychologist Rollo May, Anapol confessed her need for a mentor. She balanced her desperation with self-assurance, describing herself as a unique and occasionally brilliant, if overly idealistic, clinical psychologist who had the audacity to try to reshape American sexual culture. She enclosed her CV with an invitation for May to serve on her board of advisors. It is unclear if he ever responded. She also wrote to Robert Rimmer, lauding him for his promotion of inclusive relationships and asking him to join her board of advisors. Although she and Rimmer later formed a close professional relationship, it is unclear if he ever received the letter.[26]

Difficulty finding mentorship did not slow down Anapol's agenda. By late 1985, her thoughts on ethical non-monogamy were evolving. In October, she decided to distance herself from the term "polygamous," a word she had previously used in many of her public appearances. She was aware of its patriarchal connotations and sought a less loaded term. Various options appealed to her. She was particularly attracted to the phrases "cellular family" and "multimate relationships." She loved the connotations of the term "cellular," remarking that it united the concepts of telecommunications and biological mechanization. She had come to believe that the effort to promote ethical non-monogamy was in the same phase as feminism and gay liberation in the 1960s. She was convinced it was about to explode. Yet Anapol understood that language was important and, whatever term would replace polygamy, there needed to be a common language.[27]

By the close of 1985, Anapol adopted a new method for connecting her fellow ethical non-monogamists. The format, which she borrowed from Action Linkage, a "transformational organization" based out of Arizona, was called "many to many (or m-2-m)." Action to Action specialized in uniting people who had shared interests in alternative topics. It collected letters and articles from like-minded individuals and published them in one location. Anapol believed this method had the potential to bring cohesion to the larger community and asked her readers to begin sending in material. The adoption of the m-2-m format promoted a cross-pollination of ideas from diverse individuals who were all practicing variant forms of ethical non-monogamy. Anapol informed her readers that, while there were a host of ways in which to accomplish their shared goal of legitimizing multimate relationships, Intinet would focus primarily on networking and education. She assured her readers that the response to her call for letters had produced multiple offerings. The first was from PEP's Ryam Nearing.[28]

Back in Oregon, Nearing had continued to ramp up her educational and networking efforts. She always understood the necessity of effective outreach in accomplishing her goals. Early on, *PEPTalk* encouraged its readers to send stamped, self-addressed envelopes so that she could return postcards with information about PEP to be placed in public and university library books on the topics of group marriage, group sex, and communalism. The idea was that anyone checking out those titles would find information on PEP. By autumn of 1985, Nearing was mailing out a PEP directory that included biographies and photos of each member in hopes of establishing personal connections among her readership. She also reprinted personals, editorial letters, and features on different group marriages throughout the country in her PEP newsletter.[29]

Though Nearing was relentless in her promotion of polyfidelity, her desire to establish a more expansive network of people committed to variant forms of ethical non-monogamy outweighed her desire to promote polyfidelity exclusively. This ecumenical spirit is what initially drew her to Anapol. Anapol shared Nearing's sentiment. In her Spring 1986 newsletter, Anapol complained that one of the greatest challenges her organization faced was finding common ground among other non-monogamous "lovestyles." Alongside her lament, Anapol offered a graph. Along the x axis of the graph was a continuum from inclusivity to exclusivity. Along the y axis, she drew a line from commitment to freedom. Both traditional monogamy and swinging were on the peripheries of the graph, albeit on different ends of the commitment–freedom continuum. Anapol claimed she was interested in neither. She conveyed her reverence for Nearing's perspective, setting polyfidelity directly beside her own view, just on opposite sides of the commitment–freedom divide. According to Anapol, they were two sides of the same coin. Their only disagreement was to what extent freedom should play a role in choosing the proper multimate lifestyle.[30]

Nearing's engagement with Anapol softened her polyfidelitious rhetoric. In her spring newsletter, she published an article that argued that the choice for polyfidelity over other forms of ethical non-monogamy should be pragmatic. Though Nearing had always been a pragmatist, once she established her own organization, she had initially used it to promote polyfidelity almost exclusively. She now announced to her readers that, if she wished to pursue sexual trysts outside of her marriage, she would do so. She had tried having an open marriage when she was younger and found the endeavor unappealing. The image of family was the most enticing to her, pragmatically, romantically, and sexually. However, she told readers that her choice rested solely on her individual preferences and her own search for personal fulfillment. It would be wrong to deter others who were unsatisfied with polyfidelity. Consistent in her libertarianism, Nearing argued that while people must act according to their own nature, they should support the rights of others to do the same.[31]

Anapol followed suit. Intinet's 1986 mission statement promised to disseminate educational information and emotional support to those interested in alternative relationship options, facilitate communication among like-minded people interested in sexual-social change, and catalyze networks that could effect that change.[32] Nearing was pleased, but this did not prevent her from privately clarifying her own positions to Anapol's in correspondence. Later that summer, Nearing wrote to Anapol, disputing the way she portrayed the presuppositions of polyfidelity in her newsletter.

I've been meaning to comment on a couple of ideas in Floodtide. A while back you had a diagram locating lifestyles on a continuum. You contrasted freedom with commitment. These are not polarities to me at all. If I am free, then I can make my own choices as to relationship style. My personal choice is to focus most on the relationships which include the most commitment, but that in no way means that I am not free. I think the real contrast is between commitment and detachment or non-commitment in relationship style.

This disagreement mirrored the one between Nearing and the Kersitans a few years earlier, with Anapol on the opposite side of the argument. Whereas Kerista believed romance and passion were corruptors of utopia that should be avoided at all costs, Anapol was fearful of anything that that might undermine her passion and autonomy. Nearing stood directly in the middle of such polarities, never willing to concede that her relationships undermined her idealism or her freedom. Despite these differences, Nearing assured Anapol that she enjoyed her work and appreciated her efforts.[33]

Nearing and Anapol had more to worry about than their subtle philosophical differences. By mid-decade the AIDS crisis threatened to undermine the progress they had made. Paranoia over the new disease had seeped into the national consciousness, making suspect anything that looked like promiscuity. Many of Nearing and Anapol's readers were worried that having sex with multiple partners put them in danger of becoming infected. Nearing was in a unique position because polyfidelity promoted a closed sexual system. This meant that when it came to the transmission of sexually transmitted infections, it was an inherently safer model than other, less defined forms of ethical non-monogamy. Nearing did not capitalize on this fact to denigrate other lifestyle choices. *PEPTalk* simply warned its readership of the growing concerns the virus raised. While some chose to enter closed groups to protect themselves, others decided to prohibit sex with individuals perceived as high risk, such as gay or bisexual men and intravenous drug users. The newsletter claimed that the most important actions were to get tested and only engage with other trusted individuals who had also been tested. Some *PEPTalk* articles did mention the benefits of polyfidelity in light of such a virulent disease. However, PEP did not take a dogmatic view and intentionally tried to accommodate non-polyfidelitious perspectives.[34]

Anapol's approach to the AIDS epidemic was less clear than Nearing's. While her acceptance of lovers outside of a closed group was inherently riskier, she claimed to discourage casual sex. She taught that honesty and some degree of commitment were essential aspects of ethical sexual engagement. She admitted that having sex within a closed system was "the safest game in town." But this was only true if everyone played by the rules. Those who did not want to conform to the confines of a closed group should play safe. She told her readers that a recent study in *Psychology Today* showed that the spermicide nonoxynol-9 had been proven to kill the AIDS virus in test tubes. She advised the Intinet community to implement use of the chemical in their sex lives. While nonoxynol-9 does not stop the spread of HIV, it is important to note that she disseminated this information when understanding of HIV transmission was in its early stages. Such advice, while troubling, is understandable. More problematic was Anapol's assertion that the "emotional/mental/spiritual state of a person affects susceptibility to physical disease processes." Anapol believed that those who were mentally and spiritually healthy would be much less likely to contract any communicable diseases, including HIV. This belief was directly tied to her New Age spirituality, which colored the way she saw the threat of AIDS and led her to give advice that put her readers in serious physical peril.[35]

Some of Anapol's readers were wary of her position and let her know that polyfidelity might be the best option in the face of the very real danger AIDS imposed on the ethically non-monogamous. Phoenix, a triadic group marriage based in Los Angeles, wrote to Anapol to tell her that the responsibility to keep others safe was a heavy karmic burden, and polyfidelity was a gift for those concerned with such spiritual matters. Anapol conceded and apologized for her initial flippancy. She admitted that, regardless of her personal beliefs concerning the contraction of diseases, preventing exposure made polyfidelity a rational decision.[36]

In the summer of 1986, Nearing began advertising PEP's first major polyfidelity conference, PEPCON. The event, which she promoted as a networking weekend filled with workshops, films, games, dancing, and discussion groups, was scheduled to take place in Eugene in July of 1987. Anyone interested was to fill out a survey and mail it back. One part of the survey asked potential attendees if they wished to conduct a workshop on a matter relevant to polyfidelity. Anapol applied, hoping to use the opportunity to promote her views on the relationship between spirituality and sexuality. She wrote Nearing to tell her that she and her lover, Paul Glassco, wanted to lead a workshop on tantra. The underlying theme of their presentation was that harmonious vibrations were "the basis of music, tantric sexual practice, and enduring relationships." By giving in to these "harmonic notes" and "continuous orgasmic waves," practitioners "learn how to let go into the Tao." While it does not appear that Nearing was deeply attracted to New Age thought early on in her career, she was open to it. *PEPTalk* occasionally printed articles from writers promoting New Age literature and tantric practices. Nearing accepted Anapol's proposal. Among the workshops that *PEPTalk* promised conference attendees were ones on social contracting, cooperative parenting, sharing money, and tantra.[37]

Unfortunately, the details of the first annual PEPCON are sparsely documented. Both attendees and organizers believed it was a success. One attendee praised the conference as a place of warm fun, noting that he met people interested in forming a Best Friend Identity Cluster alongside him and his partner. More significantly, PEPCON marked the first intentional coming together of PEP and Intinet as a united force. Syntony promoted their modified Keristan ideal of polyfidelity, while Anapol and Glassco promoted sexual freedom and New Age spirituality. This cross-pollination had lasting effects. By the following autumn, *PEPTalk*'s cover story claimed that "polyfidelity is probably the alternative lifestyle most closely linked to religiosity and spirituality." This was not likely a claim the Syntonians would have made half a decade earlier when they were in throes of their struggle with Kerista.[38]

Nearing and Anapol's efforts in the second half of the 1980s birthed a small but national network. *PEPTalk*'s format continually expanded to include a larger reader's forum, giving Nearing's membership a more vocal role. In 1988, inspired by Nearing's example, PEP member Stan Major created *Touchpoint*, a contact service for anyone interested in sexual "non-exclusivity." The publication, printed in Nashville, Tennessee, was a directory that permitted members to give their location information alongside a short biography describing their interests and desires. In the pre-internet era, this was an invaluable resource for anyone seeking non-monogamous relationships.[39]

Nearing wanted to provide her readers with as much information and as many resources as possible. PEPCON was one way to do this, but it was limited in duration and difficult to attend for those living outside the Pacific Northwest. Nearing wanted to do more. In the spring of 1989, she published a second edition of her *Polyfidelity Primer*, renaming it *The New Faithful*. She turned what had been a short tabloid into a nine-chapter book detailing the pragmatism of polyfidelity. The new edition included discussions of courtship guidelines, money management, health, sex, and parenting, and it was replete with a resource section that included the works of Heinlein and Rimmer. Nearing disseminated the new edition to libraries, advertising it as an educational device as well as a means for members to connect to new people. In addition, Nearing published *Network*, a quarterly publication that allowed members to share seventy-five-word self-descriptions and gathered information on groups and resources beneficial to anyone interested in polyfidelity.[40]

By the late 1980s, Eugene had surpassed San Francisco as the epicenter of polyfidelity. As one PEP member optimistically wrote,

> The 60's brought us the dream through the works of Robert Heinlein and Robert Rimmer. The 70's brought us Kerista, the first easily observable closed group marriage of all primary partners. The 80's saw the

slow but sure gathering of people in Eugene, Oregon around the idea of polycentric lifestyles including polyfidelity. Come join us in the 90's. Between us all we can make this bird fly.[41]

Nearing was encouraged by her progress.

Anapol pressed on from her home base in Marin County. Still unable to secure a publisher for her book, she self-published *A Resource Guide for the Responsible Non-Monogamist* in 1989. The guide was an expanded compilation of resources that included articles she and others had written over the previous decade. It included practical guidance for starting local support groups, advice for effective networking, and excerpts from her newsletter. The volume also contained a host of information on tantric sexual practices. She defended the addition of tantra, arguing that methods for achieving higher consciousness through sex were crucial to the success of multipartner relationships. Most importantly, the guide was an organizational directory listing the names and addresses of nine major organizations that Anapol believed were effectively making gains for ethical non-monogamy across the nation. The listings provided each organization's contact information and a description that detailed its history and unique contributions. Some organizations, such as Southern California's Family Synergy, tended to advocate more for open relationships as opposed to group marriage. At the opposite end of the spectrum, she included Kerista. Anapol was adamant that, despite the differences between the groups, each organization was a resource for those pursuing different forms of ethical non-monogamy. None, she assured, practiced or advocated swinging. For those who were interested in such things, she added the contact information for the North American Swing Club Association.[42]

By 1990, it was clear that Nearing and Anapol's coalition was at a crossroads. During the six years that had passed since *Time* had pronounced the death of the sexual revolution, PEP and Intinet had defied that declaration, defending one of the revolution's most radical proposals by recasting non-monogamy in ethical terms. Embracing the language of moral conservatives, they claimed to be defenders of honesty, commitment, and family. These efforts had produced some tangible cohesion among their fellow ethical non-monogamists. Both Nearing's second edition of her *Primer* and Anapol's *Resource Guide for the Ethical Non-Monogamist* were evidence of their success in creating alliances across diverse factions and variant forms of ethical non-monogamy.

Despite these gains, it was clear that something was missing. Anapol best expressed this feeling in the introduction to her *Resource Guide*, where she lamented that, despite the work of those who were pioneering new "lovestyles," one of the most vexing problems within their coalition was the need for a common language. She had come to prefer the term "multimate relationships" over words like "polygamy" and "non-monogamy." Others disagreed about what word was best. She complained that the plethora of terms used to describe ethical multipartner relationships required an extensive glossary. To ensure unity, there needed to be a shared nomenclature. Fortunately for Anapol, the Zells were ready to return to public life and bring with them what she believed her and Nearing's coalition needed.[43]

During the six years that Nearing and Anapol had been collaborating, Tim and Morning Glory Zell had been on various adventures while traveling down the West Coast. After leaving St. Louis, the Zells went to Eugene, where Morning Glory hoped her ex-husband Gary might become part of their family. Although Gary was not interested in such a proposition at that time, the Zells managed to secure teaching positions at a local community college where they offered a course on "Witchcraft, Shamanism, and Pagan Religion." While teaching, the Zells became fascinated with uncovering the underlying historical events on which specific myths were based. Their research led them to the work of University of Maine biologist Franklin Dove. In 1936, Dove created a unicorn from a one-day old bull calf by surgically unattaching the calf's horn buds right after its birth and then reattaching them together in the middle of its head. Dove discovered that the two buds would then create one massive horn in place of the naturally occurring two smaller ones. He believed that earlier civilizations had also learned this trick, and their previous efforts laid the foundations for the myth of the unicorn. The Zells agreed with Dove's assessment, believing that the manipulation of nature needed to bring the unicorn into existence made it even more magical. They decided to recreate the process with goats.[44]

Failing to convince Gary to become part of their family and needing more room to raise their unicorns, the Zells decided to leave Eugene and travel south to California. They settled in the rural mountains of Mendocino County on a hippie ranch owned by a fellow neo-Pagan and began breeding unicorn goats. Their first, named Galahad, was born in early 1980. Two others, Lancelot and Bedivere, soon followed. The Zells, wanting to show off their discovery, spent the next three years traveling with the Renaissance Faire, during which time they contracted with an agent to represent them.

In the summer of 1984, the Zells' agent secured a contract with Ringling Brothers and Barnum and Bailey Circus. Unfortunately, the circus was more interested in the Zells' unicorns than it was with them and promoted the unicorns' origins as a mystery. Contractually, the Zells were unable to speak about the deal without express permission, a point that saddened them, especially after they saw the circus' poor methods of caring for their goats. Nonetheless, the unicorns became part of one of the largest publicity events in circus history and were even the subject of a comedy skit starring Martin Short on *Saturday Night Live*. Despite their reservations about the circus gig, the Zells' four-year deal was lucrative. With their tendency to prize experience over frugality, they spent most of their profits throwing neo-Pagan celebrations on their Mendocino compound and funding an excursion off the coast of New Zealand in search of mermaids (Figure 3.2).[45]

Though the Zells' eccentric escapades kept them busy, by the mid-1980s, they turned their attention back to reviving CAW, which had never officially dissolved. The Zells threw CAW festivals and even held board of director meetings during their time in Mendocino County.

Figure 3.2 Tim and Morning Glory Zell with their unicorn goat
Lancelot, 1980.
Photo courtesy of Oberon Zell.

But, aside from these sporadic celebrations and legal formalities, the
Zells spent the better part of a decade neglecting any attempts at
church growth. Without Tim's charismatic leadership, the church
had largely become defunct outside of the Zells' immediate circle.
However, when the owner of the hippie ranch they were living on
told them it was time for them to leave, the Zells decided to reenter
public life. Reviving CAW was an essential part of that decision.[46]

During their time in Oregon and Northern California, the Zells
remained non-monogamous. When traveling separately with the
Renaissance Fair, they both took other lovers. Their relationship went
through tumultuous times, and they sometimes questioned whether
they would remain together. By the time they decided to reintegrate
with society, they had years of experience navigating the pitfalls of
ethical non-monogamy. This experience had produced a practical

philosophy about how to maintain such relationships. This philosophy came with a specific vocabulary that the Zells wished to share with the world. Just as Nearing and Anapol were seeking to widen their coalition and solidify its terminology, the Zells came out of isolation, bring with them the lessons they had learned.[47]

4

Partnerships

We are taking a major step toward recreating our tribe. Toward affirming our Oneness while acknowledging our differences. Toward claiming our power to shape our own culture in the image which we desire. Toward carrying out the will of the Goddess.

—Ryam Nearing and Deborah Anapol, *Loving More Magazine* (1995)

When the Zells reemerged into public life, they brought with them a vibrant stream of ethical non-monogamy, unique in its historical origins and spiritual vision. The theological foundations of the Church of All Worlds (CAW)'s sexual ethics dated back to the early 1970s, before the initial demise of *Green Egg*. The articles published during that period were pivotal in dispersing the Zells' sexual theology within the emerging neo-Pagan community, but it was almost wholly limited to that community. In the early 1990s, Nearing and Anapol introduced the Zells' ideas to an entirely new subculture. This cross-fertilization ensured that Robert Heinlein's legacy would remain preserved within American polyamory. Many Polyfidelitous Educational Productions (PEP) and Intinet members writing to Nearing and Anapol throughout the 1980s attested to Heinlein's influence on their own transition to ethical non-monogamy. For many ethical non-monogamists, Heinlein was slowly becoming a relic from the past. The reemergence of the Zells once again secured his preeminence.

Zell published the first issue of the resurrected *Green Egg* on May Day, 1988. Robert Heinlein died seven days later, just before Zell was able to send him a copy. To honor Heinlein's life, Zell wrote a heart-felt memorandum to the science fiction master in the August issue. Alongside his eulogy for Heinlein, Zell published several letters from their personal correspondence throughout the early 1970s. The letters provided *Green Egg*'s readership with rare insight into Heinlein's mo-tivations for writing *Stranger*, which the novelist typically shared with only his wife and editor. Over many subsequent issues Zell published additional excerpts from their correspondence.[1]

Green Egg picked up where it left off in the late 1970s. The first art-icle Zell published was an updated version of his "Theagenesis: The Birth of the Goddess." The revision was only slightly altered, adopting the more popular Gaea nomenclature to refer to the goddess. This in-tentional throwback to Zell's acid-induced goddess vision projected the ethos of the magazine. Just as it had a decade earlier, Zell's gospel of ecology and goddess worship undergirded his sexual ethics. *Green Egg* went on to publish article after article detailing the sacred and ritual nature of sexual relations.[2]

Upon his reemergence on the wider American countercultural scene, Zell found he was no longer a pioneer in his attempts to tie to-gether non-Christian spirituality with sexual liberation. Throughout the late 1970s and 1980s, while the Zells isolated themselves in the forests of Mendocino, the New Age Movement had spread like wild-fire up and down the California coast. Zell was surrounded by tan-tric practitioners who seamlessly combined sex and spirituality while leaving little to no place for ancient European earth religions. New Age adherents of sacred sexuality tended to look to the non-Christian East, rather than the pre-Christian West, for their spiritual inspiration. While goddess worship was prevalent among New Age practitioners, they tended to emphasize transcendent spiritual experiences in con-trast to neo-Pagan's stress on immanence. This difference often put New Agers at odds with neo-Pagans, with the former denigrating the latter's celebration of the material world as crude. Zell experienced this discrimination firsthand when he tried to distribute *Green Egg* through the seemingly ubiquitous network of New Age bookstores that spanned the Northwest. Discouraged by the stores' rejections, he excoriated the exclusivity of the New Age community. After all, he reasoned, it was neo-Paganism that had embraced environmentalism, feminism, goddess worship, sexual liberation, and even crystal magic a decade before the emergence of the New Age movement. Despite his frustrations, Zell remained ecumenical and argued that the movements should be allies, with neo-Pagans respected as the rightful forebearers of the New Age.[3]

The Zells continued to promote their belief that sex was communal. They were committed to one another first and foremost. However, they believed that, outside of that bond, sexual connections promoted an extended unity that brought the neo-Pagan community closer together. Unlike more conservative forms of ethical non-monogamy, such as Nearing's polyfidelity, this model allowed for several diverse relationship structures outside of the primary marriage. The Zells could have multiple primaries, like Nearing, if they wished. But they were also allowed to have anything from one-night stands to substantial secondary or tertiary relationships. They were very amenable to group sex as well. Tim, who had renamed himself Otter, reminisced fondly that he and Morning Glory enjoyed "spectacular orgies that will live long in song and legend." As long as their primary relationship was conducted with integrity and honesty, peripheral relationships could remain in a state of flux.[4]

Though Zell's religion alienated him from many New Age practitioners, practical issues in his personal life drew him to Anapol. In March of 1990, Zell wrote to her seeking help. He explained that he was currently in an open plural marriage with two women and two men. He and his two wives, Morning Glory and Diane Darling, had just finished reading her *Resource Guide for the Ethical Non-Monogamist* and needed some direction. In addition to him and his two wives, his family now included Morning Glory's ex-husband, Gary. Darling, who had been Zell's mistress since 1982, officially became a part of the family in 1989, when he and Morning Glory married her in a neo-Pagan handfasting ceremony. The Zells had long felt guilty about leaving Gary behind when they first ran away together in the early 1970s. Though Morning Glory's attempts to bring Gary into the family were initially unsuccessful, she had continued to try over the years. Recently, they had introduced Darling and Gary. The two fell in love, and Gary agreed to join their group marriage. However, despite their commitments to one another, Otter felt Darling had lost sexual interest in him and that Gary resented him for stealing Morning Glory away years prior. He wondered if Anapol, as a clinical psychologist, could help.[5]

Anapol was unable to help mend the rifts in the Zells' group marriage, and the two couples later parted ways. But in the process of trying to help save his family, Anapol and Zell became friends. In 1990, they met in person in San Francisco at the Whole Life Expo, a New Age event intended to promote countercultural ideas on a large scale. Expanded Family Network, a group for the ethically non-monogamous from Berkeley that Anapol had begun working with, and *Truthseeker Magazine* cosponsored a discussion panel, Beyond the Nuclear Family: Lovestyles for the 21st Century, on which Anapol and Zell were asked to speak. The two immediately saw each other as allies. Despite their differences, they both practiced a form of ethical non-monogamy that was much more fluid than Nearing's polyfidelity, and their sexual ethics were both rooted in what they believed were ancient spiritual foundations. In addition, they were personally disposed to inclusivity, which allowed them to work with individuals across a range of perspectives. Anapol, unlike many other New Agers he had met, did not discriminate against Zell for his neo-Pagan beliefs. Their meeting marked the beginning of a long-lasting professional relationship.[6]

Despite the difficulties in their group marriage, the Zells had learned a great deal from the previous decade and a half of practicing ethical non-monogamy. In her May 1990 article, "A Banquet of Lovers: Strategies for Responsible Open Relationships," Morning

Glory immortalized these lessons in the pages of *Green Egg*. The essay was a practical how-to guide for cultivating sustainable open relationships. Presenting her recommendations in a style that was stripped of anything excessively neo-Pagan, Morning Glory argued that the two cornerstones of any sustainable open relationship were joint commitments to honesty and non-monogamy. Deceit or a preference for monogamy on the part of anyone involved was a recipe for disaster. Beyond those foundational pillars, Morning Glory encouraged partners to put their focus on their primary relationships. Primaries should always consult their counterparts before taking on new lovers. If there was tension within the primary relationship, secondary relationships should never be pursued. Potential lovers should be notified immediately of primary relationships, and, if secondary relationships become threatening to the primary ones, they must be terminated. Finally, given the spread of AIDS, it was important to always remain cautious. Moring Glory advocated what she termed the "Condom Commitment." Aside from the mutual assent of all primaries, condoms must always be used with non-primary lovers. If unprotected sex occurred with an unauthorized person, whether due to the passion of the moment or condom failure, those exposed were to quarantine until their health status was determined.[7]

While "Banquet of Lovers" conveyed the pragmatic side of the Zells' open marriage, the real significance of the essay lies in Morning Glory's use of the term "polyamorous" to describe their lifestyle. This was the first time it was used by someone within the emerging coalition, and many polyamorists credit Morning Glory with coining the term. At the end of her essay, Morning Glory referred her readers to Anapol's *Resource Guide*. Anapol introduced the term "polyamorous" to the readership she and Nearing cultivated when she republished "Banquet of Lovers" in full at the end of the first chapter of her book, *Love Without Limits*, two years later. Though the term took a while to become widely accepted, it eventually overshadowed the alternatives.[8]

During the early 1990s, Anapol worked tirelessly to promote polyamory. She accepted numerous speaking engagements ranging from panel discussions on non-monogamy and bisexuality at the University of California, Berkeley, to speaking about ethical non-monogamy at the National Sexuality Symposium. She wrote to the California legislature to advocate for sexual orientation being included under the Fair Employment and Housing Act. She appeared on numerous radio programs throughout the country. She corresponded with the American Civil Liberties Union (ACLU), established a rudimentary computer network, and appeared on daytime talk shows. All of these things she did while running Intinet Resource Center out of Marin County. Each of these endeavors connected her to a wider array of individuals and resources, whom she would then introduce to Intinet members through her newsletters and progress reports. Yet Anapol's most valuable contribution to polyamory during the 1990s was her ongoing and increasingly close engagement with Ryam Nearing.[9]

While Anapol was expanding nationally, Syntony, still comprised of Nearing and her two husbands, Barry Northrop and Allan Jensen, remained evangelists for the gospel of polyfidelity. During the early 1990s, Nearing began rethinking her plan for PEP. She and her husbands left Eugene and relocated to Hawaii. There they befriended nearby ex-Keristans. Remaining true to their ideals, Nearing hoped to establish an intentional community on the Big Island.

Despite her departure from the continental United States, Nearing remained steadfast in her national proselytization. She faithfully published her newsletter, which she renamed *Loving More*. She promoted the new edition of her *Primer* and appeared on popular talk shows such as *The Sally Jesse Raphael Show*. Nearing remained a libertarian and often promoted these political ideals at events either directly or indirectly related to the Libertarian Party. In 1991, she spoke at LA Freedom, a libertarian conference for publishers that advocated for social freedoms. Appearing alongside Robert Anton Wilson, she promoted herself as a libertarian educator whose freedoms were oppressed by both government overreach and fundamentalist Christian culture.[10]

Nearing's libertarianism, shared by her husbands, was simultaneously an asset and a liability. On the one hand, it prevented her from
becoming doctrinaire in her commitment to polyfidelity. It allowed
her to work alongside a wide range of individuals, some of whom she
disagreed with on a host of topics. It also allowed her to accept a full
range of sexual orientations as a basic human right. Despite repeatedly
emphasizing the heterosexuality of her relationship, Nearing's newsletter contained resources for non-heterosexuals and often discussed
the prevalence of bisexuality within group marriages.[11]

Though Nearing's libertarianism was often used to positive ends,
it also had negative effects. Significant among these was that her distrust for established authority made her skeptical of mainstream science. In the era of AIDS, this could be dangerous. Though she did not
deny that AIDS was sexually transmitted, throughout the early 1990s,
Nearing published several articles that were critical of contemporary
AIDS research and denied the causal link between HIV and AIDS. At
one point, her husband Allan argued that AIDS was curable, no matter
what the government said. Nearing also printed objections to these
articles from other PEP members. But, even then, she did not hide
her skepticism toward scientific consensus. She argued that, since the
government had lied about things in the past, her readers should at
least consider alternative perspectives.[12]

Nearing's efforts proved invaluable to uniting polyamorists
throughout the decade. Significant among her contributions was her
yearly PEPCON conferences. Initially held in Eugene, these provided
a meeting place for the like-minded from around the Northwest to
come together and enjoy fellowship. Although the conferences were
originally intended to focus on promoting polyfidelity, Nearing's
insatiable desire to build a national movement slowly expanded in
scope to include more free-form relationship styles. By 1991, Nearing
had drafted a social contract to which all attendees had to agree. Its
two primary components were voluntary participation in events and,
above all, a commitment to gracious social tolerance of differences
among fellow attendees. These rules were quickly put to the test.[13]

Nearing's fifth annual PEPCON, held over Labor Day weekend, 1991, at the University of California, Berkeley, was the culmination of years of networking by Nearing and Anapol. The official theme of the conference was "A Polyfidelitous Vision of the Future (Or How to Save the Family, the Planet, and Have a Good Time Doing It Too)." Convening just after Morning Glory coined the term "polyamorous," the conference brought together a diverse range of individuals and organizations. Nearing was there with her husbands to represent PEP. Anapol was accompanied by Paul Glassco, on behalf of Intinet. Phoenix, the triadic group marriage of eight years from Los Angeles that was associated with both PEP and Intinet, gave the keynote presentation, which focused on love, trust, genuineness, and "psychospiritual work." Also in attendance was Berkeley's Expanded Family Network, which by that time was closely associated with Anapol. Extending beyond the panels on mundane issues such as money management, there was also a "Coming Out" workshop led by Anapol and Glassco, as well as a clothing-optional tantra workshop.[14]

In addition to these new attendees, CAW and Kerista had come to witness the newly christened polyamorous coalition. The presence of both, alongside the newer polyamorous factions, was a testament to Nearing and Anapol's labor. Between the two of them, they had managed to convene polyamorous practitioners from different generations and ideological backgrounds (Figure 4.1).[15]

It was an uneasy union. CAW was invited to conduct the opening and closing ceremonies, as well as lead the workshop, "Alternative Spirituality for Sex Positive Lifestyles." Zell's recollection of the opening ceremony conveys some of the tensions within the conference body.

> I reached out my right hand, and Morning Glory came up on stage and took it, reciting the traits of "Two." I then reached out my left hand, and my lover Anodea came up and took it, reciting the traits of "Three." Then MG reached out her right hand and her ex-husband Gary came up, reciting the traits of "Four." Andy joined Anodea with "Five," and Diane joined Gary with "Six." And then Andy and Gary

Figure 4.1 Deborah Anapol and Ryam Nearing, early 1990s.
Photo courtesy of Loving More.

reached out their free hands to gesture expansively and inclusively to
the audience. We were not expecting what happened next, as with a
screeching of chairs, people on the ends of the front row came up on
the ends of the stage and linked hands, and everyone else joined theirs
too, until everyone ringed the entire auditorium in a big circle. Except
that there were maybe a dozen people scattered evenly throughout the
auditorium, glued to their seats, with panicked expressions. These were
the Keristans, and Jud (who wasn't there) had told them to spread out as

shills. But he hadn't told them what to do if everyone got up and made a big circle around the seats!¹⁶

Jud's absence was unsurprising. By the late 1980s, he typically avoided Kerista's public appearances, and, by 1991, internal tensions were slowly tearing the commune apart. Though Kerista's presence at PEPCON was divisive, Nearing recognized her intellectual debt to the commune. She had hoped that, despite their history of aggression, Keristans would bring something positive to the conference. Those hopes went unfulfilled, and the weekend proved Kerista's last chance to join the emerging polyamorous coalition.¹⁷

The irony of their presence at PEPCON was not lost on the Keristans. After years of desperately trying to bring Nearing into their fold, they now attended her conference where she promoted their ideas among a diverse community of ethical non-monogamists, many of whom accepted polyfidelity while rejecting the Keristan ideology from which it originated. Despite their contrarian position, Kerista gave a presentation, "Polyfidelity: Beyond the Triad," which argued for the superiority of large communal group marriages. Though this was likely aimed at undermining the legitimacy of Nearing's relationship, Nearing extended them goodwill and thanked them for their pioneering work on polyfidelity in her conference recap in her next newsletter.¹⁸

Kerista's decision to refrain from joining Nearing and Anapol's coalition undoubtedly worked in the coalition's favor. The commune was not just divisive, it was volatile. After just reaching twenty years old, Kerista's New Tribe disbanded four months after the conference. There have been numerous explanations for its disintegration. Zell believed CAW's interaction with Kerista at PEPCON that year was instrumental in the commune's demise. CAW's booth was next to Kerista's during the conference, and Keristans came over to inquire about CAW's doctrine. The Keristans boasted of their extensive social contract, which had expanded to eighty-nine rules, and asked how many rules CAW members had to follow. Zell told them that the only rule CAW members had to observe was to "be excellent" to one another. Some Keristans, according to Zell, were baffled, while others saw that it was possible to enjoy sexual liberation without the excessive baggage of Keristan ideology. Though this incident well may have led some members to question their ideology, it is unlikely this interaction had a major effect on the commune. The cracks in Kerista's foundation ran deep, and the confrontation that led to the commune's demise was a long time coming.[19]

Many Keristans had grown tired of the commune's rigidity. Over time, Jud's utopian visions had become more grandiose and detailed. In opposition to their democratic ideals, he held tight control over the inner workings of the commune. Ironically, however, it was Jud's devotion to capitalism that undermined his dominance. During the 1970s and 1980s, Kerista started several businesses. Among these was a company buying, selling, and repairing MacIntosh computers. Like Kerista's other economic endeavors, the commune members believed the business would help fund their religious expansion. Though the business grew to be worth millions, it had the opposite effect on the religion. Success meant that the Keristans had to engage more and more with the outside world. These outside interactions awoke many Keristans to the commune's oppressive tendencies, specifically regarding Jud's hegemonic control. Eve Furchgott, Jud's trusted New Tribe co-founder, eventually admitted that the commune had become a cult built around his charismatic leadership. Mutiny ensued, which ended in Jud's removal from power. Unsurprisingly, Jud disavowed the remaining members as apostates. He rejected polyfidelity as a transitional doctrine and announced that he no longer wished to be shackled by fidelity to any group, claiming he was on his way to "ultimate swinging." Emotionally exhausted, the remaining members disbanded on December 31, 1991. Despite spending their last years constantly worrying about communist expansion, the capitalist commune ironically broke up five days after the fall of the Soviet Union.[20]

Kerista's rejection of Nearing and Anapol's coalition posed no threat to the unity that PEPCON '91 embodied. The other attendees were inspired to redouble their own personal efforts, and diverse factions began brainstorming how they could join forces to effect meaningful social change. Some of these plans worked better than others. Among those ideas that did not come to fruition was CAW and Intinet's joint venture to write and produce episodes for the television show *Star Trek: The Next Generation* that featured positive depictions of polyamorous characters. Both Zell and Anapol believed that media representations were one of the best ways to normalize polyamorous relationships among mainstream Americans. *Stranger* had convinced Zell that science fiction was the best place to start. The venture did produce viable scripts. The first, "Initiation," was cowritten by Anapol and her friend Jim Heddle. In the episode, the starship *Enterprise* encounters a race of docile and loving polyamorous aliens who, due to a genetic mutation, can select their own genders. Another group of less evolved monogamous aliens, who lack the mutation and wish to rehabilitate the polys, force the polyamorous aliens to live in patriarchal nuclear families. Eventually they see the error of their ways and the two communities live in harmony. The next episode, co-created by Heddle, CAW's Diane Darling, and Otter Zell was entitled "Calling Down the Moon." It followed a primitive race of polyamorous, water-sharing, goddess-worshipping empaths, replete with baby unicorns, which the Zells promised they could supply. Morning Glory also wrote an episode that followed two crew members' romantic engagement with a polyamorous alien couple. An attempt to portray the more intimate aspects of polyamorous relationships, Morning Glory's script focused on personal interactions, as the title, "Relationship," suggests. Despite registering the episodes with the Writer's Guild of America and campaigning tirelessly for their acceptance, these episodes were eventually rejected.[21]

The failure of the Star Trek campaign did not dampen Anapol's spirits but it did prove a diversion from finishing her book. Her *Resource Guide for the Ethical Non-Monogamist* (1989) was a compilation of resources rather than the original manuscript she had been trying to complete. Energized by PEPCON '91, Anapol finally published *Love*

Without Limits: The Quest for Sustainable Intimate Relationships in June
of 1992. The nine-chapter book presented her personal method for
fostering sustainable polyamorous relationships. Much of the material
was mundane, covering issues like money-sharing, compatibility, and
child-rearing in multi-adult households. It also incorporated external
resources Anapol had collected over the years.[22]

The larger argument of Anapol's book was that most of mankind
was innately non-monogamous and that the Christian patriarchy had
imposed an unnatural form of sexual oppression on Western culture.
Though those embracing multipartner relationships were a sexual
minority, it was their right to overcome this oppression and engage
in ethical non-monogamy. This could take myriad forms, from polyfidelitious triads to open marriages that consisted of an indeterminate
number of secondary and tertiary partners. For Anapol, primary partners were unnecessary. Honesty among the parties involved and a
commitment to creating intimate sexual relationships that excluded
casual sex were the only necessary ethical components. She also argued that non-Christian spirituality was an essential component for
sustaining polyamorous relationships. She offered seven steps leading
toward sustainable and responsible non-monogamy. Most revolved
around self-healing, communication, and dealing with jealousy.
However, her fifth step stated that relational success is integrally tied
to increased flow of sexual energy. There were many tools that could
achieve this effect, among them tantric, Taoist, alchemical, and native
American traditions. Just as there is no normative family structure,
there is no single way to sexual enlightenment. Anapol preferred the
tantric approach because she believed it most directly promoted the
sacredness of sex, goddess worship, and the essential unity of existence.
However, whether these insights were gathered directly from tantra,
or through some other alternative spiritual path, she was explicit that,
"tantric knowledge is crucial to your success." Neo-Paganism was an
acceptable path. Though she still preferred other terms to Morning
Glory Zell's "polyamorous," she reprinted Morning Glory's "Banquet
of Lovers" in full at the end of her first chapter, "What Is Responsible

Non-Monogamy." Hoping to highlight the practicality of the Zells' approach, the article introduced the term to an even larger audience.[23]

Nearing was also hard at work in the aftermath of PEPCON '91. The following year, she published the third edition of her *Primer*, re-titled *Loving More: The Polyfidelity Primer*. Though it differed little from the 1989 edition, Nearing boasted that it contained "much additional material and the latest findings." The structure of the book was al-most identical, but the last two chapters were condensed into one. More significantly, Nearing removed the longer personal testimonials from the previous two editions. She replaced them with anonymous shorter testimonies gathered from people living in polyfidelitous re-lationships. These were inserted throughout the book, each correlated with the themes of their respective chapters. Nearing also promoted the exploitation of a new California law that allowed people living together to register as families. While the legal benefits were slim, she considered families preferable to domestic partnerships, which she believed inherently favored monogamy. Nearing admitted that family registration fell short of legal marriage, yet she argued that cultural recognition might foster personal contentment. She also be-lieved the registration might be a step in the direction of legal plu-ral marriage. Nearing was less interested in government recognition than in achieving cultural legitimacy. While she certainly wanted the same economic benefits marriage afforded monogamous couples, she still believed the government had no legitimate business meddling in matrimony.[24]

By the time Nearing published the third edition of her *Primer*, she had come to see polyamorous people as a persecuted sexual minority. She lamented that, while monogamy was extremely uncommon in the animal kingdom, it was the norm for humans. Despite its ubiquity, Nearing believed many individuals were not predisposed to it. She be-lieved these differences, as a part of mankind's beauty, should be cele-brated and not suppressed. It was the responsibility of those like her, living on the sexual frontier, to become examples and educators for the rest of mankind. The persecution that poly practitioners endured

was traumatic. Based on this shared struggle, Nearing believed polyamorous people should unite to mutually support one another. The
newly updated resource guide conveyed her expanded vision. The
second edition listed only two groups, PEP and The Hemlock Society,
which aided in the creation of living wills and powers of attorney. By
1992, fourteen groups appeared, including several non-polyfidelitious,
polyamorous groups, such as Expanded Family Network and the
National Organization of Sex Enthusiasts.[25]

Despite Nearing's constantly evolving ecumenism, the third edition of her *Primer* remained predominately an argument for polyfidelity. Because Anapol's *Love Without Limits* made a more general case for
polyamory, it had a wider appeal and earned her greater recognition
across the larger coalition. In the spring of 1992, Robert Rimmer, the
countercultural novelist who had befriended Tim Zell in the 1970s,
saw Nearing and Anapol appear on a talk show. Impressed, he wrote
letters to both women. He does not appear to remember receiving
Anapol's invitation to serve on Intinet's advisory board seven years
earlier. He informed her that he had just heard of her and her organization through their shared friend Robert Francoeur. He lauded
both women as role models for a new society. He praised Anapol's
new book and assured her that what she was doing was an extension
of his work in the 1960s. He wished to forward their work to literary
agents to showcase the authors as the wave of the future. Rimmer
pressed the two women, telling them that, while he enjoyed both
of their separate perspectives, he believed they should combine their
books to make something publishable for a mainstream audience.[26]

Rimmer was still a big name in polyamorous publications, often
listed just after Heinlein as central to turning many toward ethical
non-monogamy.[27] Yet, by the 1990s, his works had fallen into relative
obscurity. For years his literary contributions were largely limited to
reviews of pornography. He was unabashed in stating that he thought
Nearing and Anapol could make him relevant to a new generation.
He told them that he was currently writing a new book with the

working title *Sexual Sanity Now*, and he sent Anapol a copy of the proposal for her feedback.

The book was classic Rimmer. It argued that the federal government should promote a new sexual morality through subsidies and sex education. Sex Ed would begin during kindergarten, with sexual contact between minors limited to foreplay until their seventeenth birthday. Afterward, singles with no children would enjoy a free college education where sexual experimentation would be encouraged. The government would legalize nudity in public parks and beaches. It would institute a new media rating system that allowed the portrayal of nudity and sexual acts between heterosexuals on public television. However, queer content would be limited to pay per view and private video. The government would also legalize group marriages and fund "stress relief clinics" offering the services of federally subsidized prostitutes for a meager cost.[28]

Despite his excitement at working with Nearing and Anapol, Rimmer clearly was unfamiliar with the finer points of their thought. His conviction that the government should take the lead in the promotion of sexual ethics put him at odds with Nearing's libertarianism, and his implicit homophobia was doubtless an affront to Anapol's bisexuality. Nonetheless, both women respected Rimmer for his previous contributions to the sexual counterculture and accepted him into the coalition. Anapol published an interview with him the following autumn in Intinet's newsletter in which Rimmer promoted the ideas he had outlined in his book proposal. She portrayed him as a visionary, remarking that the years he had spent inspiring millions of baby boomers made him instrumental to the emergence of polyamory. By April of 1993, Rimmer finally accepted Anapol's long-standing offer to serve on her board of advisors, if it entailed no commitment.[29]

Despite Rimmer's prodding, Nearing and Anapol had no intention of combining their separate projects in 1992. Nearing was in Hawaii and expended most of her efforts publishing her newsletter, planning her annual conference, and constructing her own intentional community. Meanwhile, Anapol was promoting her book across the country, making radio appearances, and appearing on daytime talk shows. Despite writing a book on maintaining sustainable intimate relationships, she had trouble maintaining her own. Anapol had long believed that open relationships were a panacea, remedying the dilemma between the two polarities of commitment and freedom. Yet, by the spring of 1993, she was beginning to feel suffocated by her open relationship with Paul Glassco, to whom she was now married.[30]

By this point, Anapol and Glassco were leading Intinet together. Yet Anapol used Intinet's newsletter to vent about their relationship, chronicling their ongoing personal disagreements over numerous issues. As the passion waned between her and Glassco, she became enraptured with a new lover, Evan, to fill that void. She described the intimacies of her new relationship in explicit detail, including having sex within hearing distance of Evan's wife. She confessed that they failed to use protection in the heat of the moment. Although she had reprinted Morning Glory's "Banquet of Lovers" as a blueprint for poly ethics in her book, in practice Anapol had trouble following the advice of the neo-Pagan priestess. Morning Glory taught that individuals should forego new lovers when primary relationships were in trouble and that they should always use protection unless given the consent of their primaries to do otherwise. Anapol did neither. She reminisced that such passion took her back to her younger days, when she was unconstrained by such rules. The relationship between Anapol and Evan ended when Evan's wife became upset, a fact that brought Anapol great pain.[31]

Anapol intended to use the chronicling of her personal trysts to portray the emotional hardships associated with polyamory, and many of her readers praised her for her openness and honesty. But there was also a backlash. One reader told Anapol that, despite previously being an Intinet supporter, she and her friends were embarrassed by Anapol's "often juvenile emotional trauma and soap opera tactics," and she no longer wanted to be associated with Intinet. Rimmer, thinking in terms of professional advancement, told Anapol that, while he failed to sympathize with her position, the story would make a good book on the struggles of open marriage. Nonetheless, if he were Glassco, he would have left her already. In keeping with the spirit of openness and honesty, Anapol published both the positive and negative responses to her article in the next issue of her newsletter. Along with them she printed a second installment of the saga in which she confessed to growing weary of trying to rekindle intimacy with Glassco. Instead of focusing on rebuilding their relationship, she chased the excitement of a relationship with another new man.[32]

Anapol lacked an immediate support system. She saw Nearing when possible, but those moments were rare. PEPCON '92 lacked the universality of the previous year. The defunct Kerista was absent. Berkeley's Expanded Family Network, Anapol's nearest group of like-minded polyamorists, had also split up over personality differences. Anapol relished the friendships she formed through PEPCON, but her desire for community made her look beyond it for greater personal support. To deal with her problems, she did what was most natural to her and turned to her spirituality. The next push for unification arose from Anapol's personal struggle.[33]

In June of 1992, Timshel, a group of polyamorous clergy, met in the mountains of Pennsylvania. The group's founder, Gerald Jud, was a former pastor with a PhD in the psychology of religion from Yale. After the death of his wife, Jud had traveled to the Esalen Institute, where he was introduced to the human potential movement and tantric yoga. After becoming disenchanted with the church's unwillingness to accept the sexual practices he had discovered, Jud left the church to establish a spiritual community devoted to the unification of sex and spirit. He rejected religious dogma, taking a pluralist approach to religious truth. For Timshel, the unification of sex and spirit was not about doctrine but about the connection of the spirit and the body via tantric yoga and poly sex.[34]

Anapol was infatuated. Although she missed the first Timshel meeting in the summer of 1992 because she was taping an appearance with Nearing on *The Joan Rivers Show*, she made sure she was present for the second one in December. The group immediately impressed her. It did not hurt that she met Michael Dowd, a passionate young pastor in an open marriage, there. Anapol and Dowd had sex a few hours after meeting, and he became the subject of the second installment of the personal saga she chronicled in her newsletter. She gave him a pseudonym in her newsletter to protect him from the "crucifixion on the Poly Cross" an association with her would certainly bring. In later issues, she detailed her threesomes with Dowd and his wife, as well as another instance when she turned down her husband's request to join her and Dowd in bed. Glassco's anger over the situation exacerbated Anapol's longing to be single again. Anapol's love life aside, the Timshel meeting was a professional success. She immediately began planning a new retreat that would introduce her PEPCON friends to the East Coast clergy. As she did so, Anapol grew more ambitious and sought out the participation of leaders of other like-minded special interest groups. At the top of her list were bisexual activists.[35]

Anapol's interest in bisexual activism had many roots. At one level it was personal. She was open about her own bisexuality, and, throughout 1992, she spoke at bisexual events and made contacts within the community. She also knew that inviting bisexual women to poly events drew in more single women to balance the gender dynamic. In her own experience, heterosexual women were less apt than bisexuals to attend poly conferences.[36] Furthermore, by the early 1990s, she and Nearing had come to believe that polyamorists and bisexuals were both ostracized by other sexual minorities. As Nearing knew, discussions of poly issues immediately brought up the question of how same-sex partners in mixed-gender groups were supposed to relate to one another. That is why Nearing, despite her own heterosexuality, had given so much time to the topic of bisexuality in her newsletter and at PEPCON. In addition, both women saw that bisexuals were often rejected by both mainstream and gay communities. When Nearing and Anapol had reached out to make alliances in queer communities, they were often rejected as well. Many gay men were already practicing forms of ethical non-monogamy and taking on another controversial designation was seen as counterproductive to their fight for social acceptance. For Nearing and Anapol, the dual alienation from both the mainstream and queer communities was a point of connection shared by both polyamorists and bisexuals.

In her discussion of sexual minorities in *Love Without Limits*, Anapol listed five bisexual resources and only three for homosexuals. Given the abundance of homosexual resources compared to the paucity of bisexual ones in the Bay Area, it was clear where Anapol's allegiances lay. As she planned her conference, she intentionally sought out bisexual activist attendees. For example, she invited Jim Franzin and Loraine Hutchins to speak. Franzin was a bisexual activist on the board of the Bay Area Bisexual Network, as well as a co-editor of its publication, *Any Thing That Moves*. Hutchins, a self-identified neo-Pagan, was co-editor of the book, *Bi Any Other Name: Bisexual People Speak Out.*[37]

The "Sex and Spirit: Affirming Diversity in Patterns of Committed Personal Intimacy" retreat met at the Kirkridge retreat center in Bangor, Pennsylvania, in September 1993. What set this conference apart was that, unlike PEPCON, it was intended for leaders as opposed to new initiates. In addition to Nearing, Anapol, Jud, Franzin, Hutchins, and Rimmer, there were a host of closeted clergy desperately hoping to liberalize American sexual culture. With seventy-five attendees, the meeting was much smaller than PEPCON. Yet Anapol conveyed the status of the attendees when she remarked that "if the Moral Majority had disappeared Kirkridge that weekend, they would have temporarily succeeded in wiping out the poly movement."[38]

Given the makeup of the Kirkridge group, the program was unconcerned with remedial matters. There were no panels on managing jealousy or personal finances. Instead, it focused on challenging the hold that the Religious Right had on American culture by appealing to alternate forms of spirituality. The conference organizers dedicated two of the three days to creating vision, community, and strategies for cultural change. The middle day was devoted to networking and

cultivating spiritual practices. The latter consisted of singing and dancing, as well as nude group massage.[39]

By all accounts the conference was a success. Not only did leaders
feel emotionally recharged, but they also established lasting connections. Primary among these was the bond between Anapol, Nearing,
and bisexual activist Loraine Hutchins. Hutchins was initially skeptical of polyamorists. However, she was relieved to meet ordained
clergy who did not fear or hate her but wanted to understand and
work with her. She became convinced that straight poly people, like
so many of her queer peers, lived closeted. Within the wide-ranging
religious and sexual orientations represented, Hutchins reported that
she felt uplifted, heard, and accepted. Her decision to join Intinet's
board of advisors represented the beginning of an enduring coalition
between bisexual and polyamorous activism.[40]

In addition to the cross-pollination that occurred, one of the most
significant aspects of the Sex and Spirit retreat was that it cemented
the spiritualist ethos of Nearing and Anapol's coalition. From neo-
Paganism to the New Age, those interested in polyamory prior to the
popularization of the internet could immerse themselves in an assortment of alternative spiritualities. The conference ensured that this
remained an essential characteristic. With the addition of the Timshel
group, liberal monotheists were brought alongside pantheists, poly-
theists, and goddess worshipers. Anapol later remarked,

> What do a Catholic nun, a Jewish bisexual activist, a Hindu scientist, a
> libertarian networker, a best-selling author, a college professor, a New
> Age artist, and a renegade clinical psychologist all have in common?
> They believe that our bodies—and our erotic energies—are sacred.
> Their mission is to bring forward reverence for *eros* as the basis of the
> new movement for social change.[41]

Anapol was ecstatic about the trajectory of the coalition.

Apart from Anapol, Robert Rimmer was probably the most energized by the weekend. He immediately rekindled his campaign to
get Nearing and Anapol to merge their efforts into a single enterprise. However, instead of pressing them to cowrite a book, he was

convinced that a national magazine was what was needed. He sent a proposal to *Playboy*'s CEO, Christie Heftner, pitching his idea. Despite Rimmer's conviction that Nearing and Anapol were the perfect candidates to form an offensive front against conversative Christianity, *Playboy* rejected his idea. However, Nearing and Anapol at last wished to officially join forces. The Sex and Spirit conference convinced both women that there was a large audience on the East Coast, and, beginning in 1994, they partnered to offer a conference in Massachusetts to supplement Nearing's annual West Coast PEPCON. The two also worked as co-leaders of a women's-only retreat for polyamorous "wild women" in the spring.[42]

Anapol's desire to partner with Nearing did not stem solely from the success of the Pennsylvania retreat. After the conference, Anapol decided to leave her husband, Paul Glassco. However, the situation was complicated by their entangled private and professional lives. Glassco had been integral to Intinet's operations for years and had supported Anapol financially. Because of the nature of their relationship, Glassco believed he had a stake in the organization, which made Anapol feel as though she had few choices to disentangle their business interests. She entertained several different possibilities, including handing Initnet over to Glassco and establishing her own intentional community that could double as a Sex and Spirit retreat center. Unsure of what to do, she threw herself into a partnership with Nearing. The more time the two women spent together, the closer they became. By the end of 1994, a decade after each woman had set out separately to undermine American monogamy, they merged their operations.[43]

The first issue of *Loving More Magazine* was published in early 1995, with Nearing and Anapol serving as co-editors. While the magazine took the name of Nearing's previous newsletter, it no longer presented itself as a polyfidelitious group marriage journal. Instead, it provided information for anyone who may be "interested in evolving new relationship options, including group marriage, open dyads, intimate networks, and expanded families." In their editorial, Nearing and Anapol boasted that the magazine, the first to focus on polyamory, was a major step in unifying a new movement consisting of various ethically non-monogamous factions Nearing and Anapol had allied with over the previous decade. In addition to articles written by Nearing and Anapol, the first issue included an autobiographical account by Robert Rimmer, the instigator of the merger. As he had hoped, Nearing and Anapol had made him relevant again. Then followed a three-page article by Riff, an ex-Keritan, chronicling the lessons learned and heartaches experienced during his time as a member of the contentious commune. Joan Constantine, co-author of the 1973 book *Group Marriage* and member of the Boston poly group Family Tree, gave a recap of Nearing and Anapol's first East Coast conference held in September of 1994. Between these articles were advertisements for a bisexual conference in the Midwest, as well as the CAW's resurrected publication, *Green Egg*. Eve Furchgott, Kerista's relentless apologist and co-founder of the New Tribe, designed the cover art (Figure 4.2).[44]

Any key players who were absent or underrepresented in the first issue quickly found their voice in the subsequent issues. The second issue emphasized the alternative spiritualities that pervaded the coalition. Anapol introduced it as a tool intended to heal the rift that had occurred in society between sex and spirit. The cover story, "The Union of Sex and Spirit," was written by Timsel's Gerald Jud and summarized his own journey from traditional Christianity into polyamorous tantric spirituality. Michael Aluna (formerly Dowd), the young minster who became Anapol's lover at the Sex and Spirit conference in 1992, detailed the birth of his own extended family and the synthesis of Keristan, liberal Christian, and eastern philosophies on which it rested. Next, Anapol interviewed a tantric healer who highlighted the therapeutic aspects of tantric practice. Advertisements for Stan Dale's Human Awareness Institute and CAW's *Green Egg* also appeared. Despite their ads, full articles from CAW were absent until the fourth issue. That issue introduced Morning Glory as the person who first coined the term "polyamory" in her 1990 "Banquet of Lovers." In

Figure 4.2 The cover of the first issue of *Loving More Magazine*, 1995.
Photo courtesy of Loving More.

her piece, Morning Glory sketched the neo-Pagan underpinnings of
her own family dynamic, intimately describing the spiritual connection she experienced when having a threesome with two of her male
lovers, one of whom was a close friend of her husband.[45]

The publication of *Loving More Magazine* was a milestone for American polyamory. It unified the polyamorous factions Nearing and Anapol had allied with over the past decade and reinforced the spiritualist ethos of their national network. Diverse family models, from polyfidelity to open relating, each affirming an unlimited range of sexual orientations, were welcomed under the banner of polyamory. New Age, neo-Pagan, Hindu, Jewish, and even liberal Christian practitioners found acceptance. But as much as the early issues of *Loving More* were a testament to tolerance and ecumenism, there were seeds of dissension already present that quickly grew.

It was Anapol whom many of *Loving More*'s readership decided was the problem. Anapol's addiction to freedom had undermined all her relationships. She admitted that was what caused the failure of her first two marriages. It was also why her marriage to Glassco failed. She was never secretive about this fact and, even before co-editing *Loving More Magazine*, her desire to chronicle her sexual escapades publicly had earned the ire of many polyamorists critical of her behavior. Once Anapol decided finally to leave Glassco, she delved deeper into her search for sexual fulfillment. Had she kept the details of her sexual escapades more private, this would not have caused a problem. Yet, from the very first issue of *Loving More*, she made a point to showcase her personal experiences. This decision quickly generated fierce opposition.

Anapol's article, "On the Edge: Exploring the Polyamorous Frontier," in the first issue of *Loving More*, was a direct continuation of the "On the Path" saga she had begun in her own newsletter. But the substitution of "edge" for "path" was significant. The article detailed her life leading up to and through her relationship with Glassco. After the relationship ended, she confided that she sought a tantric lover free from any relational drama. Her search led her to engage in a wide range of sexual experimentation. At one point she was juggling twelve lovers simultaneously. The sheer number of lovers would not have offended *Loving More*'s readership. But Anapol's insistence that she wanted complete freedom, or as she put it, "all pleasure and love, no maintenance, no processing, no daily trivia" was certainly at odds with many reader's notions of commitment.[46]

Anapol might have evaded censure had she stopped after her first article. However, she continued the narrative in the next issue. There she detailed her experiences moving through a sex and spirit erotic party in San Francisco where she was "surrounded by nude and exotically costumed people getting and giving orgasms in every conceivable way after invoking various deities." For Anapol, engaging in such behavior was not a problem. The attendees were fellow spiritual seekers, many of whom she knew. She argued that the aversion many polyamorists had to such behavior was unfounded. She contended that, like handing a boa constrictor to a person with a snake phobia, such sex parties might be a remedy for sexual repression. Immersion in such an open sexual environment, she believed, could be educationally beneficial to polyamorists.[47]

Anapol's claim that polyamorists could benefit from engaging in public group sex with seemingly uncommitted people set off a firestorm among *Loving More*'s readership. Unsurprisingly, much of the criticism came from Nearing's camp. One North Carolinian wrote that they had deep reservations about the merger. After reading Anapol's articles, they were convinced that polyamory was little more than a new name for swinging. A more sympathetic reader from Oregon added that, although Anapol was within her own rights to do what she wanted, she felt she supported a lifestyle that was even more foreign to the polyamorous than was monogamy.[48]

Nearing quickly reverted to damage control. She wrote that, although such unbridled practices were foreign to those committed to polyfidelity, some people saw those connections as meaningful. In the absence of violence or deceit, it would be wrong to judge. While she and Anapol represented different perspectives, it was the purpose of their partnership to reach as many people seeking new relationship paradigms as possible. Although uniting such a wide range of people might be impossible, that was the purpose of *Loving More*. Anapol's response was more pointed. She lamented that such judgments were extremely hurtful to her and made her want to stop the work to which she had dedicated the past decade of her life. For Anapol, the spiritual nature of the group sex gathering she attended made that environment qualitatively different from swinging parties. Polyamory, she believed, should be wide enough to encompass such a sex-positive environment.[49]

The criticism deeply affected Anapol. The next issue of *Loving More* was dedicated to exploring the search for community. It claimed to highlight polyamory's desire for unity in diversity and authenticity. In the editorial Anapol lamented that, despite their ongoing search, many in the poly community still lacked the community they sought. Apparently, she was referring to herself. She announced that she was pulling out of her partnership with Nearing and that the fourth issue would be her last as co-editor. While she would continue to contribute when appropriate, she felt as though she had discovered the true nature of her own sexuality and wished to exchange polyamory for a "larger identity in a wider world." While she encouraged *Loving More*'s readership to continue supporting the magazine, she assured them that she would be much less visible in the future. In her installment of "On the Edge" that followed, she reminisced on waking up in bed with three friends. After reveling in the foursome, she traveled to a poly event where her longtime friends Stan Dale and Michael Aluna (Dowd) were speaking. There she met a new man she slept with that night. "It feels strangely familiar to be sexual with someone I've just met and may never see again. But I am a child of the sixties. I'm reverting to my old hippie era behavior," she wrote. Despite her assurance that this was not habitual, her willingness to engage in sex with strangers made her problematic to many among the coalition she had worked so long and so hard to build. After less than a year, she officially parted ways with Loving More.[50]

Polyamory did not lose Deborah Anapol in 1995. She continued advocating for polyamory in the public sphere and contributing to the magazine. She and Nearing remained friends and facilitated more events together. But she was tired. Her years of work had caught up to her. After her failed marriage to Glassco, rejection from the poly community felt like a slap in the face. Her burnout was noticeable to everyone. In a recap of that year's West Coast conference, one observer noted the drastic contrast in her demeanor. The Zells gave an impassioned keynote address, and Nearing, pregnant with her first child, was glowing. But Anapol was visibly disgruntled.[51]

Anapol's censure says as much about the nature of polyamory as it does about her. Despite its celebration of diversity, by 1995, the community had decided that there were lines that could not be crossed. Intimate commitment still defined the acceptable parameters of polyamory's sexual ethics, and anything that looked like swinging or casual sex was undoubtedly going to be contentious.

Prior to the controversy caused by Anapol, the partnerships that led to the publication of *Loving More Magazine* marked a high point in the polyamorous coalition. Reverence for relational commitment and alternative spirituality united many diverse factions, leading the Loving More coalition to believe that they were on the precipice of building a national polyamory movement. However, Anapol's fall from grace was a harbinger of deeper discord that was already present under the surface, threatening to undermine the cohesiveness needed to build a politically viable social movement.

5

Technologies

The web is relentless.

—Brett Hill, *Loving More Magazine* (1996)

Just after Deborah Anapol resigned as co-editor of *Loving More Magazine*, Nina Hartley appeared as an apologist for ethical non-monogamy on the *Jerry Springer Show*. Hartley was destined to become an icon of bisexual sex positivity. She would soon gain mainstream notoriety after her appearance in *Boogie Nights*, Mark Wahlberg's 1997 film about the porn industry. She would also go on to serve as a board member for the Victoria Woodhull Freedom Foundation for sexual freedom and give sex education talks on many college campuses. Hartley was joined by Barbara Lily, a woman with whom she had been in a long-term throuple for years. Their male lover was absent. Though he had made prior media appearances with Hartley and Lily, he resented the ridicule he endured and no longer wished to promote the lifestyle publicly. Undeterred, Hartley and Lily remained steadfast activists.[1]

Hartley's appeal was obvious. She was young, attractive, and educated, having graduated magna cum laude from San Francisco State. She was also a porn star. Hartley had shot her first movie in 1984, just as Nearing and Anapol were establishing their organizations. Her unique blend of confidence, academic achievement, and sex positivity made her a potential asset to polyamory. For many, however,

Hartley was too sex positive. Like Anapol, her more free-form approach to sexuality, particularly her willingness to make pornography, positioned her outside the ethical limits of polyamory. This was not true for all. By the late 1990s, some polyamorists wished to reframe polyamory's ethics in terms of its commitment to openness and honesty rather than by its commitment to commitment. To the chagrin of Loving More's polyfides, the second half of the 1990s saw this more libertine form of polyamory gain traction. If Loving More was going to achieve its goal of establishing a national polyamory movement, it would have to learn to accept those like Hartley better than it had Anapol.

Hartley was focused and articulate. Separating her work from her personal life, she assured the talk show audience that the bedrock of her throuple was honesty. Honesty, she argued, was also the source of the relationship's intimacy. Springer rejected the claim, countering that intimacy within marriage must be restricted to two people.[2]

The purpose of the *Jerry Springer Show* was not to debate the nuances of ethical non-monogamy. Instead, the program was intent on exploiting controversial topics to elicit shock, conflict, and discord. Susan and Mark Markwell, a poly couple promoting Intinet, also joined Hartley and Lily on stage. Despite their claim that they sought another couple for a long-term relationship, the Markwells were labeled swingers on screen, which undermined any potential for objectivity long before the show's viewership could hear any debate.

Several other guests were chosen to challenge the polyamorists. Richard David, a self-described officer in the sexual revolution, was present. David claimed he had previously been the leader of a "free love cult." Since that time, he had had a change of heart and become an advocate for the safety, stability, and trust he was now convinced only monogamy could provide. There was also Dr. Stephen Champlin, a sex therapist who charged the polyamorists with a fear of intimacy, and a fundamentalist pastor named Nestor Stroude. Stroude, joined by his wife, wasted no time attacking the polyamorists. He believed that he was being faithful to the teaching of Jesus. They, in contrast, had rejected truth, led astray by their own broken moral compasses. He charged them with selfishly breaking their marital covenant with God. Despite having been divorced, Stroude preached that sexual fidelity within marriage was the only moral option. His wife was just as austere. When Lily protested that her conscience was a trustworthy guide, Ms. Stroude assured her it had been seared by sin. When another guest countered that they were spiritual, though not Christian, and trusted the direction of their life to a higher power, she cut them off to inform them that Jesus was the only higher power.[3]

Hartley's belief that she could have a serious conversation about ethical non-monogamy on a show as sensational as *Jerry Springer* appears naïve. But she was not alone. Throughout the early 1990s, many polyamorists, including Nearing and Anapol, accepted such invitations. Despite the exploitive nature of these programs, they believed them to be a useful tool to spread their message to the widest possible audience. Like the Keristans, who appeared on Phil Donahue almost two decades earlier, many polyamorists believed that that, even in such hostile environments, they could convince others of polyamory's ethical legitimacy through reasoned argument. That rarely happened. Instead, they were met with open ridicule, disgust, and religious moralizing. Eventually most became disenchanted with trying to use mainstream television appearances to spread their message.

Nearing was one of the first to become jaded about talk shows. She and Anapol had initially found them a useful, if troublesome, tool. It was the fan mail Anapol received after her appearance on *Phil Donahue* in 1984 that convinced her to establish Intinet. Nearing followed suit, and she and her husbands made many talk show appearances throughout the 1980s and 1990s. She had even appeared alongside Anapol and Glassco on the *Joan Rivers Show* in 1992. However, her experiences became increasingly negative, and, in the late 1990s, she became convinced that such appearances were counterproductive.

As public ridicule shifted polyamorists' willingness to engage with television audiences, advancements in internet technology offered them new digital venues to network and evangelize. The internet revolution that occurred in the 1990s closely paralleled changes in the evolution of polyamory. The World Wide Web was introduced in 1990, just as Anapol and Nearing joined forces with the Zells. It became public domain in 1993, as the Sex and Spirit Conference cemented the spiritualist ethos of Nearing and Anapol's coalition. It continued to grow over the next two years and by the time the first issue of *Loving More Magazine* was published, in 1995, 18 million American homes had internet access. By the turn of the century, roughly 40 percent of adults were actively using the internet. Polyamory's co-evolution alongside the web assured that its practitioners had novel means to find the like-minded and to defend their ideas to the public.[4]

Early on the internet promoted countercultural connections. The Whole Earth 'Lectronic Link (WELL), a dial-up computer conferencing system established in the 1980s, was built to undermine hierarchical communication and create a place where virtual communities could discuss ideas without "encountering body-based forms of prejudice."[5] Early computer network systems such as USENET and the WELL connected polyamorists across the nation. Although these rudimentary networks were clunky and lacked the accessibility of current online communications, they offered email, conferencing, discussion boards, threaded forums, and online bulletin board systems that allowed polyamorists to connect and discuss controversial topics.[6]

Online outlets such as the WELL and USENET were ideal tools for polyamorists living in remote locations. Nearing relied heavily on the internet to conduct her organizational work from Syntony's home in Hawaii.[7] Many polyamorists were separated by thousands of miles and had neither the time nor the means to attend annual events such as PEPCON or the Sex and Spirit conference. Digital venues provided them with immediate, if not bodily, access to one another. Internet forum archives are filled with polyamorists' laments over the distress and alienation of being physically separated from others who shared their beliefs and interests. One polyamorist agonized over the loneliness of being poly in the rural and conservative Midwest and used the forum to propose that midwestern polys unite and start a commune in Yellow Springs, Ohio, where residents were thought to be progressive enough to leave them alone.[8]

In addition to connecting polyamorists around the country, the internet also provided them safety. Though Nearing and Anapol had devoted their lives to public advocacy, many others shared their perspective but lacked their boldness. The internet provided these polyamorists with ways to explore their sexuality. One man confessed his bisexuality to Anapol on the WELL. Though he had found self-acceptance and wished to come out to others, he did not feel he could come out to anyone outside of the WELL's community. Comfortable only in that venue, he went on at length, closely detailing his past sexual experiences and present desires. He was not alone. Libertarian engineer Richard Askins admitted that his fear of social and legal persecution prevented him and his wife from speaking publicly about their interest in polyfidelity. Though he believed Anapol was a hero, he confessed he and his wife would likely never attend a poly conference. The most they could muster was to post a personal ad on the WELL.[9]

The internet was a godsend for individual polyamorists, but it was a double-edged sword for polyamory. Though it was a safe and powerful tool for the dissemination of polyamorous ideas, relatively free from social consequences, it also undermined the central pillars on which the Loving More coalition was built. The two most contested issues were Loving More's sexual conservatism and its spiritualist ethos. The internet offered a platform for polyamorists who were underrepresented in the Loving More coalition to voice their critiques.

Alternative spirituality permeated the pages of *Loving More Magazine*. But many Polyfidelitous Educational Productions (PEP) and Intinet members lacked the coalition's penchant for spiritualism even before the merger took place. Intinet member Martin Tracy messaged Anapol about the low attendance at a Southern California Intinet meeting. While he found the meeting interesting, he believed more people might have shown up if it was not scheduled erratically according to the "principles of astrology, numerology, and intuition."

He also lamented that, while he found many people interested in forming intentional families, they were turned off by the community's tendency to tell them that, if they were serious, they should "take off [their] clothes, read *Stranger in a Strange Land*, and come to listen to our psychic lecture on tantric yoga and safe sex."[10]

Tracy was far from alone in his critique of the community's spiritualist impulse. PEP member Ken Olam vented to USENET's Triples' mailing list that the New Age ethos that had overtaken polyamory greatly bothered him. Olam, who identified as a heterosexual polyfide, admitted that, although he did not understand libertine relationship models outside of polyfidelity or group marriage, he believed that others should be free to practice such models without judgment. What vexed him was the way New Age thought had permeated the community, leaving the impression that to reject sexually restrictive social norms, polyamorists must also reject scientific evidence, rationalism, and objective truth. While his rationalist tendencies kept him from taking it personally, he felt different from most other polyamorists who readily accepted beliefs he considered "nonsensical." Nonetheless, he took solace in the fact that the online community provided him with new contacts who differed markedly from those who generally attended PEPCON. Carol Segar, another PEP member, agreed, complaining that New Age should be written "newage" so that it rhymed with sewage. While she enjoyed the tantric workshops at PEPCON for the emotional experiences and social connections they fostered, she rejected the metaphysics that undergirded them and believed they were dangerous to those who could not separate practical experience from personal belief.[11]

PEP member David Lewis complained online when one PEPCON speaker gave a presentation claiming to have channeled the writing of a new book from a being who orbited Orion. Lewis and his partner were both PhDs with a preference for more "Western minds." Nonetheless, due to their commitment to the lifestyle, they were willing to set aside their judgments concerning polyamory's New Age aspects. As Lewis was typing his complaints, he admitted he was simultaneously making plans to attend Anapol's Sex and Spirit Conference, an event he believed was sure to stretch the limits of his open-mindedness.[12]

A preference for rationalism was not the only minority opinion expressed within online poly communities. Others believed the coalition was too uptight in its sexual prohibitions. The Loving More coalition's disavowal of swinging and casual sex as incompatible with polyamory was strong. Not even Anapol's prestige had protected her from judgment. But the internet provided evidence of more lenient perspectives from the larger community. When one member mentioned that more women might be interested in polyamory if polyamorists only interested in swinging were eradicated from the group, she met with swift opposition. Another member charged her with "kink shaming." They argued that the outside world already lumped polyamory and swinging together and that such divisiveness only led to a more repressive cultural environment.[13]

Member Roy Rapoport called out the polyamorist tendency to discriminate against swingers as unjust. Though he was weary about allowing a focus on swinging to dominate the discussions on poly forums, he believed the two lifestyles were not mutually exclusive. He was in two committed relationships but also had sex on the side. He asked whether he should be labeled a swinger or a polyamorist. Should the community exile him for the sin of swinging because his morality allowed for sex outside of his committed relationships when someone else's did not? Other members shared Rapoport's sentiments. Michael Price, a doctoral student, set aside work on his dissertation to take to the computer and decry the oppressive methods of the "poly-gestapo" who were always trying to dictate the one true way. Other less polemical members admitted that the lines between the two communities were blurred, some believing that swingers were in fact polyamorists, loosely defined. The growing presence of these dissident voices evidenced a level of diversity within polyamory that the Loving More coalition had not anticipated.[14]

In addition to bringing to light the differences within the community, the internet also uncovered pockets of polyamorists that existed
completely outside of the Loving More coalition. A notable example
is Jennifer Wesp, a doctoral student in biophysics at the University
of Virginia. Wesp began using internet message boards in 1984, becoming increasingly active on them in college. She had always felt
as though she was inherently non-monogamous and was surprised
when she got to college and realized that most people did not share
her feelings. During the early 1990s, her sexual interests led her to the
USENET group alt.sex. In 1992, she began arguing with other alt.sex
members over the morality of non-monogamous relationships. She
believed relationships conducted with mutual consent and honesty
were moral, no matter the number of people involved. Predictably,
many other alt.sex subscribers disagreed. According to Wesp, it was
in the heat of these online discussions that she began searching for a
new word to describe her lifestyle. She disliked "non-monogamous"
for many reasons. It was long and thus bothersome to type. More
than that, it was a negation of a concept instead of an affirmation of
one. Hoping to create something that was shorter, more positive, and
packed more of a rhetorical punch, Wesp began a new USENET
group called alt.polyamory in the spring of 1992. Despite her long-
standing interest in ethical non-monogamy, Wesp claimed that she
had never heard of the term before.[15]

Though Morning Glory's publication of the term "polyamorous"
predates Wesp's "polyamory" by roughly two years, Wesp claims they
were coined independently of one another. The origin of the term
that has come to describe the lifestyle has remained a point of con-
tention among many polyamorists. Some argue that since the women
used different variants—Morning Glory the adjective and Wesp the
noun—both deserve recognition. Others choose sides. The *Oxford
English Dictionary* (OED) takes the literalist view and attributes Wesp
with coining the term. Her proposal for the USENET newsgroup
is cited as the term's first usage. The *OED* did, however, contact
Morning Glory, and it used some of her verbiage in the definition.[16]

Despite receiving the official credit for coining the term "poly-amory," Wesp never became a leader in the national network. When later asked about her opinions on polyamory, she responded that it was simply what worked best for her, and she wanted others to recognize it as a moral choice. However, she never wrote articles, lectured, or taught on the topic, and she did not see herself as an authority. Not long after creating alt.polyamory, Wesp became disenchanted with arguing online and stopped posting in the newsgroup. Nonetheless, the message board continues to function as a place for polyamorists to comment, learn, and argue over the ethics of polyamorous relationships. It is also where users began promoting the parrot as the unofficial mascot of polyamory. The origin of this adaptation is debated, with some appealing to the polyamorous practices of some parrot species and others referring to the phrase, "Polly wanna cracker?" The message board is currently accessible as a Google group, and its archive, dating back to its creation, is publicly accessible.[17]

Outside of her terminological contribution, Wesp is significant for two reasons. First, she represents the presence of ethical non-monogamists across the country who, while interested in polyamory, were unaware of Nearing and Anapol's endeavors. Though hard to imagine now, in the pre-Google era, the rudimentary nature of internet networks produced disjointed communities. Message board archives show that many who were active in the poly community on the WELL were unaware of what was going on in USENET groups and vice versa. When certain members of the WELL informed others of Wesp's new USENET group, alt.polyamory, many of its members had no knowledge of its existence. Anapol even wondered if it was Nearing who had started the newsgroup, and she admitted that she did not even know how to access it.[18]

Second, Wesp is significant because alt.polyamory helped solidify "polyamory" as the preferred term used among the community even when Nearing and Anapol were still reluctant to adopt it. In colloquial usage, the term "poly" preceded "polyamory." As the community debated using terms like "polygamy," "polyfidelity," and "polylove," "poly" often became shorthand for ethically non-monogamous. When Anapol reprinted Morning Glory's article "Banquet of Lovers," in her 1992 book, *Love Without Limits*, many of her readers adopted the term "polyamorous" as well as its noun form. It quickly spread from neo-Paganism into her and Nearing's network. Yet Anapol was still unsure whether it was adequate. As late as 1994, Anapol preferred terms like "polylove." Nearing, too, preferred "polylove," worrying that only "computer nerds grok polyamory." [19]

Despite Nearing's reservations, when *Loving More Magazine* was first published in early 1995, widespread accessibility to the World Wide Web ensured that the internet was no longer merely a place for computer nerds. Nearing and Anapol had overcome their reluctance and *Loving More*'s autumn issue boasted of its new website, a space where polyamory enjoyed a level playing field with all the other topics on the "electronic web." The site contained magazine articles, cover art, frequently asked questions, and links to other sites containing related issues. The site drew immediate interest and, like the WELL and USENET before it, polyamorists flocked to it to join a community, seek information, and voice concerns. Soon after, *Loving More Magazine* began publishing much of the online content in the magazine for its print readership to see. [20]

Most of *Loving More*'s online demographics were predictable. They included Heinlein fans, pagan goddess worshipers, and Wiccans. There were New Age tantrics seeking exciting spiritual connections, and there were polyfides searching for a closed group with whom they might spend the rest of their lives. Others were outliers. There was the occasional Baptist who believed that *Loving More* was accelerating the moral decline of the nation. There were also those seeking educational information. One anonymous person confessed to only visiting the site because their best friend was in a poly relationship, and, although they wanted to be happy for them, they had serious reservations and needed more information to offer their support. *Loving More* relished such inquiries, providing the visitor with information they believed would ease their worries. Remaining relevant and connected online kept Nearing's camp very busy. According to *Loving More Magazine*'s new co-editor, Brett Hill, the internet was the most poly-active space in existence. "The Web is relentless," he said. "It's on 24 hours a day to a global audience."[21]

By the late 1990s, the inundation of new voices and perspectives on the web helped to liberalize the Loving More coalition. After recovering from the community's criticisms of her sexual behavior, Anapol returned to the fold. Though she had given up her position as co-editor, by 1996, she was once again a regular contributor to *Loving More Magazine*. She continued writing articles on tantric sexual healing, now fully embracing the term "polyamory" to describe her lifestyle. In the spring of 1997, she published a new edition of her book, *Polyamory: The New Love Without Limits*, in which she credited Morning Glory with coining the term and cyberspace with popularizing it.[22]

By the late 1990s, the more liberal currents within polyamory were becoming increasingly vocal. Many of these bore a resemblance to Anapol's laissez faire approach to sex. Dossie Easton and Janet Hardy, the bisexual polyamorists who co-authored *The Ethical Slut* (1997), are the two best examples. Easton was a fifty-two-year-old marriage and family counselor with deep ties to the Bay Area BDSM community. She had turned to polyamory after escaping an abusive relationship. Rejecting sexual restrictions, she adopted what she referred to as a "creed of looseness." Hardy, writing under the pseudonym Catherine Liszt, had embraced free love in her youth before finding herself unwittingly stuck in a life of suburban monotony. After unsuccessfully trying to persuade her husband to open their marriage, she began to feel trapped. The two eventually parted ways and she, like Easton, gave up monogamy for good.[23]

Ethical Slut purported to be a practical guide to polyamory, and the book in many ways resembled much of the polyamorist literature that preceded it. It decried the hetero and mono normativity that defined American culture as vestiges of an outdated Puritanism. It provided practical guidelines for making multipartner relationships work.

It affirmed non-Christian forms of spirituality that revered sacred sexuality, specifically, Paganism, tantra, and goddess worship. It also parroted the familiar polyamorous claim that when it came to love, no matter the number of partners involved, there was more than enough to go around. Where *The Ethical Slut* diverged from most of its predecessors is that its authors made no attempt to bow to the pretense that commitment was necessary for ethical sexual intercourse. While the book's closing section, "Resources for Sluts," was filled with poly familiars such as *Green Egg, Loving More Magazine*, and The Human Awareness Institute, it also recommended the North American Swing Club Association. Though it listed Nearing in the bibliography, and it spoke of polyfidelity with reverence, it was Anapol who earned the only epigraph among the book's nineteen chapters.[24]

Ethical sluts, the authors argued, needed no reason for sexual engagement. Enjoyment and pleasure were ends in themselves. Individuals should be free to construct and maintain any relationship style that best suited them. As long as relationships were conducted with honesty, transparency, and respect for all involved, one-night stands and anonymous group sex were just as ethically valid as polyfidelitous group marriages. In Anapoldian form, Easton and Hardy argued that casual sex in public group settings could function as healthy self-exploration. Only coercion, deceit, or "sport fucking" undermined the moral status of sexual acts. Just as each sexual orientation and family structure provided diverse perspectives on sexuality, all open and honest forms of sexuality had something to teach others about sexual relationships. This included sex workers, who came under the umbrella of ethical sexual practice.[25]

The Ethical Slut was ecumenical polyamory taken to its extreme. For Easton and Hardy, there was no place for judgment or factionalism within polyamory. Instead, polyamory's goal was to normalize a "slut utopia" where sexual pluralism reigned supreme.[26] Many among *Loving More*'s more conservative readership rejected such claims. But a lot had changed in the two years between Anapol's censure and the publication of the *Ethical Slut*. Endless internet discussions made it clear that there were many polys who were willing to accept more libertine forms of polyamory. Had Anapol treaded more lightly in the early issues of *Loving More Magazine*, she would have soon met other polyamorists who shared her disposition.

Nearing gave *The Ethical Slut* a positive review in the spring 1997 issue of *Loving More Magazine*. She lauded its attempt to reclaim the term "slut" from its negative connotations and argued that the book contained many useful ideas for polyamorists. Though she was quick to point out that such sexual openness was not for her, she shared the authors' devotion to personal autonomy, responsible freedom, honesty in relationships, and the idea that sexual energy was a positive force. In the following issue, Nearing reprinted an extended excerpt from the book, and, soon after, *Loving More* offered the book for sale directly at a discounted price.[27]

As *Loving More* was liberalizing, some within its ranks were growing tired of polyamory. The best example was Eve Furchgott, the co-founder of Kerista's New Tribe. Furchgott had practiced polyfidelity for over twenty-five years. She was there when Kerista had first coined the terms "polyfidelity" and "compersion," and she had remained involved with the commune until its demise in 1991. After Kerista disbanded, Furchgott became a frequent contributor to *Loving More Magazine*. Her artwork was often displayed inside the magazine as well as on its cover. Yet despite playing such a pivotal role in polyamory's history, Furchgott had grown weary of the lifestyle.

In the winter of 1997, Furchgott penned the article, "Small Is Beautiful," detailing her transition back into monogamy. The article was a reflection on the two decades she spent with Kerista as an idealistic youth battling mainstream sexual culture. Though Furchgott did not reject the validity of polyfidelity, she admitted that many of the premises on which Kerista based its commitments were unsustainable. She now believed it was naïve of them to dismiss romantic attachments or believe that people could love non-preferentially. She hoped that contemporary polyamorists would never try to live up to such impossible standards. She confessed that, during her time with Kerista, jealousy was in fact an issue, and, after twenty-five years of flippantly dismissing those who wanted one special person to prefer them over others, she had become one of those people.[28]

Eve's youthful zeal had been tempered by her years of experience. When she was young, she was intoxicated by countercultural idealism and, for a while, Kerista's energy made polyfidelity wildly attractive. For many years the commune had staved off loneliness and boredom while providing her with a vibrant social life and a cause to believe in. But as the electricity of the communal experiment dissipated, she began to think that the traditional wisdom on which monogamy stood might be justified. Perhaps there were limits on how far the mind could stretch to accommodate new paradigms. She concluded that she could continue to fight, ignore jealousy and interpersonal politics, and try to appreciate the nuances of her lovers without comparing them. She could try to ignore her internal desire for exclusive devotion. But she now wondered if such striving was in vain. She chose to stop trying, candidly expressing her feelings for the poly community to read.

> To be told, "I love no one more than you," (unsaid: but others just as much) doesn't pack the same satisfying punch as "I love you," (unsaid: more than anyone else in the world). I know intellectually, that I am no better than others; that we humor each other in some sense when we single each other out, making perhaps much ado about nothing (or little). But that's what romance is all about! Whether wanting this kind of love is a matter of cultural conditioning or innate genetic predisposition is not important. No amount of indoctrination to feminist or other ideological rhetoric can change the fact that to me, success in love includes being the most important person in my lover's intimate life. If it's a myth, so be it. It is one I can live with.[29]

Eve knew there were consequences to her decision. She mourned the loss of stimulation that polyamory entailed and admitted to missing old lovers. But she believed the simplicity and clarity she gained in return was worth the tradeoff. A quarter-century after defying her parents' wishes for her to come back home, instead joining a sex commune in San Francisco, Eve Furchgott, the Keristan apologist and prophet of polyfidelity, embraced monogamy.

Most of the other Loving More leaders showed no signs in slowing down. Anapol continued to cast a wide net, bringing in new tantric lovers. Nearing's family had expanded as well. Just before Furchgott's turn to monogany, Nearing's family grew to five. In addition to Syntony's three original members, Nearing, Barry Northrop, and Allan Jensen, Nearing had fallen in love with Brett Hill, a man she met at the Sex and Spirit conference. Hill became the father of her child. Syntony also added a woman named Ruth to their family. Not long after Hill joined the family, Loving More relocated its headquarters from Hawaii to Boulder, Colorado, where Hill lived.[30]

The size of the Zells' family had fluctuated as well and now included five adults. Tim had renamed himself once again, setting aside Otter for Oberon, king of the fairies. By then, Oberon and Morning Glory had been together for over two decades. In the fall of 1996, they joined in a handfasting ceremony with Morning Glory's lover, Wolf Styles. A year later, the three were also living with Oberon's lover, Lisa Gabriel, and a nineteen-year-old woman named Wynter Rose, who was both Wolf's lover and Morning Glory's apprentice. The fivesome adopted the last name Ravenheart. Though the Ravenhearts admitted that their lifestyle was chaotic, they continued to prefer the sexual energy it offered rather than forego it for a simpler arrangement, as Furchgott had done. They took turns contributing a question-and-answer column in *Loving More Magazine* that provided advice for those within the poly community who were struggling with the complexities of the lifestyle (Figure 5.1).[31]

Despite the expansion of Loving More, the late 1990s remained a tumultuous time for public relations. One defining experience occurred when Nearing and her husbands agreed to appear on the popular *Geraldo Rivera Show* in 1997. The show featured college professor Barbara Foster and her husband Michael. The Fosters were both educated professionals from New York's Greenwich Village who had been in a relationship with a younger woman for the past twelve

Figure 5.1 The Zell-Ravenheart Clan, 1997. Pictured here from left to right: Wolf Styles (top), Wynter Rose (bottom), Lisa Gabriel, Oberon, and Morning Glory.
Photo courtesy of Oberon Zell.

years. That woman did not live with them in New York. Michael split his time between the women during the week, and the three spent their summers together at the Fosters' summer home in Vermont. The two women were good friends. The Fosters, who were *Loving More* contributors, had written a book on famous polyamorists in history.[32]

Appearing on the show alongside the Fosters were 1984 Playboy Playmate of the Year, Barbara Edwards, and the author of the novel *Indecent Proposal*, Jack Englehard. Edwards was presented as an expert on sexual freedom. However, she claimed that her forays into promiscuity had compromised her own marriage, and eventually the constant conflict and jealousy ended in violence and abuse. She believed that was the inevitable outcome of polyamory, and she drew on her own experience as evidence of the impossibility of healthy open marriages of any kind. She made it clear that she was sickened by the choices of her fellow guests.[33]

Englehard was a bit more sympathetic, though it was clear he was only there due to the controversial topic of his book. *Indecent Proposal* was the fictional story of a couple whose marriage is destroyed after the husband accepts an offer from a wealthy man to pay to have sex with his wife. Robert Redford, Demi Moore, and Woody Harrelson starred in a movie adaptation of the novel in 1993. Although Englehard was not a professional expert, Geraldo was very interested in his opinion. Englehard believed that polyamorists were trying to live out a literary fantasy in real life. He appealed to his Catholic upbringing as the basis of his own belief in monogamy. However, he conceded people should be allowed to choose whatever romantic arrangements they desired.[34]

Geraldo claimed he was taking the intellectual high road, yet his personal judgments were clear from the beginning. When Nearing appeared with Barry and Brett Hill, the show introduced Barry as her husband and Hill as an open boyfriend. Nearing and Barry explained that they had been married for twenty-five years. During that time, they had taken in new family members. First there was Allan, thirteen years earlier, and more recently there had been Hill and another woman. Each member of the family was faithful within their closed marriage. They were clear that they did not want the government involved in their familial relationships.[35]

Despite his claims to objectivity, Geraldo made constant remarks about the polyamorists' romantic arrangements being "New Age Three's Company," referencing the popular sit-com, and "sanctioned infidelity." He asked Hill if he was the third wheel, the fourth, or the fifth. At one point, he told Michael Foster that he could not believe that he was as attracted to his wife, Barbara, as he was to his newer younger lover sitting beside her on the stage.[36]

The audience's reactions were similar to Geraldo's. Many asked about relational logistics, curiously inquiring about who slept together, when, and how that was decided. Others said the arrangement was immoral because it violated the teaching of the Bible. When Nearing asserted that, despite having three husbands, she believed in the institution of marriage, her comment was quickly met with laughter and disbelief. When the issues of jealousy and child-rearing were raised, the conversation became heated. Barry and Hill tried to make the case that polyamory was better than the common cultural practice of serial monogamy. They cited statistics on divorce and cheating within monogamous marriages. They also appealed to the many people who they had met while publishing *Loving More Magazine* who maintained successful long-term polyamorous relationships. But the show's sensational tactics largely overshadowed their arguments. Producers interspersed the panelists' discussion segments with emotional clips from *Indecent Proposal*'s movie adaptation depicting Moore and Harrelson's marriage falling apart after she slept with Redford. Geraldo argued that the natural reaction to infidelity was rage and obsession. He pointed out that although Nearing and Barry had been married for decades, it was Hill who was the father of Nearing's two-year-old son. He asked whether that was confusing to the child. Another audience member reiterated the concern, asking whether such confusion was child abuse. They wondered if her son called her husband dad or uncle. Visibly upset, Nearing angrily responded that there was no confusion, he simply called the men by their names and that love was not abuse. Geraldo retorted that she was too smart to really believe that.[37]

Nearing's frustration was understandable. She had remained in a committed marriage to her high school sweetheart for a quarter century. Any additional commitments she had made to others were, to her, careful considerations made soberly over extended periods of time. Syntony had never rushed into new relationships. Despite hoping for a family of six, it had taken them almost a decade and a half to find their fourth and fifth. To Nearing, it was apparent that, despite the laughter of the audience, she took marriage more seriously than they did. She certainly took it more seriously than Geraldo, a fact he confirmed when he bragged that she could not tell him anything about marriage. He had been married four times and had four children by three different women. He believed her lifestyle was detrimental to her son and that, like the children of his gay neighbors, her child was in a qualitatively different position than others. Unlike having step-parents or half-brothers, they were in a league of their own.[38]

Geraldo nostalgically pined for the "old days," before the contemporary divorce crisis, when parents sacrificed their own desires and remained together for the stability for their children. Repulsed by Geraldo's hypocrisy, Nearing countered that her child was the most important thing in her life, and, if he wanted to discuss children, she was ready to "fight tooth and nail." When Barbara Edwards interrupted Nearing to tell her that all she was teaching him was that there were no moral limits in life, Nearing coldly apologized for the hardships Edwards had endured. As a dedicated activist who had spent her adult life promoting the virtues of lifelong commitment, Nearing refused to be lectured on fidelity by a Playboy playmate with a broken marriage and a talk show host with three failed marriages and children born to multiple women he was no longer with (Figure 5.2).[39]

Nearing believed the Geraldo appearance was a mistake. It must have been a relief when the producers decided not to air the episode. But that did not save Loving More from public scrutiny. Soon after, Nearing's organization became involved in a controversial court case that further scandalized polyamory on the national stage.

In fall of 1998, April Divilbiss, a young woman from Memphis, Tennessee, received a court order that transferred legal guardianship of her three-year-old daughter (from a previous relationship) to the child's paternal grandmother. April, who had recently married Shane Divilbiss, became involved with her new husband's friend, Chris Littrell, who was the best man in their wedding party. Rather than allow the rivalry to destroy their relationships, the three had decided to move in together.[40] Soon after, the three agreed to appear on the MTV program, *Sex in the 90s: It's a Group Thing*, where they described the evolution of their relationship, the realities of jealousy, and the

Figure 5.2 Ryam Nearing and her family in their home in Boulder, Colorado, 1997. Pictured from left to right: Ruth Blue, Brett Hill, Ryam Nearing, Zeke Hill, and Barry Northrop. Allan Jensen is absent.
Photo courtesy of Ryam and Brett Hill.

practicalities of living together. They disclosed that, although they all slept in the same bed, they did not all have sex, due to Littrell's heterosexuality. April's only complaint was her inability to satisfy both men sexually, a problem she believed could be remedied by adding another female to their relationship.[41]

Donna Olswing, the paternal grandmother of April's daughter, saw the MTV episode when it aired and filed for emergency legal custody of her granddaughter on the grounds that the Divilbiss household was immoral and depraved. According to Olswing's lawyer, raising a child in a home where her mother slept with two men was harmful to the child's health. April countered that, according to her pagan religion, her relationship was morally acceptable and that the court was violating her freedom of religion by imposing its own sense of morality. Loving More set up a defense fund for April and organized a benefit auction to pay her legal bills, raising roughly $20,000 to help her.[42]

The effect of the Divilbiss case on polyamory was mixed. After a two-year court battle, April gave up custody of her child to Olswing. In an open letter, she wrote that she had come to believe that the real issue was her inability to properly provide for her daughter. She admitted that she had had the child too young and that her severe financial struggles had made her realize that she was unable to provide her daughter with adequate education, healthcare, and nutrition. She believed that Olswing had used her lifestyle as an excuse to gain custody of her daughter so that she might provide her with those essentials. Though she still believed in the ethics of polyamory, she regretted bringing her daughter into a civil rights battle.[43]

Loving More interpreted Divilbiss's concession as a political loss. However, the controversy gained the attention of *Time* Magazine. In a November 1999 issue, the magazine published "Henry, Mary, Janet, and . . . ," which used the Divilbiss case to explore polyamory's growing popularity. The article was a milestone for polyamory. It had been a decade and a half since *Time* had declared the death of the sexual revolution. During that time, Nearing and Anapol had fought tirelessly to disprove that claim. Now, *Time* admitted that more and more Americans were practicing polyamory, citing Loving More as evidence. Nearing was thrilled.[44]

For many Loving More supporters, the *Time* article was the first proper portrayal of their lifestyle in a major publication. Nearing and Brett Hill, both of whom *Time* quoted at length, were happy with the way it represented them. The article highlighted the importance of Loving More, noting that it produced a magazine with a circulation of 10,000, had a successful website, and conducted two annual conferences. Although it mentioned that there was a great deal of New Age "flimflam" associated with polyamory, it claimed that it also consisted of earnest individuals who were committed to challenging the common notion that there was only one right way to organize a family. It affirmed that most polyamorists eschewed swinging for committed relationships and that each polyamorous family could devise its own set of rules as long as relationships were built on the foundations of openness and honesty. Though historically polyamory was concentrated in progressive coastal cities, *Time* argued that, over the past decade, the internet had exponentially extended its reach. There were currently hundreds of internet groups connecting poly-amorists throughout the nation. Even those in the rural Midwest now had a mechanism for meeting one another. Polyamorists could even download and display a "polypride" flag.[45]

Though *Time*'s balanced portrayal of polyamory helped spread awareness to a wider swath of the American public, it did not repre-sent a sea change in public opinion. Most media outlets continued to be unwilling to address it fairly. Talk shows remained one of the worst venues, though poly leaders still used them to evangelize. Following the publication of the *Time* article, Anapol agreed to appear on the syndicated daytime talk show, *Leeza*. Her optimism that things had changed in the wake of polyamory's increased notoriety was soon dampened when her experience paralleled that of Nearing on *Geraldo*.

The *Time* article set the context for the show's episode, and the guests pondered whether the state should have taken April Divilbiss's daughter from her. To provide a wider context for polyamory, sev-eral guests appeared, including practicing polyamorists and those who opposed the lifestyle. It was apparent from the outset that the prime directive of the show was to sensationalize polyamory. The program opened with *Loving More Magazine* contributors Sasha and Janet Lessin. The Lessins were New Age tantrics who had founded Pali Paths, a polyamorous discussion group in Hawaii. A short video showed them and another couple they were courting chanting man-tras and group kissing before retiring to the bedroom together, at which time the clip was cut off. When Leeza asked how far the ren-dezvous went, a representative from her media staff assured her that not only did it become pornographic, but that they asked her to join as well.[46]

Radio personality Tom Leykis, who was intended as the foursome's foil, joined the Lessins and the couple they were dating. Although Leykis confessed that he had never been in a polyamorous relationship, he argued that years of experimenting with promiscuity and group sex had proved to him that multipartner relationships could never entail commitment and were destined to fail. Though he believed such experimentation was acceptable for single people, it was inherently detrimental to marriage. When Lykis revealed that that he had been married four times, a polyamorous audience member pointed out his hypocrisy, arguing that he knew nothing of commitment. He countered that, while his four marriages may have failed, he, unlike the other guests, was not auditioning for the fifth every night.[47]

When Anapol appeared on stage, reference was made to the new edition of her book, *Polyamory: The New Love Without Limits.* The conversation quickly turned to the issues of morality and child-rearing. Leeza admitted that, while the nuclear family was no longer the norm, she had deep reservations about the morality of polyamory. Anapol presented her perspective in short soundbites that were difficult to take out of context. She argued that people had thrived in tribes for millennia and that the nuclear family was a modern invention. The problem, she proposed, was that contemporary society had confused sex with morality when there was no inherent connection between the two. Morals, she claimed, were about honesty. What the world needed was not a commitment to sexual fidelity, but a commitment to truth. That was the polyamorous philosophy.[48]

In addition to Anapol, there were other positive poly representations. One audience member testified that polyamory had taught them empathy and communication skills they had never possessed before. Furthermore, having multiple adults around had given their children a loving and supportive experience. The Lessins' male suitor claimed that his lifestyle had allowed him to bond with men in ways that the homophobia prevalent in society would never have allowed outside of polyamory. In the face of these testimonials, Leeza asked whether removing such a strong social restraint, like monogamy, would not naturally lead to the acceptance of bestiality and pedophilia. When Anapol assured her that the opposite was true, that what children needed was polyamory, the audience booed.[49]

Anapol's treatment on *Leeza* was the last straw for Nearing. She deeply resented watching the same ostracization take place time and time again. She now felt that such venues were inappropriate outlets for serious educational or evangelistic endeavors. She reflected on the considerable time she had devoted to meeting with talk show producers beforehand to assure that they would paint an accurate picture of her perspective during live shows. She recalled the numerous times producers had begged her to send Loving More materials ahead of the show, only for them to ignore the organization's carefully presented material when it was time for taping. Believing those efforts wasted, she lamented, "I have to thank all the pioneering brave folks who went on this tv show, although I am reminded why I'm never going to again. It's just not worth the circus atmosphere of these pieces for me."[50]

The ostracization that polyamorists endured on daytime television during the 1990s is evidence of a curious characteristic of American sexual culture in the post-60s era. Polyamorists pointed out that having serial sexual partners outside of marriage was deemed culturally acceptable. Promiscuity prior to marriage was often celebrated, and few truly lamented the destruction of the nuclear family so long as the ideal of monogamy inside of marriage was upheld. Polyamorists constantly found themselves under attack from Americans on their second, third, and fourth marriages. Clergy increasingly accepted divorce as a valid moral option. Stepparents, half-siblings, and children from multiple partners were accepted as the new norm. Despite the widespread acceptance of serial monogamy, polyamory remained anathema within the mainstream. Though half of American marriages ended in failure, the idea that people could remain indefinitely in committed relationships with multiple lovers was still so foreign that it was largely relegated to sensational daytime television.

By the late 1990s, most polyamorists had decided they no longer needed to endure public mockery. As Brett Hill had emphasized in *Time*, the internet had radically altered the communications landscape.[51] A decade earlier, there were only three or so online venues for polyamorists. By the end of the decade, there were hundreds. These would only increase in the following years as the digital world popularized polyamory to the point that the mainstream could no longer dismiss it as a dysfunctional cultural anomaly.

With the explosion of new technologies came increasingly diverse forms of polyamory. Although the Loving More coalition had liberalized in the late 1990s to include a wider array of polyamorous practices, it was increasingly unclear if it could continue to accommodate polyamory's multiple mutations. By the turn of the century, the question was whether the dissident voices fostered by the internet might be harbingers of division that would destroy polyamory as a unified concept, much less a movement.

6

Polyamories

Love is a powerful thing.

—Ryam Nearing (2002)

The dawn of the twenty-first century witnessed a quick and dramatic sea change in public opinion regarding homosexuality. The 1980s had not been kind to queer rights advocates. The culture wars that ravaged the nation took specific aim at queer issues. Right-wing defenders of traditional family values indefatigably warned that the "Gay Agenda" would destroy the moral fiber of American society. Worse, the AIDS crisis had wiped out almost an entire generation of gay men, further feeding public anxieties about queerness in general. Yet, as historian George Chauncy has noted, the twin wars queer Americans waged against both the conservative right and AIDS worked ironically in their favor as thousands came out in unprecedented numbers to defend their rights and educate the public about the misconceptions perpetuated by the "persecuting society." Their efforts in the face of such conflict eventually gave way to a general acceptance. By the late 1990s, queerness was increasingly ubiquitous, touching the lives of most Americans through friends, co-workers, and loved ones. Cultural proliferation grew exponentially as queer representation entered American homes via popular television shows like *Ellen* and *Will and Grace*. By 2000, it was becoming clear that queer Americans were winning the war for the soul of America.

Polyamory benefited from this cultural shift. Various forms of non-monogamy had long been a characteristic of many queer Americans' lives. During the 1980s and early 1990s, many gay Americans declined to publicly identify with an additional fringe identity or lifestyle sure to bring social derision. Yet as queerness became increasingly socially acceptable, more queer Americans, not just bisexuals, became comfortable taking on "polyamorist" as a designation. This added dimension further strengthened the coalition as many queer Americans began putting a name to a lifestyle they already practiced.[1]

The first Poly Pride Day was held in New York City's Central Park on September 15, 2001, four days after the 9/11 attacks. The festival was spearheaded by Justen Michael, an ambitious gay man *New York Magazine* described as "boyish." Michael had moved to New York City in hopes of finding a vibrant poly population overlapping with the city's gay community but was shocked to discover that most gay New Yorker's had no knowledge of polyamory. Not until he reached out to the city's bisexual community was he able to find information on New York's sole polyamory organization. To Michael's dismay, not only was the poly community almost completely distinct from the city's gay and lesbian population, but most of its members remained closeted. He organized the first Poly Pride Day to bridge the gap between gays and polyamorists and to encourage polyamorists to come out publicly.[2]

Michael's trouble finding polyamorists among New York's gays in the early 2000s was partially attributable to the tactics of polyamory's leaders. Loving More continued to follow the precedent set by Nearing and Anapol during the mid-1990s, seeking alliances with bisexual activists based on their shared discrimination by straight monogamists and queer communities. This approach was successful, as *Loving More Magazine*'s demographics attested. When Nearing polled her readers in the autumn of 2001, 50 percent of her respondents identified as bisexual.[3]

The turnout for the first Poly Pride Day was underwhelming. Michael decided to go ahead with the event, despite the trauma the city was experiencing, and the practical issues caused by the ensuing security high alert. Flights were cancelled, preventing most of the entertainers scheduled to perform, many out of towners, and all international attendees from getting to New York. Despite these setbacks, roughly a hundred people gathered that September day to publicly proclaim their polyamory. The following year Michael rescheduled the event for October 8, both to distance it from 9/11 and to more closely coincide with October 11, National Coming Out Day. In 2002, an estimated 150 people showed up for the second Poly Pride Day.[4]

Despite its meager beginnings, the annual Poly Pride Day represented an important step in providing a new space outside of the traditional conferences, internet chat rooms, and media appearances for polyamorists to network, proselytize, and defend their lifestyle. More significantly, it represented the emergence of a new generation of polyamorist activists. Barely in his late twenties when he organized Poly Pride in 2001, Justen Michael was no aging hippie. Unlike the Loving More coalition, the post-Reagan Information Age, rather than the counterculture of the 1960s, informed the sexual dissent that he and his peers expressed. The methods, goals, and even the nature of the polyamory this younger generation embraced often differed markedly from those who came before them.[5]

Polyamory's new generation were typically willing to work with their predecessors but were not afraid to critique their ideas. Many younger polyamorists wanted to solve the problems they saw as endemic to polyamory. Some, like Michael, wished to create deeper alliances with other sexual minorities. Others revisited long-standing divisions, hoping to tear down the remaining separations between classical polyamory and more libertine lifestyles such as swinging. Still others wished to purge polyamory of its lingering New Age and neo-Pagan heritage. Some wanted to do all three. As Nearing had done with the Keristans, these younger polyamorists wished to adopt the ideas, practices, and terminologies they deemed beneficial for their purposes and jettison those that were not. The result was multiple manifestations of polyamory, each an eclectic mix of inherited words and ideas. As digital communications continued rapidly to evolve over the first decade of the new millennium, young polyamorists disseminated these multiple strains of thought to an audience much larger than Nearing, Anapol, and the Zells had been able to reach during the preceding fifteen years combined.

In 2002, David Finch and Maureen Marovitch self-produced the documentary *When Two Won't Do*. The film follows the couple's tumultuous journey into polyamory. In the film, David is uncomfortable with polyamory and wants to settle down in a traditional marriage. Maureen feels suffocated by the idea of lifelong monogamy. Despite his reservations, David allows Maureen to take other lovers, and, at the beginning of the film, Maureen is shown in long-distance relationships with two other men, Craig and Wil.[6]

Seeking a cogent philosophy for their new lifestyle, David and Maureen undertake a journey through the world of ethical non-monogamy. First, they attend a large swingers conference in Los Angeles. David is immediately turned off by the experience and dismisses swinging as devoid of relational depth. Next, the couple visit the Ravenheart clan, where they hope to obtain sage advice from poly pioneers Oberon and Morning Glory Zell-Ravenheart. The film portrays Morning Glory as a matriarch of polyamory. Despite a revolving carousel of ten or more lovers, she always remains true to her family at home. Oberon warns Maureen that her restlessness will become detrimental to her and David's relationship if she cannot cultivate romantic relationships with lovers with whom David is comfortable. The polyamory Oberon and Morning Glory advocate is structured tightly around protecting the primacy of the inner circle while allowing for a web of secondary and tertiary lovers. Though Maureen appreciates the Ravenheart clan's insights, she is uncomfortable with the size of Morning Glory's sexual web, as well as her distinction between primaries and secondaries.[7]

After visiting the Ravenhearts, David and Maureen travel to see Maureen's long-distance lover Wil and his wife Robin. It was their first meeting with Robin, and before long difficulties emerge. Maureen

did not like being classified as Wil's secondary partner. The designation made her feel insignificant, despite her own primary relationship
dynamic with David. Robin is offended that Maureen believes she
could be her equal in the relationship. After a tense verbal exchange,
David and Maureen leave.[8]

Next David and Maureen attend Loving More's East Coast conference in New York. Nearing presents Loving More as a safe place
for everyone interested in relationships expanding beyond the nuclear
family. The conference's focus on intimacy appeals to David and he
begins to warm to the idea of polyamory. He even meets a young
woman there with whom he pursues a relationship for a short time.
However, he is shocked by her willingness to organize a group masturbation session with several of her intimate friends. He and Maureen
decline to attend.[9]

After the Loving More conference, the documentary takes a dramatic turn. Email exchanges between Robin and Maureen become
increasingly intense, undermining the relationship between the two
couples. After numerous efforts to salvage the relationship, the climax
of the film centers around a confrontational visit where Robin blames
Maureen for ruining her marriage. Though tensions temporarily cool
after Robin connects romantically with David, interactions among
the four remain emotional. Despite a seemingly pleasant end to the
visit, the last segment of the film takes a dark turn when it is revealed
that two weeks later, Robin committed suicide.[10]

The film attributes Robin's suicide to a long history of mental illness, which included prior suicide attempts dating back to her youth.
David and Maureen travel to comfort Wil, and all the parties assure
each other that Robin's suicide had nothing to do with the stresses
of polyamory. Maureen's other lover, Craig, disagrees and decides to
become monogamous again. Wil eventually comes to stay with David
and Maureen, and the movie ends with the threesome united, though
uncertain about their future.[11]

David and Maureen's documentary received mixed reviews from
polyamorists. Some of *Loving More*'s readership identified with the

struggles the film depicted and lauded it for its uncensored portrayal of the emotional complexities innate to polyamorous relationships. Others strongly disagreed, lamenting that the film did not accurately highlight the joys of the lifestyle. One subscriber wrote that the film's negative portrayal could potentially set polyamory back twenty years, believing that such depictions played into the hands of conservatives who were looking for excuses to tighten their control on nontraditional relationships.[12]

Maureen defended her film in the face of such criticisms, arguing that it was never their intention to produce a whitewashed version of polyamory for propaganda purposes. Instead, the film was meant to provoke thought and foster discussion. She believed the community was strong enough to withstand such introspection. Nearing agreed, defending Loving More's official support of the film and countering that, while the more troubling aspects of the film had caused her to have initial reservations, she valued its honesty and thought it warranted support. She felt that it accurately portrayed the controversies that existed within the community and to censor it would stifle freedom among the community. She believed each member of Loving More should watch it and judge for themselves.[13]

The controversy that surrounded *When Two Won't Do* is emblematic of the shift that occurred within polyamory in the early 2000s. Like many younger polyamorists, David and Maureen were less concerned with producing a uniform polyamory than with finding a version that was a personal fit. They were willing listen to the experiences of the older polyamorists, taking what suited them and leaving behind the rest. Though such pragmatic eclecticism had the potential for divisiveness, in David and Maureen's case, it worked in polyamory's favor, when a journalist looking to write a story on polyamory's growing popularity for *Elle Magazine* discovered the film and decided to center the piece on their experiences.

Elle published "What Its Really Like to Have Two Boyfriends (Who Know About Each Other)" in December of 2002. The piece offered mainstream print reporting on the lifestyle much like the *Time* article three years earlier but targeted to a younger audience. It mentioned the influence of both hippies and Heinlein on the older generation and discussed the difficulties of navigating sex and emotions with multiple partners. It only mentioned Robin in passing, noting that she had succumbed to her battle with mental illness. Instead, it focused on the polyamorists' devotion to one another, concluding that, despite the confusion their relationship entailed, it seemed healthier than most, lacking the neediness and volatility of many traditional relationships. *Elle* detailed polyamory's popularity among young Americans, emphasizing the differences in the new generation's approach. It used David, Maureen, and Wil as an example of younger polyamorists whose commitment to polyamory was devoid of "incense" and "intellectual flaccidity."[14]

The *Time* and *Elle* articles signalled a positive shift in media coverage on polyamory. Over the next few years countless outlets did stories on practitioners and their lifestyle. However, some older polyamorists still clung to traditional venues for proselytization. Following the *Elle* article, John Walsh dedicated an episode of his talk show to polyamory, noting the positive attention it received in *Time* and *Elle*. Walsh's show was a step up from Springer and Geraldo, but the format was much the same. By now, polyamory's most salient apologists had little interest in participating in such theatrics. *Loving More Magazine* published advice for those still willing to accept such invitations. While it claimed that those endeavors were praiseworthy, it warned that they were typically excuses for producers to sacrifice polyamorists to the public for ratings. Those warnings did not deter everyone, as the more flamboyant members of Loving More continued to accept such offers. Among them were Sasha and Janet Lessin, who had appeared with Anapol on *Leeza*. Despite previously being denigrated as hedonists and wacko spiritualists on air, they agreed to appear on the *John Walsh Show*. The results, only somewhat less sensational, were unimpressive.[15]

The fall of 2002 signaled another major change in polyamory. After eighteen years of spearheading the poly coalition, first through Polyfidelitous Educational Productions (PEP) and then through

Loving More, Ryam Nearing decided to step out of the poly limelight. Throughout the late 1990s, Nearing's domestic life had changed
substantially. For years it had consisted only of Syntony's three original members, Nearing, Barry, and Allan. The addition of Ruth and
Brett Hill in the mid-90s substantially changed their family dynamic.
Although the polyfidelitious fivesome lived together in harmony
for some time, Syntony found that their newer members had difficulty establishing lasting connections with one another. After experimenting with various living arrangements, they eventually separated.
Nearing remained with Hill, the father of her son. Barry stayed with
Ruth, and Allan departed alone. Despite their separation, the five remained close friends and still considered each other family.[16]

Due to the changes in her personal life, Nearing decided it was
time for her to retire from her position at Loving More and focus on
her family. In the October 2002 issue, she wrote a heartfelt note to
her readers telling them that she was turning the magazine over to her
longtime friend, Mary Wolf. She was grateful for the two decades she
had served the poly community through her publications and conferences. Although she would no longer continue as editor, she would
remain a consultant, an occasional contributor, and the editor of the
online discussion page. She assured her readers that while this was
goodbye, she would not really be gone. She thanked them for their
years of support and meaningful friendship, ending with the exhort-
ation, "My dreams of a world full of more loving are still my dreams.
I hope they are still yours."[17]

Loving More continued on after Nearing's resignation. Although
she contributed to the magazine over the next year, she was effectively gone by 2003. Wolf's tenure as editor proved short-lived, and the
magazine eventually fell under the leadership of Robin Trask, a self-
described "spiritual and very eclectic forty-year-old Taurean, mother
of three, astrologer, photographer, and Tantra teacher," who had stum-
bled upon polyamory via an AOL message board. Trask's leadership
further solidified the spiritualist ethos that had long been an integral
part of the Loving More coalition.[18]

Trask's spiritualist leadership dovetailed the growing division within polyamory that *Elle* had described. In the same issue that Trask introduced herself as the new editor, Wil, from *When Two Won't Do*, published an article entitled, "A Poly Skeptic Viewpoint," in which he proclaimed his membership among a subset of polys who believed that polyamory's promotion of New Age spirituality hurt its cause within the mainstream. Although some readers agreed with Wil, his article did little to alter the overall direction of Loving More. Trask staunchly represented the older Anapoldian perspective, and her contributions included astrological forecasts that took up numerous pages of *Loving More Magazine*.[19]

By 2002, poly skeptics who were unhappy with Loving More's intensified spiritualist direction had a myriad of options from which to choose. According to polyamory.org, American polyamorists had established almost 150 regional groups and websites originating in every state but Alaska. Chatrooms, message boards, and websites offered an array of avenues for those interested in polyamory to sample from its increasingly diverse flavors. This explosion provided poly skeptics with a host of new platforms on which to promote their hybrid rationalist versions of polyamory.[20]

In addition to new online groups and websites, new forms of digital media bolstered poly's popularity. In 2005, podcasting emerged as a highly effective means for young polyamorists to make their lifestyle known to the world. Many who took up this new medium exemplified polyamory's newfound eclecticism. Among the most popular of these new poly podcasters was Cunning Minx. Despite voicing an uneasiness with adopting labels, Minx was a self-described bisexual, polyamorous, kinky submissive who fully embodied the new generation's tendency to eschew rigid normative behaviors. When Minx began *Polyamory Weekly* in March of 2005, she described her content as primarily about communication, honesty, and relationships. But it was much more than that. In her own words, it was "tales from the front of responsible non-monogamy from a pansexual, kink friendly, point of view." Such themes quickly showed through as discussions about male-male-female threesomes and extended readings from BDSM erotica dominated many of her early episodes.[21]

Minx's sex-positive polyamory followed in the tradition of Easton and Hardy's *The Ethical Slut*. She recognized the diversity within the community, and the polyamory she preached was devoid of hard and fast rules or excessive moralizing. Though, for her, polyamory and BDSM went hand in hand, she realized that was not true for everyone. She rejected harsh distinctions between polyamory and swinging, urging her listeners to find solace in the communities that brought them comfort even if they sometimes overlapped. Minx claimed that such leniency was consistent with the form of polyamory she first discovered. According to that philosophy, polyamory meant stability with loved and trusted people, but also the ability to have adventures outside of that realm. She advised her listeners to embrace ideas and practices that resonated with them and discard the ones that did not. This included the spiritualist notions that were rampant among polyamorists. In one early episode, she recommended a new pagan book on polyamorous relationships with the caveat that, while she found it practically helpful, she was by no means a Pagan herself. Her pragmatic approach resonated with many young polyamorists. In 2006, *Penthouse Forum* described Minx as part of the new breed of online sex educators using the iPod to usher in the XXX wave of the future.[22]

While young polys like Minx informed a new generation about the lifestyle, some older polys adapted to the internet age as well. One of the most effective was blogger Alan M. Alan's introduction to non-monogamy followed a familiar path. Robert Heinlein's *Stanger in a Strange Land* had introduced him to alternative sexuality when he was a teenager in the early 1960s, and he had remained a non-monogamist ever since. He believed underground media channels had made the social movements of the 1960s possible and thought the same could be true for polyamory. Polyamory's online explosion during the mid-2000s convinced him it was time to do his part. In 2005, he founded the blog *Polyamory in the Media*.[23]

The benefit of Alan's blog was that it was unconcerned with promoting a specific brand of polyamory. He interspersed his commentary with his content, describing his own experiences, positions, and opinions. But what made *Polyamory in the Media* different is that it functioned as an archive where those interested in polyamory and poly-related issues could view a wide range of links to media detailing the various practices of polyamorists across the nation. In essence, it was a one-stop shop where both polyamorists and the poly-curious could acquire information about polyamory from host of sources. Readers could see how the *Baltimore Sun* covered the aging hippies and their spiritualist lovers at the latest Loving More Conference. Alongside this, they could read the work of secularist contributors to such venues such as *The Humanist* and *Free Inquiry*, which were beginning to accept polyamory as a legitimate lifestyle.[24]

Another prominent figure from the older poly generation was Dr. Ken Haslam. Haslam, a Berkeley-educated anesthesiologist and Unitarian Universalist (UU), had long been a polyamory activist. In 1999, he helped co-found the Unitarian Universalists for Polyamory Awareness (UUPA), an independent Unitarian organization created to promote acceptance of polyamory within UU congregations. The UUPA initially branded itself as a group internal to the UU and advised its members to refrain from political activism that might undermine the work of UU leaders devoted to securing marriage equality for same-sex couples. Nonetheless, their presence quickly scandalized congregations within the Unitarian Universalist Association across the country.[25] Many knew Haslam for coining the term "swolly," a word denoting those who defied easy classification into either the polyamorist or swinger camps, as well as for his work as a dedicated educator who constantly organized and spoke at polyamory events. In 2005, Haslam made one of his greatest contributions when he established the polyamory collection in the Kinsey Institute Archives at Indiana University. The archive, which was named for him, has since become a preeminent resource for historical information on American polyamory, intended for the use of future generations of scholars. Its very existence is a testament to polyamory's growing cultural legitimacy (Figure 6.1).[26]

By 2005, polyamory was reaching a critical mass. Associations with *Time, Elle,* and the Kinsey Institute meant polyamory could no longer be written off as just sensational fodder for daytime talk shows by the mainstream. However, this attention came at a price because it aroused political and religious conservatives. Prior to the mid-aughts, respected conservative cultural commentators largely dismissed polyamory as outlandish. Most agreed that the threat of ideas as radical as group marriage dissipated with the so-called death of the sexual revolution. Culture warriors such as Jerry Falwell were more worried

Figure 6.1 Dr. Kenneth R. Haslam at the Kinsey Institute.
Copyright 2017. The Trustees of Indiana University on behalf of the Kinsey Institute. All rights reserved.

about overturning abortion laws than they were about aging hippies featured on *The Jerry Springer Show*. But as polyamory continued to gain popularity online, in academic venues, and within the mainstream, conservatives eventually began to acknowledge it as a real threat. The sea change in public opinion concerning gay marriage only exacerbated this fear in the minds of many reactionary conservatives. For them, rising popular support for same-sex marriage meant that the possibility of polyamory becoming socially acceptable might not be that outlandish after all.

Notable among those who decided that polyamory was Western civilization's next great threat was conservative commentator Stanley Kurtz. Kurtz had long believed that marriage equality was a slippery slope that led to polygamy and would somehow undo the moral foundations of Western society. In 2003, he penned an article for the neocon publication *The Weekly Standard* lamenting that gay marriage was the first stop on the road to a post-matrimonial world where multiple partners were united by contract alone. In December of 2005, he followed up with the well-researched, if fallacious, article, "Here Comes the Brides." Without seeming to know much about the Loving More coalition, Kurtz reasoned that group marriage was to bisexuality what gay marriage was to homosexuality. It followed then, that if·all sexual orientations were treated fairly, bisexuality would inevitably lead marriage equality to entail group marriage.[27]

Had Kurtz known more about the Loving More coalition, he could have built a stronger historical argument. But bisexuality does not necessitate polyamory any more than a strong sex drive necessitates polygamy. Straight people can be attracted to more than one mate, and many bisexuals are monogamous. Nonetheless, Kurtz was correct that there were supporters of marriage equality who were either polyamorists or sympathetic to the their cause. As evidence, he pointed to the UUPA. Carefully noting the importance of the UU church in the history of the struggle for gay marriage, the UUPA was, for Kurtz, a clear example that marriage equality was a Trojan horse for a post-marriage polyamorous dystopia.[28]

Despite Kurtz's erroneous assumptions about bisexuality, his fears pointed to a serious conversation that had occurred within queer communities for decades. For many early queer activists, marriage equality as a political goal was a capitulation to the patriarchal heteronormative religious right-wing conservatism that had always oppressed queer communities. Yet, as the war for marriage equality became increasingly heated, many of its proponents grew weary of this older ideology. Hoping to gain the political, cultural, and economic benefits that came with legal recognition, supporters of marriage equality saw such notions as endangering the interests of the larger LGBTQ+ community. Nonetheless, there had always been a powerful stream of queer thought that had rejected legal marriage as a political or cultural end. This tradition was historically less interested in using marriage equality to usher in polyamory than it was in rejecting the state's role in marriage or, more radically, in rejecting the notion of marriage entirely.[29]

In July of 2006, an online manifesto, "Beyond Same Sex Marriage: A New Strategic Vision for All Our Families and Relationships" was posted. The document, drafted by Joseph Defilippis, the founder of the New York City based nonprofit Queers for Economic Justice, called for the recognition of family arrangements that included "committed, loving households in which there was more than one conjugal partner." Kurtz believed the statement vindicated his position. The statement, signed by hundreds of queer activists and several influential thinkers on the Left, including Gloria Steinem, Cornell West, and Judith Butler, was not specifically interested in polyamory. As *The New York Times* noted, the document stood in the older queer tradition that rejected the idea that gay marriage was a panacea that could remedy inequality among intimate relationships.[30]

The manifesto was more concerned with economic issues than with sexual liberation. It saw the debate over marriage equality as a wedge used by the Right to divide LGBTQ+ Americans, offering benefits only to a privileged few while ignoring the plight of millions who had suffered under conservative cultural and economic policies since the Reagan era. The statement proposed that marriage equality should only be the first step in the larger political agenda to extend the same economic rights offered to married people to all alternative households, whether made up of siblings, the elderly and their caregivers, non-conjugal friends, polyamorists, or others. Anything less offered undue economic privilege to an arbitrary subset of the population.[31]

In the fall of 2006, Kurtz wrote two articles for *The National Review* claiming that he had been right all along and that the "Beyond Same Sex Marriage" manifesto was proof that the true agenda of marriage equality advocates was to utilize the issue as a stepping stone to a post marriage world. For Kurtz, the manifesto's signatories were not radicals, but representatives of the coalition for marriage equality's true clandestine goals. He believed he would be vindicated after marriage equality passed and the movement that supported it shifted the so-called radicals on the periphery to the forefront in order to legalize multiple marriage.[32]

Though Kurtz was unduly paranoid about the motives of most advocates for marriage equality, poly activists were trying to gain social acceptance. In October of 2008, Dr. Ken Haslam and several other poly activists, encouraged by greater turnouts at Poly Pride, established the Polyamory Leadership Conference in order to unify leaders across the nation into a solid cultural force. However, the realization that digital initiatives were eclipsing their endeavors undercut the conference's momentum. While the conference functioned as a site for national collaboration, it soon broke into regional meetings. Eventually its leaders admitted that the internet had become the primary driver in poly activism, and support waned.[33]

The Polyamory Leadership Conference was correct in its assessment that effective activism was largely digital, and its breakup foreshadowed polyamory's dispersion. In February of 2008, *Wired* reported that the popular mainstream dating service OKCupid had evolved to include polyamorous relationships as an option for subscribers. It took this as evidence that the digital world had pushed polyamory to a cultural tipping point. According to *Wired*, the internet had not just connected polyamorists around the nation, but it had validated their worldview.[34]

Young tech-savvy polyamorists continued to use new digital platforms to creatively further their ideas. In 2008, a little-known Seattle-based actress named Terisa Greenan decided to capitalize on the new webisode craze by writing and directing twenty-one five- to ten-minute webisodes following a fictional triad through the trials and tribulations polyamorists faced. Her show, *Family*, was loosely modeled on Greenan's own experience as a polyamorist and was released bimonthly on YouTube. Though *Family*'s production budget was limited, Greenan believed the show would help normalize polyamory among a wide audience.[35]

Family was an honest attempt to showcase the struggles that polyamorists faced both in the world and in their personal relationships. It portrayed the diversity that existed within the community and the trouble polyamorists often faced relating to one another. In the show, the triad tries to connect to other polyamorists. As agnostics and atheists who are not excessively sexually adventurous, they become alienated when they find themselves surrounded by promoters of New Age spirituality and BDSM. In addition to their alienation from the larger community, the show also dealt with practical and romantic issues such as new lovers who lie about being polyamorous in order to engage in sex, potential monogamous suitors who try to tear polyamorous relationships apart, coming out to unsympathetic parents, and navigating the economic hardships of parenting and obtaining healthcare outside of legally recognized traditional marriages.[36]

Family's small production and marketing budget limited its initial reach. But the show did gain the attention of both local media outlets and the Kinsey Institute. That attention snowballed, and, in July of 2009, *Newsweek* published "Polyamory: The New Sexual Revolution?" which featured Greenan and her family.[37]

Newsweek's positive coverage detailed the diversity of family arrangements and political goals that existed within the community.

It quoted Dr. Ken Haslam, who talked openly about the emotional dangers of the lifestyle and attributed its newfound popularity to the internet. It discussed the growing discomfort polyamory was beginning to elicit from those on the Religious Right who believed polyamorists were becoming emboldened by the debate over marriage equality. Yet it argued that polyamory was a divisive issue for marriage equality advocates, many of whom felt it was a threat to their cause. Nonetheless, there were now a host of blogs, podcasts, and websites available to polyamorists and the poly-curious. While that might be "enough to make any monogamist's head spin . . . traditionalists had better get used to it," the article stated. Traditionalists, however, were not inclined to follow *Newsweek*'s advice and, in response to the article, Southern Baptist Convention president Al Mohler publicly mourned polyamory's newfound popularity as part and parcel of the postmodern condition. Following Kurtz, Mohler agreed that "polygamy" was the inevitable next step following gay marriage.[38]

By the second decade of the new millennium, many mutations of polyamory were thriving. The older generation still remained active, though less vibrant, and those searching for New Age tantrics or neo-Pagans would have little trouble finding community within polyamory's many online venues. But more vocal were younger polyamorists, many of whom rejected spiritualism as adamantly as they embraced sexual freedom. Take, for example, Bay Area polyamorous duo Shira and Gavin Katz who, in the autumn of 2011, began producing the podcast, *Pedestrian Polyamory*. The Katzes hoped to create a new American culture that normalized polyamory to the point that it became commonplace. Their show splintered off from the parent podcast, "Life on the Swingset," which indicated the Katzes' willingness to break from any poly prohibitions against casual sex.

Pedestrian Polyamory promoted itself as a down-to-earth approach to polyamory from a skeptical, rationalist, "bullshit free" perspective, and it promised to never talk about tantra, New Age, or tarot. Nonetheless, its hosts often adopted the older generation's terminology, even when it had mystical origins. An obvious example of this was their appropriation of the Keristan term "compersion," which Nearing and Anapol had popularized. Prominent San Francisco poly activist Pepper Mint also exemplified this eclectic approach when he appeared on the podcast's second episode to lament the New Age idealism of Deborah Anapol's work. "Up until recently, we didn't have any books that really came at it from a super pragmatic point of view," he said.[39]

In the summer of 2012, polyamory broke into mainstream television when *Showtime* premiered a new program, *Polyamory: Married and Dating*. The "docu-reality" was set in Southern California, where it followed two polyamorous families in their daily lives. One was a throuple from Riverside, California, that consisted of a male, Anthony, and two females, Lindsey and Vanessa. Anthony and Lindsey were married, and Vanessa was their girlfriend. All were intelligent, physically fit, young, and attractive graduate students at reputable California universities. The second family, a quad made up of two married couples, Kamala and Michael and Tahl and Jennifer, were slightly older but also fit and attractive.[40]

Married and Dating was similar to Greenan's *Family* webisodes but had a larger budget and wider appeal. The show's producer, Natalia Garcia, claimed that she wanted to show a world preprogrammed to the norms of monogamy that mature adults could carry on multiple loving relationships. However, to secure a slot on *Showtime* there had to be some sex appeal. The show graphically depicted each family engaging in group sex multiple times an episode, leaving little doubt as to why the producers cast the polyamorists they did.[41]

The gratuitous depictions of attractive polyamorists engaging in group sex makes the suggestion that *Married and Dating* was little more than the capitalist exploitation of a transgressive subculture once it reached the threshold of popularity, an interpretation that certainly bears weight. Yet, despite initial appearances, *Married and Dating* was more than Southern Californian soft-core porn. It did present the lives of real families, however beautiful and privileged. And despite its graphic sexual content, the show was not a continuous orgy. It also delved into many of the social and interpersonal problems that polyamorists face, such as dealing with intense jealousy, coming out to family members, navigating relationships with new lovers, and managing complicated sexual identities. Some cast members asked their lovers to end relationships due to jealousy or discomfort. One member of the San Diego quad came out to his conservative Jewish parents. More intimately, sex during a threesome falls apart when one member feels that they are receiving less attention, one in a series of events that leads to their separation.[42]

Another valid critique is that the bisexuality of the women in the show, often depicted explicitly in group sex situations, perpetuates a fallacious trope that all poly women want to have bisexual threesomes (or moresomes). But the show also positively portrayed male bisexuality, in a marked departure from most mainstream entertainment's tendency to suppress its depiction. The popular blog site *Gawker* admitted that, its trashiness aside, the show was likely the most humanizing depiction of the lifestyle to date.[43]

Polyamorist receptions of *Married and Dating* were understandably mixed. Poly blogger Alan M. believed the way the show humanized the cast members was an advance for the community, and any excesses in drama or salaciousness were a worthwhile tradeoff. Others disagreed, arguing that the show was a minuscule part of the community writ large and that, while the cast may be genuine, its excessive sexual content was detrimental to polyamorists and the poly-curious alike. According to this perspective, polyamorists who wished to come out after the show aired had to fight even harder against the stigma that they were only interested in group sex. Furthermore, monogamists seeking sexual stimulation might gravitate to polyamory without understanding the emotional complexities it entails and end up getting hurt or hurting others.[44]

Though the value of *Married and Dating*'s emphasis on group sex is debatable, the cast's generational differences are telling. During the first season, the Riverside throuple were not overtly spiritual, nor were they connected to any larger poly community. In one of the season's narrative arcs, Anthony is frustrated by his sense of alienation within the larger community and begins seeking out online other polys in the area. Unsurprisingly, his search leads him to the San Diego quad.[45]

Though *Married and Dating* does not overtly discuss polyamory's New Age or neo-Pagan spiritual heritage, it is clear from the start that, unlike the Riverside throuple, the San Diego quad is steeped in New Age spirituality. Kamela is especially devoted to the sacred sex tradition. Deborah Anapol affirmed this connection in a *Psychology Today* article, noting her familiarity with the San Diego community and her role in helping establish it.[46]

As the season progresses, Vanessa becomes insecure about Anthony and Lindsey's commitment to her. The couple's marriage to one another causes her to feel her place in the trouple is uncertain. So she proposes to the couple, asking them to make a lifelong commitment to her. They accept, and the three celebrate by having sex with two of their other close friends. Later, they travel to meet the San Diego quad at a potluck held at their home. Initially thinking that they were going to a sex party, the throuple are surprised to find that the gathering is focused on verbal communication and making new emotional connections rather than sex. When they tell the quad about their new commitment to one another, Kamela becomes excited. Assuring the throuple that she is experienced in both "symbolism and ceremony," she asks if she can officiate a commitment ceremony for them. They accept.[47]

In the season finale of *Married and Dating*, titled, "We Are One," Kamela unites the Riverside throuple in a handfasting ceremony. Before the ceremony begins, Anthony reflects on the meaning of their commitment, noting that while the law will not recognize it, they are dedicating the act to those who cannot get married, whether they are in same-sex or plural relationships. After all, he reasons, "who the fuck gives a shit about the law, when it comes to personal relationships."[48]

Kamela's decision to use the handfasting ritual to unite the Riverside throuple is depicted as one option among many, chosen because it resonated with them. None of the ritual's meaning or pagan history is explained, other than a quick comment that it is thought to pre-date Christianity. The simple ritual involved the three exchanging vows and promising to live a life of perpetual honesty with one another. Kamela then proclaimed their bravery as poly pioneers.[49]

Kamela may have been correct about the bravery of the Riverside throuple, but they were hardly pioneers. When the throuple handfasted for *Showtime*'s viewership, it had been almost forty years since Oberon and Morning Glory Zell's handfasting at the Gnostic Aquarian Festival when the local Minnesota newspapers reported on the polyamorists exchanging their blood and vowing to remain united as God and Goddess throughout any future incarnations that may exist. Without the Zells, it is unlikely that there ever would have been a handfasting ceremony uniting a beautiful young throuple of UC grad students on premium cable in 2012. Stripped of the deeper ritual and symbolism present in the Zells' ceremony, the throuple's handfasting was another example of the new generation's appropriation of the older one's work and ideas, stripped of their historical context.

Showtime's decision to downplay mysticism and play up sex was undoubtedly calculated. Sex sells. But trying to make New Age or neo-Pagan spiritualism palatable to premium cable subscribers nationwide is risky. Nevertheless, by 2012, a sex-positive version of polyamory retaining small remnants of its spiritualist history was on the air. For many polyamorists, this was a huge cultural win.

If sociologist Elizabeth Sheff is correct, many Americans who watched *Married and Dating*'s glamorized version of polyamory from the comfort of their own homes were already polyamorists. In 2013, Sheff published *The Polyamorists Next Door*, the first academic book exploring the nascent polyamory community. Sheff initially approached her research as a participant observer, beginning her fifteen-year study on polyamorous communities after falling in love with a polyamorous man. She was introduced to Loving More in 1995, and, by the time she began her doctoral dissertation at the University of Colorado, the organization had relocated to Colorado as well.[50]

Though Sheff's personal attempt at polyamory ended in heart-break, her insightful scholarship gained her recognition as a leading expert on American polyamory even before the publication of her book. Much of her early research focused on Colorado's Loving More community. Her later studies took her to the Midwest and to the East and West Coasts, where she interviewed dozens of polyamorists she met at private poly potlucks and on internet forums.[51]

Sheff came to several conclusions about American polyamory, most of which are natural extensions of its history. Sheff noted that polyamory is practiced in a variety of ways. While it was difficult to decipher how many people were polyamorous, there were different family forms, sexual orientations, and levels of exclusivity. Despite this variety, Sheff reported that American polys tended to be "white, well educated, liberal, and middle to upper class." She also noted the presence of a large bisexual community, especially among women, and the relative paucity of gays and lesbians. While most were not religious, she found significant minorities of Pagans and members of the UU church, with some Jews, Buddhists, and Christians mixed in.[52]

Sheff's claim that polyamorists tended to lean politically liberal is unsurprising. The post-Reagan era differed greatly from the 1960s and 1970s. By the late 1990s, the culture wars had polarized Americans largely along two political fronts. Issues important to polyamorists, such as environmentalism, sexual liberation, and social justice, led many to identify as liberals. The libertarian ethos that undergirded the thought of the Zells, Kerista, and Nearing was dissipating. Despite many polys still believing that that government should stay out of personal relationships, there was a decisive liberal shift. Even Nearing, who was often engaged in libertarian politics during her youth, wrote these activities off as a passing phase. In her own mind, she had always been more of a progressive at heart.[53]

Sheff's claim that polyamorists, aside from smatterings of Pagan and UU minorities, tend to lack religious affiliation is also unsurprising. That had been the growing historical trend for most of the length of Sheff's study. If she had conducted her research a few years earlier, it would likely have been the inverse. Her finding that polyamory consisted almost entirely of affluent, well-educated whites is significant. Sheff attributes this to the fact that this demographic has the unique ability to challenge social norms. She believes their social and financial standing affords them the privilege of indulging in transgressive lifestyles without fear of social ruin.[54]

Sheff's work produced a sociological justification of Nearing and Anapol's thirty-year-old claims. She dismissed the claim that polyamory was inherently detrimental to children, arguing that fluidity made it better suited to the post-1950s world. Society was no longer made up of straight white male breadwinners who supported stay-at-home mothers taking care of babies. Even those who strove for that ideal often found it economically unfeasible. Polyamory, she argued, offered potential relief in the form of shared economic resources, increased emotional support for adults, a greater number of positive role models for children, and the potential for greater bonding between adult men.[55]

Sheff's assessment of polyamory was largely positive, but it was not without qualification. Despite evidence of polyamory's many benefits, she was frank about its shortcomings. An abundance of adults could turn a home into an overcrowded atmosphere and space. Though most children had little trouble accepting their poly parents, external social stigma made polyamorous families vulnerable to common ridicule and invasive investigations from Child Protective Services.[56]

Sheff believed that polyamorists who properly implemented practical relational tools could overcome most of polyamory's shortcomings. Honest and clear communication, emotional protection, responsible partner selection, and the prioritization of children could effectively deter polyamory's negative side effects. Social stigma, however, was a systematic issue. In her discussion, Sheff revealed her sympathy to the sentiment set forth by the drafters of the 2006 "Beyond Same-Sex Marriage Statement." Though she did not cite the statement, she affirmed that society must "come to grips" with the wide spectrum of familial formations that existed. Contrary to conservative critiques, she believed recognition of those realities would not undermine Western civilization, but instead produce a more flexible and better adapted society. She believed shaping public policy in the mold of a heterosexual monogamous myth from seventy years ago was tragic. Rather, society should construct public policy based on rational ethics, not religious tradition, putting the economic well-being of children first regardless of family structure.[57]

The Polyamorists Next Door depicted an adaptive poly community that spanned the nation. *The Atlantic* cited it as evidence that polyamorists had been stigmatized and in fact had a lot to teach monogamists when it came to honesty, communication, and resilience. But Sheff's celebration of polyamory's prevalence did not overshadow her portrayal of the difficulties that accompanied the lifestyle. She believed polyamory was in need of a practical ethics that transcended traditional religious morals. The issue was where to find ethical direction.

In 2013, those looking for a practical guide to polyamorous ethics for the contemporary world were likely to be disappointed. Anapol's *Love Without Limits* was over two decades old, and, despite a new edition in 1997, it still promoted tantra as the key to poly success. *The Ethical Slut* had promoted itself as a guide, but it was more an argument for the possibility of responsible freedom than a systematic manual. Though Sheff understood the need for such work, she was a sociologist, not a philosopher, psychologist, or self-help author. She was no longer even polyamorous herself.[58]

Polyamorists Franklin Veaux and Eve Rickert sought to fill the need for an updated ethics with their *More Than Two: A Practical Guide to Ethical Polyamory* (2014). The book was funded by a crowdsourcing effort and supported by several influential polyamorous activists, including Sheff, Cunning Minx, Dr. Ken Haslam, and Bay Area activist Pepper Mint. As a practical guide, it greatly expanded on the foundation provided by Easton and Hardy in *The Ethical Slut*. Hardy wrote a foreword to the book, claiming that, if she and Easton were slutty big sisters with their heads in the clouds, then the authors of

More Than Two were wise next-door neighbors with their feet on the ground.[59]

The authors of *More Than Two* respectfully explained that, while American polyamory's original organizers were "commune-oriented pagans or New Age spiritualists," those labels did not fit the majority of polyamorists in the new millennium. With this change in religious demographic, there was a need for an updated ethics that was useful to all polyamorists. To fill this need, they offered a rights-based ethics founded on consent, honesty, and personal agency, devoid of appeals to spiritualism. Veaux described it as a self-conscious attempt to rationally transcend both religious tradition and cultural expectation.[60]

The philosophy of *More Than Two* was practical, but not philosophically pragmatic. At nearly five hundred pages, it covered every aspect of polyamory, from respecting the emotional rights of spouses' lovers to coming out to children. To introduce an objective normative ethics without appealing to transcendent realties, Veaux and Rickert presented relational tools based on the respect for the rights of all parties involved in polyamorous relationships. Clear and direct communication without lies of omission were key to the system. Self-care, self-efficacy, personal autonomy, and an emphasis on all partners—whether primary, secondary, or further removed—being unique individuals with inviolable rights were the key themes. The authors' rights-based approach led them to reject ethical systems that produced interpersonal abuses. In doing so, they hoped that contemporary polyamorists could move past rules-based approaches to a polyamory that favored primary couples to the emotional detriment of other lovers. This approach garnered praise from the larger poly community, with Alan M. heralding it as just what polyamory's second, more mainstream generation needed.[61]

The publication of Sheff's *The Polyamorists Next Door* and Veaux and Rickert's *More Than Two* represents the culmination of a shift in polyamory that was under way when the Loving More coalition first united in the mid-1990s. Anapol, Nearing, and the Zells' vision of a community destined to use alternative spirituality to overthrow the

Judeo–Christian ethics of the Religious Right was no longer dominant. In place of that unified vision, ubiquitous and diffuse streams
of agnostics, atheists, secularists, and swingers all claimed to be polyamory's rightful heirs. As the flame wars of the early internet message
boards had proved, these currents were always present. But now they
were legion, making futile any attempts to meld polyamory's multiple mutations into one. They were also more effective than their
forebears. No longer relegated to sensational daytime talk shows,
polyamory became a hot topic for mainstream media and academic
inquiry. As the wider swath of American polyamory dispensed with its
mystical heritage, this young generation acquired and benefited from
a cultural currency the previous generation had coveted. This process
ensured that, by the second decade of the twenty-first century, there
was not so much a polyamory movement as there was a movement
of polyamories.[62]

Afterword

When Franklin Veaux and Eve Rickert published *More Than Two* in 2014, it had been thirty years since Nearing and Anapol had first begun their work and forty since the Zells had united in handfasting. By then, Nearing and her husbands had long since retired from public life, though they remain alive and well. Nearing is still with Brett Hill. Barry and Ruth also still live together, not far from Allan Jensen. They are all still close, despite having moved into separate houses.[1]

Though Nearing left the poly limelight of her own accord, time has taken other members of polyamory's founding generation. In May of 2014, *The Huffington Post* reported that the priestess of the Church of All Worlds, Morning Glory Zell-Ravenheart, had passed away after an almost decade-long battle with cancer. It credited her with popularizing polyamory in the early 1990s and reprinted a lengthy quote from Oberon.

> My beloved has passed beyond the veil. She drew her final breath at 5:42 yesterday afternoon. Her handmaidens, students and priestesses prepared her body and dressed her in her beautiful Sea Priestess robes. She is now lying in grace in the Temple for a few days until we take her body to its final resting place in the Earth. It's been an incredible week—grief and joy intermixing like a lava lamp. So many beautiful people gathered around, taking care of everything. That's all I can really say right now . . . I can barely type.[2]

When Morning Glory passed, she and Oberon had been in a polyamorous marriage for four decades. Their union, however odd to outside observers, was a testament to commitment and endurance.

When I met Oberon for lunch in Santa Cruz in February of 2018, he was living with friends in Bonny Doon, California, not far from Robert Heinlein's old home. He was an eager storyteller, excited to talk about his adventures over the years. Although he was pushing seventy-five, he bragged that his loud lovemaking with his current girlfriend annoyed his housemates. But when the topic of Morning Glory came up, his eyes fell, and he became visibly emotional. He assured me that their relationship was unparalleled. No one had, or could, replace her. Four years after her death, he still lived in the shadow of her passing. No one else was there through everything, he told me. There was no longer anyone to laugh at his jokes or finish his stories (Figure A.1).

Not long after Morning Glory's passing, the polyamory community lost Deborah Anapol as well. She had continued contributing to *Loving More Magazine* long after Nearing's departure. Though Anapol's spiritualist approach to polyamory had fallen out of favor with many of the younger generation, she continued to be a guiding light for those committed to the sacred sex tradition. After releasing the second edition of *Love Without Limits* in 1997, she went on to publish *Compersion: Meditations on Using Jealousy as a Path to Unconditional Love* (2004), *The Seven Natural Laws of Love* (2005), and *Polyamory in the 21st Century* (2010). That year she was also awarded the Vicki Sexual Freedom Award from the Woodhull Freedom Foundation.[3]

In addition to her career as a writer and poly educator, Anapol continued working as a relationship coach, tantric teacher, and sexual healer. She passed away unexpectedly in her sleep on August 18, 2015, after spending the day meditating with friends in London, where she was leading a workshop. According to those present, she had spent the night showing them a film about ecstatic death and reflecting on the possibility of intentionally letting go into it. "If you live your life orgasmically, then your death will also be orgasmic," she reportedly said right before she went to sleep. The next day, Alan M. shared the news. He mourned the loss of "a founding mother of the polyamory

Figure A.1 Oberon Zell, Santa Cruz, California, 2018.
Photo by the author.

movement" and posted a picture of her alongside Ryam Nearing. Robin Trask at Loving More also wrote a eulogy thanking her for her contributions and lamenting that many of polyamory's younger generation were unaware of her trailblazing work.[4]

While poly's older generation lost significant figures, its new generation found themselves in a radically changing world. In the June 2015 civil rights case, *Obergefell v. Hodges*, the US Supreme Court ruled that under the Due Process and Equal Protections clauses of the Fourteenth Amendment, it was unconstitutional to deny same-sex couples the right to get married. The case was a landmark decision, in the spirit of *Loving v. Virginia*, which had extended marriage rights to multiracial couples, half a century prior. Although marriage equality was already the law of the land in thirty-seven of the fifty states, *Obergefell* effectively ended a decades-long legal struggle by ensuring the same for residents of the other thirteen. LGBTQ+ activists all over the nation rejoiced over such a significant and meaningful victory.[5]

The Obergefell decision was not easily won. The 5–4 vote was a close call. According to Chief Justice John Roberts, the Constitution was void of any theory of marriage, and it was not the place of five federal lawyers to impose their opinion on the people. He commented that, while marriage equality supporters may have cause to celebrate, the Constitution had nothing to do with it. In addition, it was his opinion that the jump from opposite-sex to same-sex marriage was much greater than from monogamy to multiple partners, and he thought that the decision might later be used to make a case for polyamory.[6]

An analysis of the Supreme Court's majority opinion shows that a jump to polyamory might be a bit more complex than Roberts believed. The majority opinion of the *Obergefell v. Hodges* decision was deeply monogamist. On the one hand, it admitted that the legal understanding of marriage had changed over time. Coverture and arranged marriages were no longer acceptable, and mixed-race marriages had been made legitimate. Nonetheless, the Court based its decision to protect same-sex marriage on continuity, rather than discontinuity. Its rationale rested on four premises. The first was that marriage is inherent to personal autonomy, the third was that marriage safeguards children and families, and the fourth was that marriage is a keystone of the American social order. However, the language of the second premise made explicit the Court's position. It stated that same-sex marriage was a fundamental right because to marry supports a "two-person union like any other in its importance to the committed individuals." The opinion ends with the affirmation that "in forming a marital union, two people become something greater than they once were."[7] In order to secure the same legal protections, future polyamorists will have to reject one of the fundamental premises on which the *Obergefell* decision rests, as well as its concluding sentiment.

For most polyamorists this does not matter. Aligned with most of their forbearers, polyamorists seem to be, at least for the moment, largely content with keeping their private relational lives just that. While this perspective is not universal, Elizabeth Sheff has argued that it is the dominant opinion across the community.[8]

This tendency not to challenge marriage laws may change in the future. It is possible that a future poly coalition will arise that sees legal marriage as a worthy goal. But it will soon be a decade since the legalization of same-sex marriage, and Stanley Kurtz's fears have yet to be realized. There has been no large-scale reordering of the marriage equality coalition where marriage abolitionists move to the center and become the face of a new movement. Most legal challenges that have occurred mirror that of the San Diego throuple who each secured their names on their child's birth certificate. They have been modest, incremental, and non–precedent setting.

The flipside to Kurtz's fears seeming unfounded, is that the signers of the Beyond Same-Sex Marriage Statement have remained disappointed. Despite their cogent critiques of same-sex marriage as a political end, advocates have won few tangible victories. There are those who remain committed to the statement's principles. In 2008, Nancy Polikoff published a book expounding the concerns set forth in the statement. New York University professor Lisa Duggan has also pointed out how those in non-traditional relationships are uniquely vulnerable in times of tragedy. Despite their calls to address the social inequalities the current institution of marriage perpetuates, there has been no cohesive large-scale movement to extend equal economic, legal, or social protections to those outside the boundaries of matrimony.[9]

In the fall of 2016, a decade after the original publication of the Beyond Same-Sex Marriage Statement, a select group of the original signers convened at a conference in Manhattan to discuss the statement's legacy. Although they continued to hold out hope for a post-marriage society, they confessed that the mainstream gay rights movement refused to follow their lead and current policies have ignored the document. They admitted that, although the statement is still taught in queer studies programs around the country, it had been a political failure.[10]

The lack of activism to either extend or abolish marriage may stem partially from pragmatic concerns. In 2017, the Canadian Polyamory Advocacy Association declared November 23 the first Polyamory Day to commemorate a 2011 Supreme Court decision that decriminalized polyamory in British Columbia. According to the Canadian Supreme Court, so long as polyamorists did not try to legally formalize their unions, they remained outside the censure of anti-polygamy and anti-bigamy laws. The 2017 celebrations were successful, garnering international recognition. Perhaps unaware of Justen Michaels's 2001 Poly Pride Day, influential polyamorists associations all over the world have regarded November 23, 2017, as the first international Polyamory Day.[11]

In America, pragmatic concerns have taken a more regressive turn. During the Trump administration, many activists interested in such issues felt as though they had to protect gains already made rather than pour energy into new initiatives that might fare better under progressive leadership. Federal discrimination against trans persons also struck them as a more pressing concern. Fears of legal regression concerning sexual autonomy were exacerbated by the US Supreme Court's June 2022 decision to overturn *Roe v. Wade*. Not only did this decision remove federal protection for abortion access but it also called into question the future of gay marriage, queer acts, and even access to birth control.[12]

Although polyamorists have not publicly waged a political war for marriage access or abolition, polyamory has continued to spread. Most young Americans using a smartphone have encountered some form of ethical non-monogamy. The gay hookup app *Scruff* recently added polyamory to its list of selectable relationship statuses and even a site as sexually innocuous as *Facebook* offers open relationships as a possible option. For dating apps that have not expanded to include such options, popular polyamory websites encourage their readers to post their polyamorous status in their taglines and bios. In addition, new dating apps specifically for the ethically non-monogamous have emerged. Any American using dating apps to pursue intimate connections is now only a few swipes away from encountering someone practicing polyamory. This rapid growth, coupled with its tendency to remain silent in the political sphere, has led one commentator to refer to polyamory as "the most quietly revolutionary political weapon in the United States."[13]

As polyamory continues to spread throughout American culture, it has found new and unlikely venues. In June of 2018, evolutionary psychologist Dr. Geoffrey Miller appeared on the popular podcast *Making Sense* to discuss the benefits of polyamory. One of America's best-known public intellectuals, *Making Sense*'s host, Sam Harris, gained nationwide attention for his assaults on the evils of religion in the wake of 9/11. In the years that followed, his sustained attacks on religion and irrationality earned him a spot, alongside Richard Dawkins, Daniel Dennett, and Christopher Hitchens, as one of the "Four-Horsemen of the new atheism."[14]

Miller, who is a tenured professor at the University of New Mexico, is a prolific and respected evolutionary psychologist who specializes in sexual selection. In the fall of 2017, he began teaching a course "Polyamory and Open Sexuality." In his syllabus, he lamented polyamory's lack of legal protections, despite new research suggesting that more than 50 percent of millennials surveyed no longer accept monogamy as an ideal, potentially pushing the number of young Americans practicing some form of ethical non-monogamy higher than that of those who identify as LGBTQ+. The class, offered to undergraduate and graduate students, was promoted as an excellent primer to prepare those going into clinical psychology for the realities of relationships in the modern world.[15]

During his interview with Harris, Miller, who is himself a poly-amorist, proposed that historically monogamy has been a "wildly successful way to take hominid pair bonds and update them for agri-cultural and industrial civilizations in ways that work for most peo-ple most of the time, pretty well." But, according to Miller, many of the social and environmental circumstances that helped ritualize monogamy and turn it into a societal norm are no longer relevant. Not bound by the same agricultural and industrial factors, the social atmosphere and technological advances of the contemporary world have produced a type of "Cambrian Explosion of different relation-ship patterns" with which American youths are experimenting. While Miller believes that many of these variant forms of ethical non-monogamy will certainly prove unsustainable, forms of polyamory may remain and coexist with monogamy in American society.[16]

Having a respected evolutionary psychologist advocate for poly-amory's benefits to one of America's most well-known and outspoken atheists is a testament to how far polyamory has come. Yet some might argue that Miller's social standing frees him to make such claims, echoing Elizabeth Sheff's argument in *The Polyamorists Next Door* that polyamory has historically been a phenomenon among well-off white Americans because they are socially and financially free enough to be sexually transgressive without suffering devastating social con-sequences. Despite Harris's popular appeal and Miller's scientific ex-pertise, they are in fact two highly educated, affluent white men.

But as polyamory continues to grow in popularity, its demographics are expanding as well. In February of 2019, *The Ethical Slut* co-author Janet Hardy appeared alongside Elizabeth Sheff on the *NPR* podcast *1A*. In the episode, "The New Sexual Revolution: Polyamory on the Rise," Hardy, who is still lovers with her co-author Dossie Easton, reflected on the fact that, although they were both free love hippies from the 1960s and 1970s, their contemporary readership was vastly more diverse. Sheff agreed, noting that a lot of young people practiced polyamory but did not wish to identify as a polyamorist, primarily due to the word's association with aging hippies.[17]

Appearing alongside Hardy and Sheff were Ron Young, the founder of the organization Black and Poly, and Crystal Farmer, the editor of the organization's website, blackandpoly.org. Farmer is also founder of the Gastonia Freedom School, a school for minority children with special needs in Gaston County, North Carolina, and she is the committee coordinator for Polyamproud, an international coalition of influential polyamorists representing a wide array of racial and gender identities that have assembled to rethink the symbolic representation of polyamory in public.[18]

Young and Farmer's appearance with Hardy and Sheff underscored polyamory's spread across racial lines. Young and Farmer also represent the growing diversity in relationship models characteristic of younger polys. Young rejected adherence to any one fixed relationship model. He claims his relationships are fluid, lacking hard edges. Farmer claims to be solo poly. For her, this means that, while she maintains multiple ongoing sexual relationships, she is her own primary. She lives alone and has no plans for marriage or asset-sharing (Figure A.2).[19]

The most significant aspect of Black and Poly's approach is the way it uses polyamory as a political weapon for the black community. On its website, the organization argues that love and family are God-given rights misrepresented to minorities as unattainable commodities by an oppressive society. For Young, polyamory is an unlikely means of defense against such social tyranny.

> As a people, disenfranchisement, mass incarceration, with Jim Crow-like laws after release, substandard schools, and gentrification has diametrically cut us off from basic human necessities in this country. . . . Polyamory may be many things to many people, but, as a black man, I see it as an opportunity to break free from the chains that have bound us for so many years. . . . By coming together, pooling resources, protecting each other, and making our homes a true place of refuge from

Figure A.2 Crystal Byrd Farmer, Gastonia, North Carolina, 2021.
Photo courtesy of Crystal Byrd Farmer.

the tyranny that has plagued us for so many years, we can elevate ourselves to a place where we too can "afford" LOVE and FAMILY.[20]

Young effectively flips Sheff's theory on its head. Instead of polyamory functioning as a social luxury that oppressed communities cannot afford, it becomes a tool to dismantle that oppression. This pragmatic utilization of polyamory as a means for justice within black communities illustrates how polyamory can serve entirely new functions within different communities.

Geoffrey Miller's evolutionary metaphor is appropriate. Polyamory is going through a type of Cambrian Explosion. The rapid evolution of a host of diverse polyamories that has occurred since the mid-1990s is much like that prehistoric evolutionary event that produced much of the biological diversity on earth today. If the post-modern social and technological environment has made this explosion possible, polyamory's genetic history should not be forgotten. Take, for instance, Jillian Deri's *Love's Refraction: Jealousy and Compersion in Queer Women's Polyamorous Relationships*, published by the University of Toronto Press in 2015. Without the contributions of women such as Ryam Nearing, Deborah Anapol, and Morning Glory Zell, there would be no such guide to queer feminist polyamory published by a reputable university press with a subtitle containing a word divined from a Ouija board by a sex commune in San Francisco the 1970s. Compersion, seen from this perspective, functions much like the whitewashed version of the handfasting ceremony *Showtime* depicted to its viewers and the libertarian impulse that leads most polyamorists to reject the fight for legal marriage rights. All are examples of how, despite the variations present in contemporary American polyamory, each manifestation retains inherited traits from common ancestors.[21]

Notes

ABBREVIATIONS

CAWA   Church of All Worlds Archives

EUSARA   Emory University Stuart A. Rose Archives

KIA   Kinsey Institute Archives

HCBLSCA   Hamilton College Burke Library Special Collections Archives

RHAUCSC   Robert Heinlein Archives, University of California, Santa Cruz

UCSBA   University of California, Santa Barbara Archives

INTRODUCTION

1. Faith Karimi "Three Dads, a Baby and the Legal Battle to Get Their Names on the Birth Certificate," *CNN* (March 6, 2021), https://www. cnn.com/2021/03/06/us/throuple-three-dads-and-baby-trnd/index. html and Marisa Dellatto, "Gay Poly Throuple Makes History, Lists Three Dads on a Birth Certificate," *New York Post* (March 1, 2021), https://nypost.com/2021/03/01/poly-throuple-makes-history-3-dads-on-a-birth-certificate/. For their own account of their struggles, see Ian Jenkins, *Three Dads and a Baby: Adventures in Modern Parenting* (Hoboken: Cleis Press, 2021).

2. Sarah M. Moniuszko, "HGTV Features First-Ever Throuple on House Hunters: Viewers Share Praise, Express Shock." *USA Today* (February 13, 2020), https://www.usatoday.com/story/entertainment/tv/2020/ 02/13/hgtv-house-hunters-throuple-episode-thrills-shocks-viewers/ 4747049002/, Tim Fitzsimons, "What's a Throuple? House Hunters Episode Puts Polyamory on the Radar," *NBCNews* (February 14, 2020), https://www.nbcnews.com/feature/nbc-out/what-s-throuple-house-hunters-episode-puts-polyamory-radar-n1137286.

3. Samantha Cooney, "What Monogamous Couples Can Learn from Polyamory, According to Experts," *Time Magazine* (August 27, 2018), https://time.com/5330833/polyamory-monogamous-relationships/ ; Olga Khazan, "Multiple Lovers Without Jealousy," *The Atlantic* (July 21, 2014), http://www.theatlantic.com/health/archive/2014/07/multiple-lovers-no-jealousy/374697/; Stacey Woods, "I Heard Someone Describe Compersion as 'The Opposite of Jealousy.' Huh?" *Esquire* (September 2014), 76; Zachary Zane, "Who Really Practices Polyamory? *Rolling Stone* (November 12, 2018), https://www.rollingstone.com/culture/culture-features/polyamory-bisexual-study-pansexual-754696/; Christopher Ryan, "Are We Designed to be Sexual Omnivores," *TED* (February 2013), https://www.ted.com/talks/christopher_ryan_are_we_designed_to_be_sexual_omnivores#t-24512.

4. American Psychological Association. Division 44, Task Forces. Consensual Non-monogamy Task Force. https://www.apadivisions.org/division-44/leadership/task-forces/. Brandon Showalter, "APA Launches Task Force on 'Consensual Non-monogamy,' Calls Polyamory a 'Marginalized Identity,'" *The Christian Post* (July 9, 2019) https://www.christianpost.com/news/apa-launches-task-force-on-consensual-non-monogamy-calls-polyamory-a-marginalized-identity.html; M. L. Haupert, Amanda N. Gesselman, Amy C. Moors, Helen E. Fisher, & Justin R. Garcia, "Prevalence of Experiences with Consensual Nonmonogamous Relationships: Findings from Two National Samples of Single Americans" *Journal of Sex & Marital Therapy*, 43, no. 5 (2017).

5. Mark Regnerus, *Cheap Sex: The Transformation of Men, Marriage, and Monogamy* (New York: Oxford University Press, 2017), 178–184. Regnerus's discussion of polyamory is troubling. He uses polyamory interchangeably with non-monogamy, though the two notions are clearly distinct. He engages sparsely with the sociological research on poly communities, straw-manning polyamory based on his personal interpretations of popular journalism.

6. Mimi Schippers, *Beyond Monogamy: Polyamory and the Future of Poly Queer Sexualities* (New York: New York University Press, 2016), 15. In contrast to Regnerus, Schippers does not put sex at the center of poly relationships and gives special attention to asexual poly relationships. She argues that polyamory's focus on romance, commitment, and familial stability has caused it to lose its subversiveness and become heteronormative. See Mimi Schippers, *Polyamory, Monogamy, and American Dreams: The Stories We Tell About Poly Lives and the Cultural Production of Inequality* (New York: Routledge, 2020), 2–4, 112, 127, 133.

7. Josh Bote, "What You Need to Know About Polyamory, Including Throuples, but Were Too Afraid to Ask," *USA Today* (February 14, 2020). https://www.usatoday.com/story/news/nation/2020/02/14/polyamory-everything-you-need-know-throuples-communication/4759860002/.

8. Research on polyamory in the international community, though sparse, is growing. For an example, see Janet Bennion, "Polyamory in Paris: A Social Network Theory Application," *Sexualities* 25, no. 3 (March 2022): 173–179.

9. Nancy Cott, *Public Vows: A History of Marriage and the Nation* (Cambridge: Harvard University Press, 2002), 3.

10. Bronski adopts the term "persecuting society" from British historian R. I. Moore and applies it to sexual culture throughout American history. See Michael Bronski, *A Queer History of the United States* (Boston: Beacon Press, 2011), 16–18. For coverture and the American moral establishment, see David Sehat, *The Myth of American Religious Freedom* (New York: Oxford University Press, 2011), 51–69, 97–100.

11. Polygamy is ethical non-monogamy in the sense that its practitioners typically provide an ethical system to justify its practice. The polyamorist critique of polygamy is really of polygyny, where men may have multiple spouses, but women cannot, rather than the more general term polygamy, which is gender-neutral in meaning but typically polygynous in practice. For a history of early American polygamy, see Sarah M. S. Pearsall, *Polygamy: An Early History* (New Haven: Yale University Press, 2019). For an academic critique of polygyny, including the persistence of patriarchal familial structures, see Rose McDermott, *The Evils of Polygyny: Evidence of Its Harm to Women, Men, and Society*, edited by Kristen Renwick Monroe (Ithaca: Cornell University Press, 2008). For more descriptive and nuanced views, see Cardell K. Jacobson and Laura Burton, eds., *Modern Polygamy in the United States: Historical, Cultural and Legal Issues* (New York: Oxford University Press, 2011). For polyamorist rejection, see Mimi Schippers, *Beyond Monogamy*, 16. For a criticism of that rejection, see Schippers *Polyamory, Monogamy, and American Dreams*, 36.

12. Abigail Adams to John Adams, March 31, 1776. National Archives, https://founders.archives.gov/documents/Adams/04-01-02-0241. For a discussion of the true intent of Abigail's letter to her husband, see Gordon S. Wood, *Friends Divided: John Adams and Thomas Jefferson* (New York: Penguin Press, 2017), 134–136.

13. Elizabeth Cady Stanton et al., *Declaration of Sentiments and Resolutions* (Seneca Falls, 1848), https://liberalarts.utexas.edu/coretexts/_files/resources/texts/1848DeclarationofSentiments.pdf. For a discussion of the drafting and significance of the Declaration of Sentiments, see Harriet Sigerman, *Elizabeth Cady Stanton: The Right Is Ours* (New York: Oxford University Press, 2001), 43–57.

14. For an analysis of the pre-feminist woman's movement, see Nancy Cott, *The Grounding of Modern Feminism* (New Haven: Yale University Press, 1987), 16–20. For a more expanded history, including the women's movement's tenuous relationship with black suffrage, as well as its political and moral conservatism, see Christine Stansell, *The Feminist Promise* (New York: Modern Library, 2010), 61–136.

15. "Free love" was first coined by the religious reformer John Humphrey Noyes in 1848, when he established the Oneida Community, a perfectionist utopian communal experiment that practiced "complex marriage," a form of sexual communism where all male community members were thought to be "spiritually married" to all female community members. See Ellen Wayland-Smith *Oneida: From Free Love Utopia to the Well-Set Table* (New York: Picador, 2016); Anthony Wonderley, *Oneida Utopia: A Community Searching for Human Happiness and Prosperity* (Ithaca: Cornell University Press, 2017), 99–107; and Holly Jackson, *American Radicals: How Nineteenth Century Protest Shaped the Nation* (New York: Crown, 2019). For a broader history of nineteenth-century free love, see John C. Spurlock, *Free Love: Marriage and Middle-Class Radicalism in America, 1825–1860* (New York: New York University Press, 1988). For a newer, gendered analysis that focuses on the contributions of the movement's women, see Joanne E. Passet, *Sex Radicals and the Quest for Women's Equality* (Urbana: University of Illinois Press, 2003).

16. For an example,e see Deborah Anapol, *Polyamory in the 21st Century: Love and Intimacy with Multiple Partners* (Lanham: Rowman and Littlefield, 2010), 45–48.

17. For a detailed exposition of Bohemian culture, including the influence of Emma Goldman, see Christine Stansell, *American Moderns: Bohemian New York and the Creation of a Century* (New York: Metropolitan Books, 2000).

18. For the larger cultural changes in the 1920s, see Ronald Allen Goldberg, *America in the Twenties* (Syracuse: Syracuse University Press, 2003) 83–100. For the bourgeoning gay culture in the 1920s, see George Chauncey, *Gay New York: Gender Urban Culture, and the Making of the Gay Male World* (New York: Basic Books, 2019). For the greater shifts in sexual

culture during the 1920s, see John D'Emilio and Estelle Freedman, *Intimate Matters: A History of Sexuality in America* (Chicago: University of Chicago Press, 1997), 241–274 and John C. Spurlock, *Youth and Sexual Culture in the Twentieth Century United States* (New York: Routledge, 2016). For a sustained argument for not only putting sexuality at the heart of the culture wars but for beginning those wars in the 1920s, see R. Marie Griffith, *Mortal Combat: How Sex Divided American Christians and Fractured American Politics* (New York: Basic Books, 2017).

19. Cott, *Public Vows*, 168. Margot Canaday, *The Straight State: Sexuality and Citizenship in Twentieth Century America* (Princeton: Princeton University Press, 2009), 130–133.

20. Historian Kevin Schultz calls the easily identifiable strict norms that defined the "moral righteousness" of American family life during the postwar era as "The Rules." See Kevin M. Schultz, *Buckley and Mailer: The Difficult Friendship that Shaped the Sixties* (New York: W. W. Norton and Company, 2015), 49–53. For the effect of the Cold War on the production of sexual consensus, see Elaine Tyler May, *Homeward Bound American Families in the Cold War Era* (New York: Basic Books, 2008) and Miriam G. Reumann, *American Sexual Character: Sex, Gender, and National Character in the Kinsey Reports* (Berkeley: University of California Press, 2005), 8–12. For a survey of the state's increasing surveillance of sexuality, see Jessica R. Pliley, *Policing Sexuality: The Mann Act and the Making of the FBI* (Cambridge: Harvard University Press, 2014) and Margot Canaday, *Straight State*. For the systematic persecution of homosexuality, see Daniel Hurewitz, *Bohemian Los Angeles: And the Making of Modern Politics* (Berkeley: University of California Press), 115–159; Lilian Faderman, *The Gay Revolution: The History of the Struggle* (New York: Simon and Schuster, 2015), 13–52; and David K. Johnson, *The Lavender Scare: The Cold War Persecution of Gays and Lesbians in the Federal Government* (Chicago: University of Chicago Press, 2004).

21. For overarching analyses of the American counterculture, see Christopher Gair, *The American Counterculture* (Edinburgh: Edinburgh University Press, 2007); *Imagine Nation: The American Counterculture of the 1960s and 1970s*, edited by Peter Braustein and Michael William Doyle (New York: Routledge, 2002); and Nadya Zimmerman, *Counterculture Kaleidoscope: Musical and Cultural Perspectives on Late Sixties San Francisco* (Ann Arbor: University of Michigan, 2010). For hippie culture, see Micah L. Issitt, *Hippies: A Guide to an American Subculture* (Santa Barbara: Greenwood Press, 2009); Timothy Miller, *The 60s Communes: Hippies and Beyond* (Syracuse: Syracuse University Press, 1999); and Timothy

Miller, *Hippies and American Values* (Knoxville: University of Tennessee Press, 2012).

22. For new religious movements and the counterculture, see Carole Cusack, *Invented Religions: Imagination, Fiction, and Faith* (Burlington: Ashgate, 2010).

23. The counterculture's relationship to politics is varied. As Timothy Miller points out, most hippies were not exceptionally interested in political organization or Marxist theory. However, they were typically anti-capitalist, anti-establishment, and anti-war. When they were not politically withdrawn, both their sympathies and actions caused many observers to see them as overlapping with the New Left to a great extent. The history I present here highlights a strain of hip culture that was both anti-socialist and at times pro-war. For a discussion, see Miller, *Hippies and American Values*, xix–xxiv.

24. For an analysis of the cultural shifts of the 1970s, see Bruce Schulman, *The Seventies: The Great Shift in American Culture, Society, and Politics* (New York: Free Press, 2001).

25. The paucity of historical research on bisexuality is baffling in light of contemporary academic interest in sexuality. Even Steven Angelides's *A History of Bisexuality* is less a history of the bisexual movement than it is a chronicling of its erasure within queer theory. See Steven Angelides, *A History of Bisexuality* (Chicago: University of Chicago, 2001).

26. For 1960s liberation movements, see Terry H. Anderson, *The Movement and the Sixties: Protest in America from Greensboro to Wounded Knee* (New York: Oxford University Press, 1995). For a history of the post 1960s culture wars, see James Davidson Hunter, *Culture Wars: The Struggle to Define America* (New York: Basic Books, 1991); Lisa McGirr, *Suburban Warriors: The Origins of the New American Right* (Princeton: Princeton University Press, 2001); and Andrew Hartman, *War for the Soul of America: A History of the Culture Wars* (Chicago: University of Chicago Press, 2015).

CHAPTER I

1. Sydney Ahlstrom uses the term "harmonial religion" to refer to forms of piety that seek to unite spiritual composure, physical health, and other aspects of human well-being, interpreting such harmony as flowing "from a person's rapport with the cosmos." He admits that this is a diffusive impulse that has many diverse manifestations and roots reaching back through the centuries. Syncretic in nature, such traditions often

entail rites and rituals, have charismatic leaders, and may also appeal to an ancient past. For a discussion, see Sydney Ahlstrom, *A Religious History of the American People*, 2nd ed. (New Haven: Yale University Press, 2004), 1019–1020.

2. The interplay between new religious movements and sexual ethics within the counterculture is complex. The Jesus Movement incorporated the dress and slang of the counterculture with a more traditional Christianity that supported sexual traditionalism. In its darkest manifestations, countercultural religion could produce deadly mind control, coercion, and violence, as was the case with the infamous Manson Family murders. Yet, on the other end, many young Americans incorporated neo-Pagan, Native American, Buddhist, Hindu, Sikh, Jain, and Sufi concepts to formulate novel ethical systems that prized peace while rejecting sexual traditionalism. In the face of Christianity's waning hegemony, others created new religious movements seemingly unattached to any previous established religion. See *The 60s Communes*, 92–127 and Cusack, *Invented Religions*, 1–5. Gretchen Lemke-Santangelo has argued that the combination of psychedelics and countercultural religion allowed young women to carve out spaces of autonomy and begin rethinking the strictures of patriarchy present in both traditional religion and the sexual ethics that emanated from it. Gretchen Lemke-Santangelo, *Daughters of Aquarius: Women of the Sixties Counterculture* (Lawrence: University of Kansas, 2009), 5, 113–136.

3. See Heinlein to Lurton Blassingame, October 21, 1960, in Robert Heinlein, *Grumbles from the Grave*, edited by Virginia Heinlein (New York: Ballentine Books, 1989), 227–231 and Heinlein to Harmann B. Deutsch, July 19, 1961, Robert Heinlein Archives, University of California Santa Cruz. (hereafter RHAUCSC). For a detailed view of Heinlein's life and work, see William H. Patterson, *Robert A. Heinlein: In Dialogue with His Century,* vol. 1 (New York: Tor, 2010) and *Robert A. Heinlein: In Dialogue with His Century,* vol. 2 (New York: Tor, 2014).

4. Robert Heinlein, *Stranger in a Strange Land* (New York: G. P. Putnam's Sons, 1961).

5. Robert Heinlein, *Grumbles*, 235–236. Oberon has had numerous names during his long tenure. His birth name was Tim Zell. His other names include Otter Zell, Otter G'Zell, Oberon Zell, Oberon Zell-Ravenheart, and the initials OZ.

6. For a survey of Rand's thought and influence, see Jennifer Burns, *Goddess of the Market: Ayn Rand and the American Right* (New York:

Oxford University Press, 2009). For Rand's larger influence on the counterculture, see pages 259–260.

7. Helen A. Berger, Evan A. Leach, and Leigh S. Shaffer, *Voices from the Pagan Consensus: A National Survey of Witches and Neo-Pagan in the United States* (Columbia: University of South Carolina Press, 2003), 1–15. Margret Adler, *Drawing Down the Moon: Witches, Druids, Goddess-Worshipers, and Other Pagans in America Today* (New York: Penguin, 1986), 3–7.

8. John C. Sulak, *The Wizard and the Witch: An Oral History of Oberon Zell and Morning Glory Zell: Seven Decades of Counterculture, Magick, and Paganism* (Woodbury: Llewellyn, 2014), 15–16, 20. I rely heavily on this oral history which is composed of many firsthand accounts from both Oberon and his wife, as well as a host of their other friends and acquaintances.

9. Lance Christie, "The Origin of ATL," inserted in Letter from Tim Zell to Robert Heinlein February 4, 1972, RHAUCSC; Lance Christie, "On CAW/ATL Origins, Influences and History," undated; Oberon Zell-Ravenheart, "A Personal History of the Church of All World," June 18, 2011, Church of All Worlds Archives (hereafter CAWA).

10. See Lance Christie, "The Origin of ATL" (November 10, 1967), inserted in Letter from Tim Zell to Robert Heinlein February 4, 1972, RHAUCSC; and Sulak, *The Wizard and the Witch*, 30–1.

11. Sulak, *The Wizard and the Witch*, 31.

12. Oberon Zell-Ravenheart, "A Personal History of the Church of All World," June 18, 2011. CAWA.

13. Sulak, *The Wizard and the Witch*, 37. Lance Christie, "The Origin of ATL" (November 10, 1967), inserted in Letter from Tim Zell to Robert Heinlein February 4, 1972; and Tim Zell, "The Fulton Years" (November 3, 1966), inserted in Letter from Tim Zell to Robert Heinlein February 4, 1972, RHAUCSC.

14. "Note from the Editors," *The Atlan Torch: The University of Oklahoma Edition*, September 26, 1966, 1, University of California Santa Barbara Archives (hereafter UCSBA). Tim Zell, "Unholy Rollers," *The Atlan Torch: The University of Oklahoma Edition*, September 26, 1966, 2–4, UCSBA; R. L. Christie, "An Answer to Tim Zell," *The Atlan Torch: The University of Oklahoma* Edition, October 1, 1966, UCSBA.

15. Lynne Bartow, "BaAuH2O for President," *The Atlan Torch*, November 11, 1963, UCSBA; Sulak, *The Wizard and Witch*, 3;. R. L. Christie, "Censorship," *The Atlan Torch*, September 24, 1966, UCSBA.

16. Tim Zell, "The Fulton Years," November 3, 1966, inserted in a letter from Tim Zell to Robert Heinlein February 4, 1972, RHAUCSC; Tim

Zell, "The Measure of a School," and Rich Hileman, "The Woods," *The Atlan Torch*, April, 21. 1965, UCSBA.

17. Sulak, *The Wizard and Witch*, 46.

18. Oberon Zell-Ravenheart, "A Personal History of the Church of All World," June 18, 2011, CAWA; Lance Christie, "On CAW/ATL Origins, Influences and History," undated, CAWA.

19. Ibid.

20. Oberon Zell-Ravenheart, "A Personal History of the Church of All World," June 18, 2011, CAWA.

21. Tim Zell, *Green Egg* 1, no. 1 (March 1968): 1.

22. Tim Zell, *Green Egg* 2, no. 13 (January 1969): 1; Tim Zell, *Green Egg* 1, no. 5 (May 1968): 1.

23. Margot Adler, *Drawing Down the Moon: Witches, Druids, Goddess Worshippers, and Other Pagans in America Today* (New York: Penguin, 1997), 293.

24. Ibid., 276.

25. Ibid., 293–294.

26. Oberon Zell, Email to the Author, November 10, 2016.

27. Sulak, *The Wizard and the Witch*, 49; Oberon Zell-Ravenheart, "A Personal History of the Church of All World," June 18, 2011, Kinsey Institute Archives (hereafter KIA).

28. Adler, *Drawing Down the* Moon, 251.

29. Ibid., 47–60; Margaret Alice Murray, *The Witch-Cult in Western Europe* (Oxford: Oxford University Press, 1921), 9–16. For a discussion of the shortcomings of Murray's thesis, see Michael York, "Invented Culture/ Invented Religion: The Fictional Origins of Contemporary Paganism" *Religio: The Journal of Alternative and Emergent Religions* 3, no. 1 (October 1999): 135–146. For Graves, see Robert Graves, *The White Goddess: A Historical Grammar of Poetic Myth* (New York: Farrar, Straus, and Giroux, 1948), 189–194, 476.

30. Adler, *Drawing Down the Moon*, 63.

31. Oberon Zell-Ravenheart, "Green Egg: The 40-Year-Old Hippie," in *Green Egg Omelette: An Anthology of Art and Articles from the Legendary Pagan Journal,* edited by Oberon Zell-Ravenheart (Franklin Lakes, Career Press, 2009), xiii; and Tim Zell, *Green Egg* 3, no. 22 (February 1970): 1; Tim Zell, *Green Egg* 3, no. 22 (February 1970): 1. See also "Common Themes of Neo-Pagan Religious Orientation Abstracted from Meetings of the Ecumenical Council of Themis Califia South Members, Summer 1970," in *Green Egg* 4, no. 43 (Samhain 1971): 11–12

and W. Holman Keith, "Council of Themis," in *Green Egg* 4 no. 44 (December 1971).

32. Tim Zell, *Green Egg* 3, no. 22 (February 1970): 1.
33. Sulak, *The Wizard and Witch*, 66.
34. Ibid., 68–69.
35. Ibid., 69.
36. Ibid., 70.
37. Ibid.
38. Tim Zell, "TheaGenesis: The Birth of the Goddess," in *Green Egg Omelette*, 90–94.
39. Ibid.
40. Tim Zell, "Biotheology: The Neo-Pagan Mission," *Green Egg* 4, no. 41 (Lugnhasadh 1971): 67–68.
41. Tim Zell, "Ego-Ethos: The Ethics of Self-Actualization," *Green Egg* 5, no. 49 (October 1972): 1–4.
42. Oberon Zell, Email to the author, September 11, 2017.
43. Letter from Tim Zell to Robert Heinlein (February 4, 1972), RHAUCSC; Julie Carter and Tim Zell, "Ero-Theology: Sexual Communion as Worship," *Green Egg* 4, no. 45 (February 1972): 11–14; Tim Zell, "EroEthics: Neo-Pagan Sexual Morality" *Green Egg* 5, no. 46 (March 1972): 1–4.
44. Sulak, *The Wizard and Witch*, 85; Zell, "40-Year-Old Hippie," *Green Egg Omelette*, xiv; Oberon Zell-Ravenheart, "A Personal History of the Church of All World," June 18, 2011, CAWA; Editorial Giggles, *Green Egg* 4, no. 42 (November 1971); Editorial Giggles, *Green Egg* 4, no. 44 (December 1971).
45. Zell originally wrote Heinlein in September of 1971, but, still intimidated, he did not mail it until after the New Year. Letter from Tim Zell to Robert Heinlein, January 18, 1972, RHAUCSC. See also Letter from Robert Heinlein to Tim Zell (February 28, 1972), RHAUCSC. Zell eventually published letters from their ongoing correspondence in *Green Egg* after Heinlein's death. See *Green Egg* 82, 85, and 89.
46. For a concise summary of Rimmer's life and work, see "Robert Rimmer," in *Sex from Plato to Plagia,* vol. 2. Edited by Alan Soble (Westport: Greenwood Press, 2006), 929–932.
47. Letter from Robert Heinlein to Tim Zell, January 20, 1972, and Letter from Tim Zell to Robert Heinlein, February 2, 1972, RHAUCSC.
48. For a brief bio of Wilson and a discussion of his relationship to Discordianism, see "Making the Donkey Visible: Discordianism in the Works of Robert Anton Wilson," in *The Handbook of New Religions*

and Cultural Productions edited by by Carole Cusack and Alan Norman (Leiden: Brill Publishing, 2012), 421–440.

49. Oberon Zell-Ravenheart, "A Personal History of the Church of All World," CAWA; Mary Lou Gust, "Bewitching Rites," *Minnesota Daily*, Tuesday April 16, 1974, reprinted in *Green Egg* 7, no. 63 (June 21, 1974): 17; Robert Anton Wilson and Robert J. Shea, "Anarchism and Crime," *Green Egg* 7, no. 62 (May 1974). Compare Robert Anton Wilson, "Crowley, Leary, and Genetics," *Green Egg* 6, no. 60 (February 1974): 5–7 and "Paleopuritanism and Neopuritanism: A Neurosemantic Analysis," *Green Egg* 7, no. 65 (September 1974): 13–14.

50. Tim Zell, "Editorial Giggles," *Green Egg* 6, no. 55 (June 21, 1973); Sulak, *The Wizard and Witch*, 89–95.

51. Tim Zell, "Editorial Giggles," *Green Egg* 6, no. 55 (June 21, 1973).

52. For a concise autobiographical account, see Sulak, *The Wizard and the Witch*, 103–119.

53. Ibid., 109–114.

54. Ibid., 114–119.

55. Ibid., 117.

56. Ibid., 117–125.

57. Ibid., 124–125. The entire Handfasting Ceremony and details are printed in *Green Egg*. See Morning Glory and Time Zell, "Neo-Pagan Handfasting Rite . . . Church of All Worlds," *Green Egg* 7, no. 63 (June 1974): 9–12.

58. Larry Adcock, "Rites of Energy Arousal Open Witches Conclave," *St. Paul Pioneer Press*, Friday April 12, 1974, reprinted in *Green Egg* 7, no. 63 (June 1974): 13–14.

59. Gust, "Bewitching Rites," 17.

60. Sulak, *Wizard and the Witch*, 126.

61. Morning Glory G'Zell, "The Ordination of Moring G'Zell As Priestess of the Church of All Worlds," *Green Egg* 7, no. 65 (September 1974): 7.

62. See especially Thad and Rita Ashby, "The Yoga of Sex," *Green Egg* 7, no. 67 (December 1974): 5–7; J. G. Calander, "Nudity in the Church," *Green Egg* 8, no. 75 (December 1975): 28; and Carl Jones, "Sexual Magic: The Natural Dynamic," *Green Egg* 8, no. 75 (December 1975): 29.

63. Morning Glory G'Zell, "PRINCIPIA DISCORDIA, or How I Found the Goddess and What I Did to Her When I Found Her," *Green Egg* 7, no. 64 (August 1974): 20; Tom Williams, "Keeping the Flame Alive: The Preservation and Transmission of *Green Egg*," in *Green Egg Omelette*, xix.

64. Ibid.

65. Adler, *Drawing Down the Moon*, 312.

66. For a discussion of the role of secularism and pragmatism in counter-cultural new religious movements, see Cusack, *Invented Religions*, 8–12.

CHAPTER 2

1. For the Summer of Love, see Mark Harris, "The Flowering of the Hippies," *The Atlantic*, September 1967, https://www.theatlantic.com/magazine/archive/1967/09/the-flowering-of-the-hippies/306619/. For the decline of Haight-Ashbury, see Nadya Zimmerman, *Countercultural Kaleidoscope* (Ann Arbor: University of Michigan Press, 2011), 3, 165–167 and David Farber, The Intoxicated State/Illegal Nation: Drugs in the Sixties Counterculture," in *Imagine Nation: The American Counterculture of the 1960s and '70s*, edited by Peter Braunstein and Michael William Doyle (New York: Routledge, 2002), 32–35. For the Diggers, see Christopher Gair, *The American Counterculture* (Edinburgh: Edinburgh University Press), 128–129. For Death of the Hippie parade, see Timothy Miller, *The Hippies and American Values* (Knoxville: University of Knoxville Press), xiii; and Zimmerman, *Countercultural Kaleidoscope*, 166.
2. For the post-1960s evolution of American communes, see Timothy Miller, *Communes in America: 1975 and Beyond* (Syracuse: Syracuse University Press, 2019).
3. Robert Heinlein, *Grumbles from the Grave*, edited by Virginia Heinlein (New York: Del Rey, 1989), 236.
4. Robert Anton Wilson, "The Religion of Kerista and Its 69 Positions" *FACT*, July/August 1965, http://www.kerista.com/nkerdocs/raw.html
5. "Nab 7 During Interracial Free Love Frolic in NYC," *Jet Magazine*, October 1958, 28.
6. See Wilson, "The Religion of Kerista," and Leonard Freitag, *History of the Communal Utopian Spiritual Movement*, 1984, http://www.kerista.com/dauhistory5.html, also "Nab 7 During Interracial Frolic."
7. Wilson, "The Religion of Kerista."
8. For an interesting description of early Keristan sexual ritual, see Sylvan Porter, "The Kerista Cult or Sex on the Half Shell: Explaining a Beatnik Re-Hash of Some Moldy Love Theories," *Man to Man*, January 1967, http://www.kerista.com/mantoman.php. Also Yo, "Yo Says Hi! Only 1 Rule and William a Butterfly," January 8, 2010, http://www.kerista.com/nonspeak/yoo.html. When a sexually transmitted infection was introduced to the group, it typically made its rounds to most members. See Wilson, "The Religion of Kerista." and Frietag, *History of the Communal*.

9. It appears Ginsburg was sexually involved with at least one of Kerista's members. For Ginsburg's perspective, also see Letter from Allen Ginsberg to Gary Snyder (October 26, 1964) in *The Selected Letters of Allen Ginsberg and Gary Snyder, 1956–1991*, edited by Bill Morgan (Berkeley: Counterpoint, 2008), 77. Also Bill Morgan, *I Celebrate Myself: The Somewhat Private Life of Allen Ginsberg* (New York: Penguin Books, 2006), 393.

10. Porter, "The Kerista Cult," and Wilson, "The Religion of Kerista."

11. Porter, "The Kerista Cult," and Frietag, *History of the Communal.*

12. Wilson, "The Religion of Kerista," and Frietag, *History of the Communal.*

13. Frietag, *History of the Communal.* Throughout Keristan history, members interpreted the alphabet board in various ways. Some downplayed its ability to tap into the realm of the transcendent, while others strongly embraced it. Jud, though willing to wield it as a weapon, appears to have believed it legitimate. Later members remembered that although Jud was dismissive of most personal critiques, he was more apt to listen to a message that originated from the board. See *Far Out West: Inside California's Kerista Commune*, directed by Travis Chandler and Dan Greenstone (2021) https://www.amazon.com/Far-Out-West-Californias-Kerista/dp/B099CGC3CF.

14. Wilson, "The Religion of Kerista," and Frietag, *History of the Communal.* Even Eve, "The Erotic Evolution of Kerista: Pushing Out the Frontier of Sexual Liberation," *Kerista Journal of Utopian Living* 3, no. 3 (Winter 1987): 8

15. "19 Arrested in Raid by Narcotics Police," *The New York Times,* October 18, 1964, http://www.nytimes.com/1964/10/18/19-arrested-in-raid-by-narcotics-police.html?_r=0; Frietag, "History of the Communal."

16. Jud Presmont, "Kerista Commune Follow Up Questionnaire," 1994, Emory University Stuart A. Rose Archives (hereafter called EUSARA).

17. The Purple Submarine, "Why Utopian Eyes? Introduction to the First Issue," *Utopian Eyes* 1, no. 1 (January 1974): 1. For Eve's own recollection of her arrival in San Francisco, see Even Eve, "Where Have All the Hippies Gone," *Utopian Eyes*, 1 no. 1 (January 1974): 4–7.

18. Even Eve, "Glossary #2 of Keristan English," *Kerista: Advanced Practical Scientific Utopian Theory* 2, bk. 1 (Summer 1982) http://www.kerista.com/poly.html. In my private correspondence with Eve, she said that she remembers it being another member, Geo Logical, who coined the term "polyfidelity." Geo believed it was Eve who coined the term.

19. Alphabet Board Log, December 4, 1973–January 9, 1974. See particularly December 4–9, 1973, and December 13, 1973. EUSARA. See also

Letter from Bluejay Way to Friend (undated), Hamilton College Burke Library Special Collections Archives (hereafter HCBLSCA).

20. Alphabet Board Log, December 24–27, 1973. EUSARA. Even Eve, "Glossary of Keristan English Part 1," *Scientific Utopianism and the Humanities* 1, no. 4 (Spring 1985), http://www.kerista.com/kerdocs/glossary.html.

21. Alphabet Board Log, December 22 and 28, 1973. EUSARA.

22. "Building a Commune in San Francisco," *Mother Earth News*, July/August, 1974, https://www.motherearthnews.com/nature-and-environment/kerista-commune-zmaz74jazhol and "Kerista Commune: New Tribe Timeline," http://kerista.com/timeline.html.

23. "Diet for a Utopian Planet," *Utopian Eyes* 1 no. 1 (December 1974): 17. Letter from Way to Ryam Nearing, May 16, 1981. HCBLSCA. "The Sleeping Schedule," http://www.kerista.com/ss.html, as well as Letter from Way to Mary, Lynn, Allan, and Barry, May 16, 1981. HCBLSCA.

24. Even Eve, "A Relgious Rap on Religious Raps," *Utopian Eyes* 1, no. 1 (December 1974): 41–43. Bluejay Way "Perspective: Perfection," *Utopian Eyes* 1, no 2 (Spring 1975): 8–9.

25. "The Utopian Social Contract of Kerista," *Utopian Eyes* 1, no. 4 (Autumn, 1975), 3–9; also Even Eve, "The Erotic Evolution of Kerista," *Kerista: Journal of Utopian Living* 3, no. 3 (Winter 1987): 10–11. See the obituary of Paula "Qes" Mitchell, kerista.com.

26. John D. Greenwood, *A Conceptional History of Psychology: Exploring the Tangled Web* (Cambridge: Cambridge University Press, 2015), 268. Compare The Storefront Classroom Family, "Great Minds: Immanuel Kant," *The Storefront Classroom: A Utopian Newspaper* 5, no. 4 (October/November, 1977): 1, 7, and "Introduction: The Significance of the Social Contract," *Utopian Eyes* 1, no. 4 (Autumn 1975): 1.

27. Fredrick Perls, Ralph Hefferline, and Paul Goodman, *Gestalt Therapy: Excitement and Growth in Human Personality* (Highland: *Gestalt Journal Press*, 1994), xix.

28. Ibid., xxii–xxiii, and "The Gestalt Growth Co-op: A Cooperative Approach to Self-Esteem Enhancement, Character Development, Improved Interpersonal Communication and Creative Conflict Resolution." EUSARA. For Perls at Esalen, see Jeffrey J. Kripal, *Esalen: America and the Religion of No Religion* (Chicago: University of Chicago Press, 2007), 157–165.

29. Kerista, "Social Contract Consciousness: The Basic 17 Standards," http://communalsocieties.hamilton.edu/islandora/object/hamLibCom%3A5685?solr_nav[id]=af36fd0b5f30d87ddd6c&solr_nav[page]=

o&solr_nav[offset]=o#page/1/mode/1up/search/social + contract+ Ibid. For a particularly interesting look into the psychological stress that the unrelenting drive for purity could induce, see Larry Hamelin, "And to No More Settle for Less Than Purity: Reflections on the Kerista Commune," *Praxis: Politics in Action* 1, no. 1 (August, 2013): 58–73.

30. Kipseeks, "My Ins and Outs with Kerista," 2003, http://www.kerista.com/speak/kip1.html.

31. Roger Knull, "My Brief Encounter with Kerista: An Outsider's Account," November 23, 2005, http://www.kerista.com/nonspeak/rio.html.

32. Bluejay Way, "Recent Major Changes," *Utopian Eyes* 2, no. 3 (Summer, 1976): 6–8. "The Eco-Village," *The Utopian Classroom* 4, no. 2 (June–July): 76.

33. Erik Cohen, "The Paradox of the Kibbutz," *Built Environment* 3, no. 12 (December 1974): 617–620. For a concise description of the classical Kibbutz, see Melford E. Spiro, "Utopia and Its Discontents: The Kibbutz and Its Historical Vicissitudes," *American Anthropologist* 106, no. 3 (September 2004): 556–568.

34. "Exploring Utopias: The Kibbutz," *The Storefront Classroom* 5, no. 4 (October-November 1977): 1.

35. Jud Presmont, "Getting Rid of Hangups Through Cooperative Living," and "More About the Utopian World Peace Plan of Kerista," *Utopian Eyes* 2, no. 3 (Summer 1976): 19–24.

36. Ibid.

37. "University of Utopia," *The Storefront Classroom* 7, no. 3 (August/September 1979): 1.

38. Virginia Adams, "Getting at the Heart of Jealous Love," *Psychology Today* (May 1980): 43.

39. Phil Donahue transcript (July 1, 1980). The recording of the show as well as the transcript is located within the Kinsey Institute Archives. The transcript can also be found at https://www.kerista.com/kerdocs/donahue.html

40. Ibid.

41. Deborah Anapol, *Polyamory in the 21st Century* (Lanham: Roman & Littlefield, 2010), 58–59. Will Mahoney to the Purple Submariners, November 5, 1982, and Bluejay Way to Stan Dale, December 18, 1982. HCBLSCA.

42. Will Mahoney to the Purple Submariners, November 5, 1982; Will Mahoney to Zia, Way, and Other Keristan Islanders, February 3, 1983;

Way to Will Mahoney, December 19, 1982; and Way to Gloria Steinem, December 18, 1982. HCBLSCA.

43. Allan and Lynn went through a few early attempts at establishing a pol-yfidelitous community before Jensen settled down without Lynn. For a concise history of his early journey, see Jensen, "Ten Years," *PEPTalk*, 2. KIA. Allan Jensen to Kerista Village, July 23, 1979, and Jud to Allan, Lynn, and Joey, October 1, 1978. HCBLSCA.

44. Jensen, "10 Years," 2. Mary Northrop to Bluejay Way, March 16, 1981. HCBLSCA. Also, Barry Northrop, "Best Friend Bee-Bop," PEPTalk for the Polyfidelitious (Summer 1987), 1. KIA. Cerro Gordo was a com-mune based in Cottage Grove Oregon during the 1970s and '80s. Its primary concern was ecological friendliness. For information on Cerro Gordo, see Timothy Miller, *The 60s Communes: Hippies and Beyond* (Syracuse: Syracuse University Press, 1999), 140–141.

45. Barry Northrop to the Purple Submariners, February 25, 1981. HCBLSCA.

46. Mary to Way, March 16, 1981. HCBLSCA.

47. Tye to Barry, Mary, and Allan, March 11, 1981. HCBLSCA.

48. Mary to Tye, March 16, 1981, and Mary to Eve, Way, Jud, Loki, Lil, and Everyone, April 27, 1981. HCBLSCA.

49. Ibid.

50. Tye and Way to Barry, May 30, 1981. HCBLSCA,

51. Barry to Kerista, August 2, 1981, and Tye and Way to Barry, May 30, 1981. HCBLSCA.

52. Jud to Ryam, June 2, 1981. HCBLSCA.

53. Ryam to Geo, March 7, 1982; Ryam to Tye, March 8, 1982; and Zia to Ryam, Allan, and Barry, March 21, 1982. HCBLSCA.

54. Ryam to Jud, March 26, 1982. HCBLSCA.

55. Way to Ryam, March 30, 1982; Ryam to Way, April 7, 1982; and Tye to Ryam, April 13, 1982. HCBLSCA. The debate over the nature of para-digms bled from Kerista's correspondence with Ryam into their ever-expanding list of ideological commitments. It was number seventy-eight in the 1983 version of Eighty-Four Standards and forty-six in the an-onymous later version of eighty-eight standards. See Even Eve, "Social Contract of the Gestalt-o-Rama Do-It-With-Friends Mental Health System," excerpted from *Polyfidelity: Sex in the Kerista Commune and Other Related Theories in How to Solve the World's Problems* (San Francisco: Performing Arts Society, Inc., 1984), and "The 88 Standards of the Gestalt-o-Rama Growth Co-op and the Kerista Tribe." EUSARA.

56. Ryam to Tye and Way, November 5, 1982, and Tye to Syntonians and Joanie, December 24, 1982. HCBLSCA.

57. Jud to Ryam, March 10, 1983. HCBLSCA. For Jud's political views, see "The Question of Parity: Soviet Intentions from the Perspective of Both Hawks and Doves," and "Spook Story: The KGB According to De Borchgrave and Moss," *The Storefront Classroom* 8, no. 4 (October–November 1980): 1–5.

58. See incomplete letter to Ryam, March 21, 1983; Tye to Ryam, March 25, 1983; Tye to Ryam, April 4, 1983; Tye to Ryam, April 23, 1983; and Tye to Will Mahoney, April 4, 1983. HCBLSCA.

59. Ryam to Tye, August 14, 1985. HCBLSCA.

CHAPTER 3

1. Much has been written on the post-1960s fracture of American society. See Terry Anderson, *The Movement and the Sixties: Protest in America from Greensboro to Wounded Knee* (New York: Oxford University Press, 1995); James Davidson Hunter, *Culture Wars: The Struggle to Define America* (New York: Basic Books, 1991); Lisa McGirr, *Suburban Warriors: The Origins of the New American Right* (Princeton: Princeton University Press, 2001); *The Hidden 70s: Histories of Radicalism* edited by Dan Berger (New Brunswick: Rutgers University Press, 2010); Daniel Rodgers, *Age of Fracture* (Cambridge: Belknap Press, 2011); and Andrew Hartman, *War for the Soul of America: A History of the Culture Wars* (Chicago: University of Chicago Press, 2015).

2. For the sexual revolution. see Beth Bailey, *Sex in the Heartland* (Cambridge: Harvard University Press, 1999). For the argument that sex was central to the culture wars, see Marie Griffith, *Mortal Combat: How Sex Divided American Christians and Fractured American Politics* (New York: Basic Books, 2017). For divorce rates, see Kristin Celello, *Making Marriage Work: A History of Marriage and Divorce in the Twentieth Century* (Chapel Hill: University of North Carolina Press). For American retreat from the sexual revolution, particularly in the realm of queer acceptance, see George Chauncey, *Why Marriage* (New York: Basic Books, 2004) 37–51.

3. John Lee, "The Revolution Is Over: In the '80s, Caution and Commitment are the Watchwords." *Time Magazine*, April 9, 1984, 74–84.

4. Rodgers, *Age of Fracture*, 145.

5. Linda Grant, *Sexing in the Millennium: Women and the Sexual Revolution* (New York: Grove Press, 1994), 11, 255; Chauncey, *Why Marriage*, 37–51.

6. Family Synergy "Statement of Purpose" Flyer and Family Synergy "Who Are We," Flyer, undated; Orange County Family Synergy, "Calendar of Events," 5, no. 8 (November 1979), KIA; Deborah Anapol, *A Resource Guide for the Responsible Non-Monogamist* (Mill Valley: Intinet Resource Center, 1989), KIA.

7. Deborah Anapol, *Polyamory in the 21st Century: Love and Intimacy with Multiple Partners* (Lanham: Rowman and Littlefield, 2010), 59–59.

8. For short early histories, see "P.E.P. Activities" in *PEPTalk*, Winter 1984, 6 and "Anniversary Time," *PEPTalk*, January 1990, 2, KIA.

9. Ryam Nearing, "Something Old, Something New," *PEPTalk*, Spring 1985, 1–3, KIA, for an example of Nearing's engagement with fundamentalist detractors see "Ryam Nearing Talks to Pali Paths (January 1995) (DVD), KIA. For the clearest articulation of Nearing's political views, see her appearance at the libertarian conference, L.A. Freedom '91 (DVD), KIA.

10. Ryam Nearing, *The Polyfidelity Primer* (Eugene: PEP Productions, 1984), 1, KIA.

11. Ibid.

12. Ibid., 3, 7.

13. Ibid., 4, 6.

14. "P.E.P. Activities," *PEPTalk,* Winter 1984, 6, KIA.

15. Deborah Anapol to Rollo May, Sept 15, 1985, KIA; "Women Who Run with More Than One Lover or Mate: Women and Polyamory with Deborah Anapol and Ryam Nearing," 90s (DVD), KIA.

16. Deborah Anapol, "Polygamy: Another Lifestyle," *In Context*, Summer 1985, 38–39.

17. Deborah Anapol to Jean Nagger, September 19, 1984, and Deborah Anapol to Maria Carvainis, April 24, 1985, KIA.

18. Deborah Anapol to Jean Nagger, September 19, 1984, KIA; Donahue Transcript #01175 Cincinnati, Ohio (1984), KIA.

19. Ibid. Deborah Anapol, *Intinet Newsletter*, December 1985, 2, KIA.

20. Deborah Anapol *Intinet Newsletter*, October 1985, 2; and Deborah Anapol to "Friend," KIA.

21. Playboy Channel, *Women on Sex*, "Sex Without Jealousy" Show #26, Michael Trikilis Productions, Inc., May 29, 1985 (DVD), KIA.

22. Ibid.

23. Ibid.

24. Ryam Nearing, "Polyfidelity on Playboy," *PEPTalk*, Summer 1985, 3, KIA.

25. Deborah Anapol, *Intinet Newsletter*, September 1985. KIA.

26. Deborah Anapol to Rollo May, September 15, 1985, and Deborah Anapol to Robert Rimmer, July 12, 1985, KIA.

27. Deborah Anapol to James A. Siefkes, October 18, 1985, and Deborah Anapol to William, October 14, 1985, KIA.

28. Deborah Anapol *Initnet Newsletter*, November 1985, and *Intinet Newsletter*, December 1985, 1, KIA.

29. Randy Burns, "Library Seeding Project," *PEPTalk*, Summer 1985, 5, KIA; Ryam Nearing, "The First P.E.P. Membership Directory," *PEPTalk*, Autumn 1985, 2–3. For personals, see page 6, KIA.

30. Deborah Anapol, *Initnet Newsletter*, May 1986, KIA.

31. Ryam Nearing, "Fidelity: Only If It's Fun for You." *PEPTalk*, Spring 1986, 2–3, KIA.

32. Deborah Anapol *Intinet Newsletter*, April 1986, KIA.

33. Ryam Nearing to Deborah Anapol, August 26, 1986, KIA.

34. "AIDS Risk," *PEPTalk*, Spring 1986, 3, KIA; Allan Jensen, "AIDS Again," *PEPTalk*, Spring 1987, 5, KIA.

35. Deborah Anapol, *Intinet Newsletter*, September 1985, and Deborah Anapol, *Intinet Newsletter*, October 1985, KIA.

36. Deborah Anapol, *Intinet Newsletter*, October 1985. KIA.

37. "PEP Conference '87," *PEPTalk*, Summer 1986, 7; Deborah Anapol, "PEPCon Workshop Sign-Up," KIA. Mycall Sunanda, "The Evolution of Primal Sufi Tantralini," *PEPTalk*, Winter 1986, 3, KIA; "PEPCON '87," *PEPTalk*, Summer 1987, 7, KIA.

38. Walter Powell "PEPCON Notes," *PEPTalk*, Autumn 1987, 3. Also Shirley Reeves, "And More PEPCON Notes," *PEPTalk*, Autumn 1987, 3, KIA. Randy Burns, "Spirituality, Polyfidelity, and Community," *PEPTalk*, October 1988, 1, KIA.

39. "Ads and Connections," *PEPTalk*, October 1988, 11, KIA; *Touchpoint* 1, no. 4 (October 1988) and *Touchpoint* 3, no. 3 (July 1990), KIA.

40. Ryam Nearing, *The New Faithful: A Polyfidelity Primer* (Eugene: PEP Productions, 1989), 68; Ryam Nearing, "The New Primer," *PEPTalk* (July 1989), 2; "Someone Is Looking for You," *PEPTalk*, October 1989, 2, KIA.

41. Walt Powell, "Eugene: A Geographical Center for Polyfidelity," *PEPTalk* (July 1989), 8.

42. Deborah Anapol, *A Resource Guide for the Responsible Non-Monogamist* (Mill Valley: Intinet Resource Center, 1989), KIA.

43. Ibid.

44. Sulak, *The Wizard and Witch*, 142, 160–162; Frank Throne, "Unicorn no Longer Fabulous; Biologist Has Produced One," *Science Newsletter* 29, no. 78 (May 16, 1936): 312–313.

45. Sulak, *The Wizard and the Witch*, 144, 163–165, 219. For the unicorns in popular media, see Danika Fears, "That Time Ringling Bros. Claimed It Had Real Unicorns," *New York Post*, March 2, 2017, https://nypost. com/2017/03/02/how-unicorns-became-stars-of-the-greatest-show-on-earth/, and *Saturday Night Live* "News Segment: Nathan Thurm," https://www.hulu.com/watch/273991. Oberon's life, including the creation of his unicorns and his search for mermaids, is the subject of Danny Yourd's 2017 documentary, "The Wizard of OZ."

46. Sulak, *The Wizard and the Witch*, 223.

47. Ibid., 171, 186.

CHAPTER 4

1. Oberon Zell, "It Was 20 Years Ago Today," in *Green Egg Omlette*, edited by Oberon Zell-Ravenheart (Franklin Lakes: The Career Press, 2009), xvi; Otter G'Zell, "In Memorium," *Green Egg* 21, no. 82 (August 1988): 4–5.

2. See Anodea Judith, "Eros and Ritual" *Green Egg* 22, no. 85 (May 1989): 6–7, and D. Rose Hartman, "Why Sex Centric Religion Moved Underground and What to Expect When It Surfaces," *Green Egg* 25, no. 96 (March 1992): 16,17.

3. Otter G'Zell, "Niggers of the New Age," *Green Egg* 23 (August 1990): 2.

4. Otter, G'Zell to Deborah Anapol, March 7, 1990, KIA.

5. Ibid.

6. Deborah Anapol, Intinet Resource Center Progress Center Quarterly Report (Summer 1990), KIA.

7. Morning Glory Zell, "A Banquet of Lovers: Strategies for Responsible Open Relationships" *Green Egg* 23, no. 89 (May 1990): 12–13. For frank insight into the Zells' relationship, see Sulak, *The Wizard and the Witch*, 171, 186.

8. Deborah Anapol, *Love Without Limits: The Quest for Sustainable Intimate Relationships* (San Rafael: Intinet Resource Center, 1992), 13–17.

9. Deborah Anapol, Intinet Resource Center Quarterly Progress Report, Winter 1990 and Spring 1991, KIA; 9th District Assemblyman Bill Filante to Deborah Anapol (May 16, 1991), KIA; Deborah Anapol, Intinet Resource Center Quarterly Progress Report, Spring 1991, KIA;

Deborah Anapol, Intinet Resource Center Quarterly Progress Report, Winter 1990 and Spring 1991, KIA.

10. Barry Northrop, "Polyfidelity Hits Network TV: Small Minds in the Big City," *PEPTalk*, Spring 1991, 3, KIA; Ryam Nearing, "Polyfidelity on Video" *Loving More*, Winter 1992, 2, KIA; LA Freedom '91 (DVD), KIA. Syntony moved to Hawaii in 1990. See Ryam Nearing, "The Big Island," *Loving More* 29 (Winter 1992): 3, and Ryam Nearing to Deborah Anapol, December 9, 1992, KIA.

11. For example, see "Book Reviews" and "The Latest Greatest Bisexual Resources," *Loving More* 27 (Summer 1991), 5, KIA.

12. Jack Johnston, "Debunking HIV as the Cause of AIDS," *Loving More* 32 (Autumn 1992): 3, 6–7, KIA; Allan Jensen, "AIDS: A Radical View," *PEPTalk*, July 1990, 5, KIA; Lyn Ehrnstein, "AIDS Awareness," *Loving More* 33 (Winter 1993): 8–10. KIA.

13. Ryam Nearing, "PEP's 5th Annual Conference," *Loving More* 29 (Winter 1992): 3, KIA.

14. 5th Annual PEPCon Promotional flyer, 1991, KIA; Deborah Anapol, "Polyfidelity Conference Strikes a Chord," *Floodtide* 3, Fall 1991, 1, KIA.

15. Ibid.

16. Oberon Zell, Email to Author, November 10, 2016.

17. Ryam Nearing, "PEP's 5th Annual Conference," *Loving More* 29 (Winter 1992): 4, KIA.

18. Ryam Nearing, "Aloha," *Loving More* 29 (Winter 1992): 2, KIA.

19. Oberon Zell, Email to the author, November 10, 2016.

20. Jud Presmont, "Comic Sketch of the Kerista Schism" and Jud Presmont, "Kerista Commune Follow Up Questionnaire," 1994, EUSARA. There are several ex-Keristan accounts that detail the inner workings of the commune that eventually led to its demise. See Even Eve, "Whatever Happened to Kerista?" *Communities Journal* 80/81 (Spring/Summer 1993) http://www.kerista.com/what.html; Kipseeks, "My Ins and Outs with Kerista," 2003, http://www.kerista.com/speak/kip1.html; and Mitch Slomiak, "Community: The Darkside Part 1 and 2," *Best of Loving More* 1, no. 1 (1997): 19–27, KIA.

21. Deborah Anapol, "Media Campaign," *Floodtide* 3, no. 1 (Fall 1991), 2; James Heddle and Deborah Anapol, *Star Trek Script* "Initiation," November 17, 1991, KIA; James Heddle, Diane Darling and Oberon Zell, *Star Trek Script* "Calling Down the Moon," November 16, 1991, KIA; Morning Glory Zell, *Star Trek Script* "Relationship," undated, KIA; Deborah Anapol to Writers Guild of America, January 1, 1992, KIA.

22. Deborah Anapol, *Love Without Limits: The Quest for Sustainable Intimate Relationships* (San Rafael: Intinet Resource Center, 1992), 163–171, KIA.

23. Ibid., 13, 35–36.

24. Ryam Nearing, *Loving More: The Polyfidelity Primer* (Captain Cook: PEP Publishing, 1992), frontmatter, 13, 25, 29, 34, 42–44, KIA.

25. Compare Nearing, *Loving More*, 80–88; with Ryam Nearing, *The New Faithful: The Polyfidelity Primer* (Eugene: PEP Publishing, 1989), 68.

26. Robert Rimmer to Deborah Anapol, May 5, 1992; Robert Rimmer to Ryam Nearing, June 5, 1992; Robert Rimmer to Deborah Anapol, June 2, 1992; Rimmer to Ryam Nearing, June 5, 1992; and Robert Rimmer to Deborah Anapol and Paul Glassco, July 13, 1992, KIA.

27. The references litter the primary sources. For an explicit statement, see Nearing, *Primer*, 80. Two of the three extended testimonials in Nearing's second edition reference Heinlein and Rimmer side by side. Nearing's husband Allan Jensen was the only one that did not, appealing to Kerista instead. Nearing, *New Faithful*, 13–61.

28. Robert Rimmer to Deborah Anapol, May 5, 1992, and Robert Rimmer to Deborah Anapol, June 2, 1992, KIA.

29. Deborah Anapol, "Robert Rimmer Today," *Floodtide*, Fall 1992, 1; Robert Rimmer to Deborah Anapol, April 26, 1993, KIA.

30. Ryam Nearing, "TV Time Again," *Loving More* 32 (Autumn 1992): 2, KIA.

31. The detailing of the saga began in Deborah Anapol, "On the Path: Searching for Poly Love," *Floodtide*, Spring 1993, 1, 3, 12–13, KIA.

32. "Letters," *Floodtide*, Summer 1993, KIA; Robert Rimmer to Deborah Anapol, April 26, 1993, KIA; Deborah Anapol, "On the Path for Polylove Part 2," *Floodtide*, Summer 1993, 8, KIA.

33. Deborah Anapol, "PEPCON a Success," and "Expanded Family Dissolves," *Floodtide*, Winter 1992, 9, KIA.

34. Gerald Jud, "The Union of Sex and Spirit," *Loving More* 1, no. 2 (Spring 1995): 4–5, KIA.

35. Deborah Anapol, "On the Path for Polylove: Part 4," *Floodtide*, Winter 1993, 7–10, KIA. Compare Deborah Anapol to Jerry and Rusty Annette, June 3, 1993, with Deborah Anapol, "On the Path for Polylove Part 2," *Floodtide*, Summer 1993, 8, KIA.

36. Deborah Anapol to Jerry, June 22, 1993, and Deborah Anapol to Jerry and Rusty et al., July 29, 1993, KIA.

37. Anapol, *Love Without Limits*, 91–92; "Editorial," *Anything That Moves: Beyond the Myths of Bisexuality* Premiere Issue (1991), KIA; *Bi Any Other*

Name: Bisexual People Speak Out, edited by Lani Ka' Auhumanu and Loraine Hutchins (Los Angeles: Alyson Books, 1991).

38. Sex and Spirit: Affirming Diversity in Patterns of Committed Personal Intimacy, Sexuality and Spirituality Program, KIA; Anapol, "Special Report: Summer of Conferencing," *Floodtide*, Winter 1993, 1, KIA.

39. Lorraine Hutchins, "Sexuality/Spirituality Conference Forms a New Coalition," September 22, 1993, KIA.

40. Ibid. Also see Deborah Anapol, *Floodtide*, Winter 1993, 5, KIA.

41. Deborah Anapol, "The Body Sacred Celebrating Diversity Sexuality and Spirituality: Press Release," KIA.

42. Robert Rimmer to Christie Hefner, October 4, 1993; Robert Rimmer, "Loving More Magazine Proposal"; and Deborah Anapol to Bob Rimmer, February 1, 1994, KIA.

43. Deborah Anapol to Ryam Nearing, October 8, 1993; Deborah Anapol to Jim, January 14, 1994, KIA; Deborah Anapol, "PEP and Intinet Join Forces to Create *Loving More Magazine*" *Floodtide*, Winter 1994, 1, KIA.

44. The first issue was released in winter of 1995. However, Nearing's dating system began with winter and ended in fall. See Contents, *Loving More Magazine*, Winter 1995, frontmatter, 1–2, 10–15; Robert Rimmer, "Keeping Life Exciting at 78," *Loving More Magazine*, Winter 1995, 4–5; and Riff, "To Love Is to Abide," *Loving More Magazine*, Winter 1995, 8–10, KIA.

45. Deborah Anapol, "About This Issue," *Loving More Magazine*, Spring 1995, 2; Gerald Jud, "The Union of Sex and Spirit," *Loving More Magazine*, Spring 1995, 4–7; Michael Aluna, "Panfidelity and the Birth of the Aluna Clan," *Loving More Magazine*, Spring 1995, 10–11; Deborah Anapol, "Tantra and Sexual Healing: An interview with Victor Gold," *Loving More Magazine*, Spring 1995, 13–15; Morning Glory Zell, "Family of the Heart," *Loving More Magazine*, Fall 1995, 24–25, KIA.

46. Deborah Anapol, "On the Edge: Exploring the Polyamorous Frontier," *Loving More Magazine*, Winter 1995, 23–25, KIA.

47. Deborah Anapol, "On the Edge: Exploring the Polyamorous Frontier," *Loving More Magazine*, Spring 1995, 22–23, KIA.

48. "Viewpoint," *Loving More Magazine*, Summer 1995, 32, KIA.

49. Ibid.

50. Deborah Anapol, "On the Edge: An Ongoing Exploration of New Paradigm Relating," *Loving More Magazine*, Fall 1995, 27, KIA.

51. Terry Brussel Gibbons, "West Coast Conference Report: Volunteer Opportunities Abound," *Loving More Magazine*, Fall 1995, 20, KIA.

CHAPTER 5

1. *The Jerry Springer Show*, "Non-monogamous Relationships" (1996), KIA.
2. Ibid.
3. Ibid.
4. "World Wide Web Timeline," Pew Research Center, March 11, 2014, http://www.pewinternet.org/2014/03/11/world-wide-web-timeline/.
5. Fred Turner, *From Counterculture to Cyberculture: Stewart Brand, the Whole Earth Network, and the Rise of Digital Utopianism* (Chicago: University of Chicago Press, 2006), 159.
6. Deborah Anapol, "Computer Network," *Floodtide*, Summer 1992, 4, KIA.
7. Ryam Nearing and Deborah Anapol, "Polyamory: A Personal and Historical Retrospective," *Loving More Magazine*, Winter 2003, 13, KIA.
8. LKELLY@DESIRE.WRIGHT.EDU, Triples message, September 8, 1993, KIA.
9. Harry Alan Benjamin Shapiro to Deborah May 15, 1991, and Richard Adkins to Paul and Deborah, July 14, 1991, WELL logs, KIA.
10. Email from Martin Tracy to Deborah Anapol, March 4, 1993, WELL logs, KIA.
11. Ken Olum, Triples Message, September 8, 1993, and Carol Segar, Triples Message, September 8, 1993, WELL logs, KIA.
12. David Lewis, Triples Message, Sept 15, 1993, WELL logs, KIA.
13. Lynsa, Triples Message February 25, 1994, WELL logs, KIA.
14. Roy Rapoport, Triples Message February 26, 1994; Michael T. Price, Triples Message, February 26, 1994; and Lynsa, Triples Message, March 2, 1994, KIA.
15. Kenneth Haslam, audio interview with Jennifer Wesp, KIA.
16. For a concise history of the debate, see Alan M. "Polyamory Enters the Oxford English Dictionary and Tracking the Word's Origins," January 6, 2007, https://polyinthemedia.blogspot.com/2007/01/polyamory-enters-oxford-english.html.
17. Haslam, interview with Wesp, KIA; Google Groups, "alt.polyamory," https://groups.google.com/forum/#!forum/alt.polyamory. For years the parrot served as a symbol for polyamory as an internet mascot and as a symbol worn physically as a pin or a t-shirt. See Alan M. "The Polyamory Flag Is a Grim Confusing Failure. Let's Do Better," *Polyamory in the News*, July 27, 2020, https://polyinthemedia.blogspot.com/search?q=parrot and Alex West, "A List of Poly Symbols," May 11, 2002, http://www.hevanet.com/alexwest/parrots/symbolist.html.

The popularity of the parrot waned as other symbols were adopted. The most notable is the heart superimposed with the infinity symbol. See Dee Morgan, "What Does the Infinity Heart Signify," *Polyamproud*, September 3, 2022, https://www.polyamproud.com/post/what-does-the-infinity-heart-signify.

18. Anapol to 75300.642@compuserve.com, June 11, 1992, WELL logs, KIA. Although Anapol was on the USENET Triples mailing list, it appears she was not initially active within the newsgroups.

19. Anapol to @hardy@panix.com February 24, 1994, WELL logs, KIA.

20. Brett Hill, "On-line Community," *Loving More Magazine*, Fall 1995, 30–31, KIA.

21. Ibid. Also Brett Hill, "Website Update," *Loving More Magazine*, Spring 1996, 29 and "Website Report" *Loving More Magazine* (Winter 1996), 28, KIA.

22. Deborah Anapol, *Polyamory: The New Love Without Limits* (San Rafael: Intinet Resource Center, 1997), 5.

23. Dossie Easton and Catherine A. Liszt, *The Ethical Slut: A Guide to Infinite Sexual Possibilities* (San Francisco: Greenery Press, 1997), 10, 16.

24. Ibid., 133.

25. Ibid., 252–255.

26. Ibid, 265.

27. Ryam Nearing, "Review: *The Ethical Slut*," *Loving More Magazine*, Spring 1997, 30; Dossie Easton and Catherine A. Liszt, "*The Ethical Slut*" *Loving More Magazine* (Summer 1997): 4–6; and "About This Issue," *Loving More Magazine* (Summer 1998): 2, KIA.

28. Eve Furchgott, "Small is Beautiful," *Loving More Magazine*, Winter 97/98, 16–17, KIA.

29. Ibid, 17.

30. Ryam Nearing, "About This Issue," *Loving More Magazine*, Summer 1996, 2–3, KIA.

31. The Ravenheart Family, "Poly Advice," *Loving More Magazine*, Spring 1998, 14–15, KIA.

32. The Geraldo Rivera Show, unaired episode, 1997, KIA.

33. Ibid.

34. Ibid.

35. Ibid.

36. Ibid.

37. Ibid.

38. Ibid.

39. Ibid.

40. Woody Baird, "Pagan Mother Battles Custody," January 11, 1999, Associated Press, http://www.polyamorysociety.org/Yahoo-Divilbl iss_Article.html; and Divilbiss, "Open Letter," http://www.polyamory society.org/Divilbiss_Families_Case_Ends.html.

41. MTV, *Sex in the 90s: It's a Group Thing*, https://www.youtube.com/watch?v=stbnbDQ97Yk.

42. "Judge Rules," *Loving More Magazine*, Summer 1999, 2, 3, and 12, KIA. Also Baird, "Pagan Mother" and Divilbiss, "Open Letter."

43. Divilbiss, "Open Letter."

44. Barry Northrop, "Legal Update," *Loving More Magazine*, Summer 2000, 2, KIA; John Cloud, "Henry, Mary, Janet, and . . ." *Time Magazine* November 7, 1999, http://content.time.com/time/magazine/article/0,9171,33866-1,00.html.

45. "About This Issue," *Loving More Magazine*, Winter 2000, 2. Cloud, "Henry, Mary, Janet, and . . ." The Poly Pride flag was first introduced by Jim Evans in 1995. It has three bars of color: blue, red, and black. In the center there is a gold π symbol. According to Evans, the blue represents openness and honesty among partners, red represents love and passion, black represents solidarity with those closeted to the outside world, and gold represents the value placed on attachment, whether friendly or romantic, as opposed to purely physical relationships. Though Evans initially chose the π symbol because it began with P, it was easy to type, and because queer movements had a history of using Greek letters, later polyamorists have argued that π's infinite decimal representation symbolizes infinite love. See Jim Evans, "Polyamory, Pride Flags, and Patterns of Feedback," August 23, 2016, http://jimevansmusic.blogs pot.com/2016/08/polyamory-pride-flags-and-patterns-of.html   and Lauren Pineda "Polyamory: What Is It and Why Does the Flag Have the Phi Symbol?" *Rare* https://rare.us/rare-life/polyamory-flag/.

46. *Leeza Show*, Polyamory (December 15, 1999), KIA.

47. Ibid.

48. Ibid.

49. Ibid.

50. Liberated Christians, "Leeza Show on Polyamory—Some Lessons Learned," http://www.libchrist.com/poly/leezashow.html. Also see Megan Hurston, "Network of Many Loves: A History of Alternative Media in the Polyamory Movement" (PhD Dissertation, University of Colorado, 2016), 143, https://scholar.colorado.edu/cgi/viewcontent.cgi?article=1034&context=jour_gradetds.

51. Cloud, "Henry, Mary, Janet, and . . ." *Time Magazine.*

CHAPTER 6

1. Larry Gross has argued that the final years of the twentieth century saw queer Americans become a permanent part of the visible American cultural cast. Larry Gross, *Up from Invisibility: Lesbians Gay Men, and the Media in America* (New York: Columbia University Press, 2001), xv–xvi, 156–201. For a concise history of the shift in American thinking on homosexuality, including the reasons for that shift, see Chauncy, *Why Marriage*, 40–58.
2. Deb Schwartz, "Mes Cheris Amours," *New York Magazine*, October 21, 2002, http://nymag.com/nymetro/urban/features/n_7833/; "Poly Pride: An Interview with Justen Michael," *Loving More Magazine*, Summer 2001, 19–20, KIA.
3. "Status Report: Poly Survey," *Loving More Magazine*, Fall 2001, 2, KIA.
4. "Poly Pride 2002: Questions and Answers with Justen Michael," *Loving More Magazine*, Summer 2002, 18–19, KIA.
5. Polyamorists now observe Polyamory Day on November 23. This is in large part because earlier efforts, such as Justen Michael's, initially failed to create a large-scale movement. Thus, many polyamorists are likely unaware of that history. See Zoe Duff, "Polyamory Day," *Canadian Polyamory Advocacy Association*, November 23, 2011, https://polyadvocacy.ca/polyamory-day-2020/ and Alan M., "Today Is Polyamory Day!" *Polyamory in the News*, November 23, 2022, https://polyinthemedia.blogspot.com/search?q=polyamory+day+.
6. *When Two Won't Do*, directed by David Finch and Maureen Marovitch. Montreal: Picture this Productions, 2002.
7. Ibid.
8. Ibid.
9. Ibid.
10. Ibid.
11. Ibid.
12. "Letters About the Video," *Loving More Magazine*, Winter 2002, 2–3, KIA.
13. Ibid.
14. Sarah Miller, "What Its Really Like to Have Two Boyfriends (Who Know About Each Other)," *Elle*, December 20, 2015, https://www.elle.com/life-love/sex-relationships/a32307/what-its-like-to-have-two-boyfriends/.

15. John Ullman, "Doing a Media Interview? Make Sure It's Not Poly In, Garbage Out," *Loving More Magazine*, Summer 2002, 15; *The John Walsh Show* (DVD); and Janet Kira Lessin, "Lessins Learned on the John Walsh Show," *Loving More Magazine*, Winter 2003, 4–5, KIA.

16. Ryam Hill, email to author, January 24, 2019.

17. Ryam Nearing, "Editor's Note," *Loving More Magazine*, Fall 2002, 2, KIA.

18. Robin Trask, "Editor's Note," *Loving More Magazine*, 33, 4–5, KIA.

19. Wil Taylor, "A Poly Skeptic Viewpoint," *Loving More Magazine*, Winter 2004, 19; "Letter to the Editor," *Loving More Magazine*, Summer 2005, 3; Robin Trask, "The Poly Astrological Calendar," *Loving More Magazine*, Summer 2005, 32–34; and Robin Trask, "The Poly Astrological Forecast," *Loving More Magazine*, Winter 2006, 30–32, KIA.

20. "Local Poly Resources," Polyamory.org November 20, 2005, KIA.

21. Cunning Minx, "Poly Origin Story," *Polyamory Weekly*, Podcast Audio, March 10, 2005; Cunning Minx, *Polyamory Weekly* 42 Audio Podcast, January 24, 2006.

22. Cunning Minx, *Polyamory Weekly* 40 Audio Podcast, January 10, 2006; Cunning Minx, *Polyamory Weekly* 39–43 Audio Podcast, January 3–31, 2006, KIA; and Rachel Kramer Bussel, "High Tech Sex: Are Podcasts the Future of Porn?" *Penthouse Forum*, February 2006, 55.

23. Megan Hurson, "Networks of Many Loves: A History of Alternative Media in the Polyamory Movement" (PhD dissertation, University of Colorado, 2016), https://scholar.colorado.edu/cgi/viewcontent.cgi?article=1034&context=jour_gradetds.

24. Alan M., "Polyamory in the Media," September 2005 Archive, https://polyinthemedia.blogspot.com/2005/09/

25. Unitarian Universalists for Polyamory Awareness, "Polyamory and the UUA Principles and Purposes," February 2005, KIA; "Board Announces Important All-Church Meeting," *Steepletalk* 7, no. 5 (March 4, 2001):1, KIA.

26. "Kenneth R. Haslam Collection on Polyamory," https://kinseyinstitute.org/news-events/news/2019-01-24-haslam-polyamory.php, and Alan M. "Ken Haslam on Sex and Sensibility," December 18, 2009, https://polyinthemedia.blogspot.com/search?q=haslam+.

27. Stanley Kurtz, "Beyond Gay Marriage," *The Weekly Standard*, August 4, 2003, https://pages.pomona.edu/~vis04747/h21/readings/Kurz_Beyond_gay_marriage.pdf , and *The Weekly Standard*, "Here Comes the Brides," December 26, 2005, https://www.washingtonexaminer.com/weekly-standard/here-come-the-brides

28. Kurtz, "Here Comes the Brides."

29. For a succinct history of the complexities of the marriage debate within queer communities, see Chauncey, *Why Marriage*, 87–136. For a popular commentary, see Anemona Hartocollis, "For Some Gays, a Right They Can Forsake," *The New York Times*, July 30, 2006, https://www.nytimes. com/2006/07/30/fashion/sundaystyles/30MARRIAGE.html?pag ewanted=1&_r=2.

30. "Beyond Same Sex Marriage: A New Strategic Vision for All Our Families and Relationships," Unmarried Equality, http://www.unmarr ied.org/beyond-same-sex-marriage/.

31. Ibid. Also, "Beyond Same Sex Marriage: A New Strategic Vision for All Our Families and Relationships," *Monthly Review*, August 8, 2006, and Hartocollis, "For Some Gays, a Right They Can Forsake."

32. Stanley Kurtz, "The Confession: Have Same Sex Marriage Advocates Said Too Much," *The National Review* October 31, 2006, https://www. nationalreview.com/2006/10/confession-stanley-kurtz/, and "The Confession II: "Conservative" Proponents of Same-Sex Marriage Are About to Be Overtaken by Radicals," *The National Review*, November 1, 2006, https://www.nationalreview.com/2006/11/confession-ii-stan ley-kurtz/.

33. The Polyamory Leadership Network: Dedicated to Information Sharing and Mutual Aid Within the Polyamory Network, "About the Polyamory Leadership Network," https://polyamoryleadership network.org/about-the-polyamory-leadership-network/ and Second National Polyamory Leaderships Summit (March 1–2, 2009), Draft Minutes, KIA.

34. Regina Lynn, "Internet Pushed Polyamory to Its Tipping Point," *Wired*, February 29, 2008, https://www.wired.com/2008/02/sexdrive-0229/.

35. Alan M., "Family Polyfolks Interviewed on Radio," *Polyamory in the Media*, March 12, 2009, https://polyinthemedia.blogspot.com/2009/ 03/family-polyfolks-interviewed-on-radio.html.

36. All webisodes of *Family* are written and directed by Terisa Greenan and can be found on YouTube at https://www.youtube.com/watch?v= G2-MTs_Lsog&list=PLq7goNqijXWCB_rnOde9dTWi34PLXz AEC&index=1. See also Hurson, "Networks of Many Loves," 179.

37. Jessica Bennet, "Polyamory: The New Sexual Revolution?" *Newsweek*, July 28, 2009, https://www.newsweek.com/polyamory-next-sexual-revolution-82053.

38. Ibid. Al Mohler, "Polyamory: The Perfectly Plural Post-modern Condition," *The Christian Post*, August 10, 2009, https://www.christ

ianpost.com/news/polyamory-the-perfectly-plural-postmodern-con-dition-40185/.

39. Shira and Gavin Katz, *Pedestrian Polyamory*, Episode 2, "Talking with Pepper Mint," October 18, 2011.

40. Alan M., "Q&A with Polyamory Producer Natalia Garcia," *Polyamory in the Media,* September 29, 2012, https://polyinthemedia.blogspot.com/2012/09/casting-call-for-possible-2nd-season-of.html.

41. Natalia Garcia, quoted in Alan M., "Casting Call for Possible Second Season of Showtime's Polyamory," *Polyamory in the Media,* September 25, 2012, https://polyinthemedia.blogspot.com/2012/09/casting-call-for-possible-2nd-season-of.html.

42. *Polyamory: Married and Dating,* "Radical Honesty," Season 1, Episode 6, directed by Natalia Garcia, BermanBraun Productions, August 16, 2012, and "Triggers," Season 2, Episode 2, directed by Natalia Garcia, BermanBraun Productions, August 22, 2013.

43. See *Polyamory Married and Dating,* "Coming Around," Season 2, Episode 7, directed by Natalia Garcia, BermanBraun Productions, September 26, 2013, and Rich Juzwiak, "Showtime's Polyamory Is Trashy, Profound, and the Best Reality Show on TV," July 26, 2012, https://gawker.com/5929318/showtimes-polyamory-is-trashy-profound-and-the-best-reality-show-on-tv.

44. Alan M., "The Showtime Polyamory Series: Taking Stock," *Polyamory in the Media*, October 26, 2012, https://polyinthemedia.blogspot.com/search/label/Showtime%20Season%201, and Shaun McGonigal, "Coming Out Poly in Light of Mainstream Images," *Poly Skeptic*, October 2, 2012, https://polyskeptic.com/2012/10/02/coming-out-poly-in-light-of-mainstream-images/.

45. *Polyamory: Married and Dating,* "We Are One," Season 1, Episode 5, directed by Natalia Garcia, BermanBraun Productions, August 23, 2012.

46. Deborah Anapol, "Polyamory: Married and Dating," *Psychology Today*, July 20, 2012, https://www.psychologytoday.com/us/blog/love-without-limits/201207/polyamory-married-and-dating.

47. *Polyamory: Married and Dating,* "Radical Honesty."

48. *Polyamory: Married and Dating,* "We Are One."

49. Ibid.

50. Elizabeth Sheff, *The Polyamorists Next Door* (Lanham: Rowan and Littlefield, 2014), x.

51. Ibid.

52. Ibid., 2–19.

53. Ryam Hill, Email to Author, January 10, 2019.

54. Sheff, *Polyamorists Next Door*, 31–36.

55. Ibid., 191–215.

56. Ibid., 217–254.

57. Ibid., 283–286.

58. Olga Khazan, "Multiple Lovers Without Jealousy: Polyamorous People Still Face Plenty of Stigmas, but Some Studies Suggest They Can Handle Certain Relationship Challenges Better Than Monogamous People Do," *The Atlantic*, July 21, 2014, https://www.theatlantic.com/health/archive/2014/07/multiple-lovers-no-jealousy/374697/; Sheff, *Polyamorists Next Door*, 275.

59. Franklin Veaux and Eve Rickert, *More Than Two: A Practical Guide to Ethical Polyamory* (Portland: Thorntree Press, 2014), 11–14.

60. Ibid., 31, and Franklin Veaux, "More Than Two: Guest Post on Ethical Polyamory from Franklin Veaux," The Orbit: Atheism Activism, Culture, September 27, 2013, https://the-orbit.net/greta/2013/09/27/more-than-two/.

61. Veaux and Rickert, *More Than Two*, 58–60, 80–81, 236, 425–427, 460; Alan M., "*More Than Two* Reviews and Getting It into Libraries," *Polyamory in the Media*, July 1, 2014, https://polyinthemedia.blogspot.com/2014/07/.

62. Christopher Ryan, "Are We Designed to be Sexual Omnivores?" TED: Ideas Worth Spreading, February 2013, https://www.ted.com/talks/christopher_ryan_are_we_designed_to_be_sexual_omnivores, and Susan Dominus "Is an Open Marriage a Happier Marriage," *The New York Times*, May 5, 2017, https://www.nytimes.com/2017/05/11/magazine/is-an-open-marriage-a-happier-marriage.html.

CHAPTER 7

1. Barry Northrop, email to the author, March 13, 2019, and Ryam Hill, email to author, January 16, 2023.

2. Antonia Blumberg, "Morning Glory Zell-Ravenheart Dead: Pioneering Pagan, Polyamory Leader Dies at 66," *The Huffington Post*, May 19, 2014, https://www.huffpost.com/entry/morning-glory-zell-dead_n_5324410.

3. "Vicki Sexual Freedom Awards," Woodhull Freedom Foundation, https://www.woodhullfoundation.org/vicki-sexual-freedom-awards/

4. Alan M. "Deborah Taj Anapol, 1951–2015," *Polyamory in the Media*, August 19, 2015, and Robin Trask, "The Passing of a Polyamory Trailblazer," https://www.mynewsletterbuilder.com/email/newsletter/1412432001.

5. Adam Liptak, "Supreme Court Makes Gay Marriage a Right Nationwide," *The New York Times*, June 26, 2015, https://www.nytimes.com/2015/06/27/us/supreme-court-same-sex-marriage.html.

6. Ibid, and *Obergefell et al. v. Hodges et al.*, June 26, 2015, 29. For Roberts on multiple marriage, see his dissent, 20–21, https://www.supremecourt.gov/opinions/14pdf/14-556_3204.pdf.

7. *Obergefell et al. v. Hodges et al.*, June 26, 2015, 28.

8. Sheff, *The Polyamorists Next Door*, 173.

9. See Nancy D. Polikoff, *Beyond Straight and Gay Marriage* (Boston: Beacon Press, 2008), and Lisa Duggan, "Beyond Marriage: Democracy, Equality, and Kinship for a New Century," *The Scholar and Feminist Online* 10.1–10.2 (Fall 2011/Spring 2012), http://sfonline.barnard.edu/a-new-queer-agenda/beyond-marriage-democracy-equality-and-kinship-for-a-new-century/.

10. "The Beyond Marriage Statement: Reflections 10 Years Later," October 2, 2016, http://aftermarriage.clags.org/sessions/10-years-after-beyond-marriage/.

11. Zoe Duff, "Polyamory Day," *Canadian Polyamory Advocacy Association*, November 23, 2011, https://polyadvocacy.ca/polyamory-day-2020/, and Alan M., "Today Is Polyamory Day!" *Polyamory in the News*, November 23, 2022, https://polyinthemedia.blogspot.com/search?q=polyamory+day+.

12. Julie Rovner, "Foes of Trump's Restrictions on Family Planning See Law on Their Side," *NPR*, February 8, 2014, https://www.npr.org/sections/health-shots/2019/02/28/698646797/foes-of-trumps-restrictions-on-family-planning-clinics-see-law-on-their-side; Heather Marie Stur, "Donald Trump's 'Trans Ban' Reverses More Than 70 Years of Military Integration," *The Washington Post*, January 29, 2019, https://www.washingtonpost.com/outlook/2019/01/29/donald-trumps-trans-ban-reverses-more-than-years-military-integration/?utm_term=.4b7b8ec8f646; and Nina Totenberg and Sarah McCammon, "Supreme Court Overturns Roe v Wade, Ending Right to Abortion Upheld for Decades," *NPR*, June 24, 2020, https://www.npr.org/2022/06/24/1102305878/supreme-court-abortion-roe-v-wade-decision-overturn.

13. Olivia Goldhill, "Polyamorous Sex Is the Most Quietly Revolutionary Political Weapon in the United States," *Quartz*, December 20, 2018, https://qz.com/1501725/polyamorous-sex-is-the-most-quietly-revolutionary-political-weapon-in-the-united-states/; Gabrielle Smith, "The Best Dating Apps for Non-Monogamous Folks, Right This Way," *Cosmopolitan*, February 1, 2022, https://www.cosmopolitan.

com/sex-love/a33626157/best-polyamorous-dating-apps/;   Madeline
Howard, "The 9 Best Polyamorous Dating Apps You Can Download
Right Now: Plus, What to Put on Your Profile If You're on a More
Traditionally Monogamous App," *Women's Health*, April 14, 2021,
https://www.womenshealthmag.com/sex-and-love/a36108639/best-
polyamorous-dating-sites-apps/.

14. Andrew Anthony, "Sam Harris: The New Atheist with a Spiritual Side,"
The Guardian, February 6, 2019, https://www.theguardian.com/books/
2019/feb/16/sam-harris-interview-new-atheism-four-horsemen-
faith-science-religion-rationalism.

15. Geoffrey Miller, "Polyamory and Open Sexuality: Course Syllabus,"
August 23, 2017, https://www.primalpoly.com/courses-taught.

16. Sam Harris, "Transformations of Mind," *Making Sense 128*, June 4, 2018.

17. Joshua Johnson, *NPR 1A*, "The New Sexual Revolution: Polyamory on
the Rise," February 17, 2019.

18. Farmer's work ties together a host of polyamorists from different backgrounds and experiences. For her personal work in education, see
Gastonia Freedom School, https://gastoniafreedom.org/about-us/.
Polyamproud's work has predominately focused on producing a demo-
cratically selected reimagined Polyamory Pride flag to replace the outdated one designed by Jim Evans in 1995 that has drawn derision from
many within the polyamory community; see Polyamproud.com. For a
history of the debate surrounding the Polyamory Pride Flag, see Alan
M., "The Polyamory Flag Is a Grim, Confusing Failure. Let's do Better,"
Polyamory in the News, July 27, 2020, https://polyinthemedia.blogspot.
com/search?q=poly+flag.

19. Johnson, "The New Sexual Revolution."

20. Ron Young, "Welcome to Black and Poly," April 3, 2019. Blackandpoly.
org

21. Jillian Deri, *Love's Refraction: Jealousy and Compersion in Queer Women's
Polyamorous Relationships* (Toronto: University of Toronto Press, 2015).

Index

For the benefit of digital users, indexed terms that span two pages (e.g., 52–53) may, on occasion, appear on only one of those pages